Air Force Tac Recce Aircraft

NATO and Non-aligned Western European Air Force Tactical Reconaissance Aircraft of the Cold War

Paul J. Wagner,
CMSGT, USAF, Retired

The contents of this work including, but not limited to, the accuracy of events, people, and places depicted; opinions expressed; permission to use previously published materials included; and any advice given or actions advocated are solely the responsibility of the author, who assumes all liability for said work and indemnifies the publisher against any claims stemming from publication of the work.

ISBN: 978-1-4349-9458-5
Printed in the United States of America

First Printing

For more information or to order additional books,
please contact:
RoseDog Books
701 Smithfield Street
Pittsburgh, Pennsylvania 15222
U.S.A.
1-800-834-1803
www.rosedogbookstore.com

This book is dedicated to my father Ted Wagner Jr. who inspired my love of aviation and gave me the work ethic to do my best; my mother Margaret who encouraged my writing; my wife Cathy who tolerated my absences when I sequestered myself in my office to write; and my grandson Joey, who is a true aviation enthusiast.

Cover Photo

Image 001, RF-4C Phantom II of the 67th Tactical Reconnaissance Wing, Bergstrom Air Force Base, Texas (Photo courtesy of the USAF)

Picture Acknowledgments

All artwork and pictures are © copyright by the author except for those provided by the following photographers and organizations, as identified in the captions, and cannot be duplicated and used without their prior written approval:

Air Force Historical Research Agency (AFHRA)
Air Systems Command/Historical Office (ACS/HO)
Alastair McBean
Anders Presterud
Andries Waardenburg
Bruno Althaus
Chris Muir
Daniele Faccioli
Defense Visual Information Center (DVIC)
Den Pascoe
Diego Bigolin
Dirk Jan de Ridder
Giuseppe Tonelotto
Ian Howat
Ian Powell
Jan Lidestrand
Jimmy Lescalle
John Dunn
John P. Stewart
Joop de Groot
Jorge Manuel Antâo Ruivo
Keith Blincow
Lockheed Martin

Luis Rosa
Michael Schmidt
Mick Bajcar
National Museum of the USAF (NMUSAF)
Nicolas Laroudie Dijon
Piotr Biskupski
Pulido Romera
Robert Lundin
Roberto Yanez
Stephen Boreham
Steve Murray
Steve Williams
Tom Houquet
Tor Karlsson
Trevor Thornton
Vic Flintham
Ville Jalonen
Werner Horvath
Willie Metz

Contents

Introduction

Between 1948 and 1989, the North Atlantic Treaty organization (NATO) and non-aligned Western European air forces operated more than fifty different tactical reconnaissance (Tac Recce) aircraft in support of allied and Western European air and ground combat commanders. With the exception of the TR-1A, these aircraft were derived from existing air force combat and training aircraft developed, manufactured and used during the Cold War. Despite their contribution, most Tac Recce aircraft have received no more recognition than a footnote in aviation history. Seldom do the references to Tac Recce aircraft merit more than a couple lines in an obscure paragraph.

This book is a comprehensive review of all Tac Recce aircraft produced and operated by NATO and Western European air forces during the Cold War. Each chapter focuses on a specific aircraft and includes information on the aircraft's history, development, physical description, sensors, operators, and capabilities. All countries, units, aircraft, weapon systems, and manufacturers referenced in this book, are referred to by their the name and/or designation, they were known by during the Cold War.

The aircraft in this book includes a mix of armed multi-mission aircraft, such as the Harrier GR.Mk.1/3, and unarmed specialized Tac Recce aircraft, such as the RF-4C/E Phantom II. Since World War II (WW II), if a requirement was issued for a new Tac Recce aircraft, manufacturers modified existing combat and training aircraft to accommodate the large film based cameras and electronics of that era. The challenge for the manufacturer was to modify the aircraft design and retain the performance characteristics required to satisfy the operational mission requirements while incorporating the Tac Recce mission equipment into an existing and already full airframe. This left the manufacturer two options; either limit the sensor suite, or remove any offensive and defensive weapons systems, avionics and electronic systems

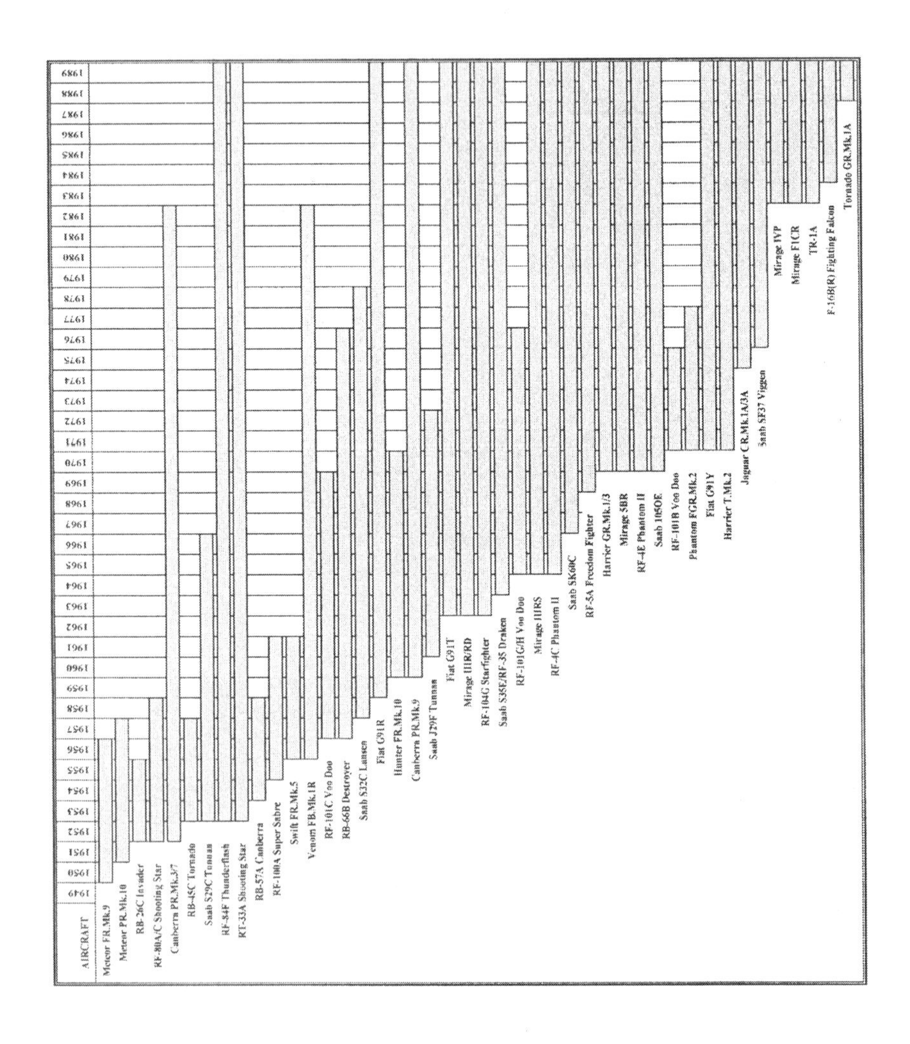

Figure 001, Chronology of NATO and Non-Aligned Western European Air Force Tac Recce Aircraft During the Cold War

deemed non-essential for the Tac Recce mission. However, the selected approach frequently depended on the philosophy of the military service responsible for issuing the requirement for the new Tac Recce aircraft.

Image 002, Lockheed F-5 Lightning, is the unarmed photographic reconnaissance version of the P-38 Lightning fighter used by the USAAF in World War II and used by the French AF from 1943 - 1952. (Photo courtesy of the Air Force Historical Research Agency [AFHRA])

Within Europe, the accepted approach or standard focused on a multi-mission capability. As a result, most European Tac Recce aircraft developed during the Cold War retained some, if not all of their defensive and offensive armament. However, during the early 1950's the United States Air Force (USAF) made a conscious decision to procure only unarmed Tac Recce aircraft. This decision was based on lessons learned from WW II and the Korean Conflict. USAF officials recognized that given an opportunity, aircrews conducting armed reconnaissance missions preferred to shoot targets using offensive and defensive weapons, not cameras. As a result, the USAF developed specialized Tactical Reconnaissance Squadrons and Wings (TRS/TRW), which focused on the acquisition, processing, exploitation, and reporting of tactical targets for United States (US) and NATO air and ground commanders during the Cold War. During the early years of the Cold War, as the US produced the majority of the Tac Recce aircraft used by NATO air forces, many Western European air forces adopted the American Model for Tac Recce units.

During the latter half of the Cold War, advances in technology resulted in smaller, lighter and more capable sensors and electronics. This led to the development of podded reconnaissance systems. Sometimes the pods were modified from existing wing pods, such as external fuel tanks; and sometimes they were custom pods designed for installation under the aircraft fuselage or on the wing pylons. The use of reconnaissance pods significantly reduced the time and cost required to modify an existing airframe to perform the Tac Recce mission. In addition, the use of podded sensors allowed the manufacturer to retain the aircraft's offensive and defensive weapon systems.

A limited number of countries procured combat aircraft capable of performing reconnaissance missions, but did not use them in the reconnaissance role. For example, the US built RF-5A Freedom Fighter was procured by the Greek AF, and the Italian built Fiat G91R was procured by the Portuguese AF; however, these aircraft were assigned to strike and ground attack units, and never employed by those air forces in the Tac Recce role.

During the forty-two years of the Cold War, Tac Recce mission requirements continued to evolve and expand. As part of this process, Tac Recce units were tasked to conduct peacetime reconnaissance and surveillance missions in support of national and strategic intelligence requirements. Early in the Cold War, this included over flights of denied airspace using long-range, high-altitude aircraft not normally associated with Tac Recce units, such as the USAF RB-45C Tornado and the Royal Air Force (RAF) Canberra. Later, selected high-altitude, supersonic aircraft, such as the RF-100A Super Sabre, conducted a limited number of over flights of Eastern European nations. During the Berlin Crisis of the early 1960's RF-101C Voodoos flew reconnaissance missions in the air corridors that connected Berlin to West Germany. With the advent of long-range, standoff surveillance sensors in the 1970s and 1980s, Tac Recce aircraft had the capability to conduct surveillance missions of the Eastern European border regions without having to conduct flights into denied air space.

Prior to the introduction of jet powered Tac Recce aircraft in the early 1950s, Western European and US air force Tac Recce units, employed armed and unarmed surplus WW II photographic-reconnaissance aircraft. These aircraft permitted Western European and US air force Tac Recce units to train the aircrews and ground personnel required to staff the Cold War air force Tac Recce units. While these aircraft are not described in this book, I believe it is important to recognize the aircraft used by these air forces during the early years of the Cold War. The following is a list of the Western European countries and US units with air force reconnaissance mission requirements and the surplus WW II aircraft they used between 1945 and 1955:

- French AF — F-5A/B/F/G Lightning — 1943 - 1952
- USAF, 160th TRS — F-6 Mustang — 1944 - 1947
- Turkish AF — Spitfire PR.Mk.XI — 1944 - 1954
- Turkish AF — Spitfire PR.Mk.XIX — 1944 - 1954
- French AF — Mosquito PR.Mk.XVI — 1945 - 1953
- Swiss AF — Mosquito PR.Mk.IV — 1945 - 1954
- USAF, 45th TRS — F-6 Mustang — 1946 - 1948
- RAF, No. 2 Sq — Spitfire PR.Mk.XI — 1946 - 1950
- RAF, No. 13 Sq — Mosquito PR.Mk.XVI — 1946 - 1953
- RAF, No. 58 Sq — Mosquito PR.Mk.XVI — 1946 - 1953
- RAF, No. 81 Sq — Mosquito PR.Mk.XVI — 1946 - 1953
- RAF, No. 81 Sq — Spitfire PR.Mk.XI — 1946 - 1954
- Royal Norwegian AF — Spitfire PR.Mk.XI — 1946 - 1954
- RAF, No. 540 Sq — Mosquito PR.Mk.XVI — 1947 - 1953
- Belgium AF — Spitfire FR.Mk.XIV — 1947 - 1954
- Royal Danish AF — Spitfire PR.Mk.XI — 1947 - 1955
- Swedish AF — Spitfire PR.Mk.XIX (S-21) — 1948 - 1955
- Swedish AF — F-6 Mustang (S-26) — 1948 - 1955

Meteor FR.Mk.9

Image 003, Royal Air Force (RAF) Meteor FR.Mk.9, s/n VZ611, low-altitude photographic-reconnaissance aircraft on training flight in Great Britain. (Photo copyright by Vic Flintham)

The first of the new generation of post World War II Tac Recce aircraft in Europe was the Meteor FR.Mk.9. Derived from the Meteor F. Mk.8 interceptor; the Meteor FR.Mk.9 is NATO's the first jet powered Tac Recce aircraft. The Meteor FR.Mk.9 is a single-seat, twin-engine, fighter-reconnaissance aircraft designed and manufactured for the RAF by Gloster Aircraft Co. Ltd. The aircraft is designed for low to medium-altitude, day-only, photographic-reconnaissance missions. The prototype Meteor FR.Mk.9 first flew on 23 March 1950.

A single-seat, armed photographic-reconnaissance aircraft; the Meteor FR.Mk.9 has a blunt nose and a cigar-type fuselage, which tapers sharply as it nears the tail. The single-place cockpit is located just forward of the wing's leading edge and is covered with a moveable single-piece canopy that slides aft for pilot ingress and egress. Additional fuel can be carried on a flush mounted fuel tank under the fuselage centerline position with a capacity of 216 US gal (818 ltr/180 Imp gal). The Meteor FR.Mk.9 retains the four, British Hispano Mk.5, 20 mm cannon in the nose. The retractable, tricycle landing gear has a single-wheel nose gear and one wheel on each main gear. The two non-afterburning Rolls Royce Derwent-8 turbojet engines are housed in wing-mounted nacelles midway between the fuselage and wing tips. The engine intakes and exhaust extend forward and aft of the wing. The wings are low-mounted on the fuselage, with an equal-tapered leading and trailing edges, blunt tips and a tubular pitot sensor on the left wing tip. There is one underwing hardpoint outboard of the engine on each wing for external fuel with a capacity each of 120 US gal (454 ltr/100 Imp gal). The horizontal stabilizer has an unequal backward tapered leading and trailing edge with blunt tips, and is mid-mounted on the unequal backward tapered vertical stabilizer with a rounded tip.

Image 004, Meteor FR.Mk.9, s/n WH791, on display at the Newark Air Museum, UK. Note the flat optical sensor windows on either side of the nose and the circular sensor window in the nose cone. This aircraft was an engine test bed for Rolls Royce. (Photo copyright by Steve Murray)

The nose of the Meteor FR.Mk.9 was extended 9 in (0.2 m) to permit installation of a rotating, remote controlled F.24 camera. The modified nose contour includes one forward-oblique and two side-oblique optically transparent camera windows just forward of the nose-mounted cannon.

Delivery of the production Meteor FR.Mk.9 began in July 1950. Gloster produced a total of 126 Meteor FR.Mk.9s, some of which equipped the following RAF reconnaissance squadrons in support of NATO during the Cold War:

- RAF, No. 2 Squadron (Sq) Meteor FR.Mk.9 1950 - 1956
- RAF, No. 79 Sq Meteor FR.Mk.9 1951 - 1956

While several Meteor fighter variants have survived; are flying, on display, or in storage, only two examples of the Meteor FR.Mk.9 still exist today.

Table 001, Meteor FR.Mk.9 Technical and Performance Specifications)

DIMENSIONS:			
Wing Span:	37 ft 2.0 in	11.33 m	
Length:	44 ft 3.0 in	13.49 m	
Height:	13 ft 10.0 in	4.22 m	
Wheel Track:	10 ft 5.0 in	3.18 m	
Wheel Base:	13 ft 4.0 in	4.06 m	
Wing Area:	350.0 ft^2	32.51 m^2	
POWERPLANT(S):			
Number of Engines / Designation:	Two (2) Rolls Royce Derwent 8 turbojets		
Maximum Power / Thrust per Engine:	3,500 lbs st	1,588 kg st	
FUEL CAPACITY:			
Internal Fuel Capacity:	504 US gal	1,909 ltrs	420 Imp gal
External Fuel Capacity:	456 US gal	1,727 ltrs	380 Imp gal
Total Fuel Capacity:	961 US gal	3,636 ltrs	800 Imp gal
WEIGHTS:			
Empty:	10,790 lbs	4,894 kg	
Maximum Take-Off:	15,700 lbs	7,122 kg	
Maximum Wing Loading:	44.9 lbs/ft^2	219.0 kg/m^2	
PERFORMANCE:			
Max Level Speed at Sea Level:	592 mph	953 kmh	514 kts
Max Level Speed at Altitude:	575 mph @ 20,000 ft	925 kmh @ 6,096 m	499 kts @ 20,000 ft
Nominal Cruising Speed:	414 mph	666 kmh	360 kts
Initial Rate of Climb at Sea Level:	7,000 ft/min	2,134 m/min	
Service Ceiling:	44,000 ft	13,411 m	
Maximum / Ferry Range:	710 mi	1,143 km	617 nm

Data File for the Meteor FR.Mk.9

Meteor PR.Mk.10

Image 005, RAF Meteor PR.Mk.10, s/n WB165, high-altitude, photographic-reconnaissance aircraft assigned to 541 Squadron. Note the absence of the four nose cannon. (Photo copyright by Vic Flintham)

Developed in a parallel with the Meteor FR.Mk.9, Gloster Aircraft Co, LTD produced a single-seat, twin-engine, unarmed photographic-reconnaissance version of the Meteor F.Mk.8 known as the Meteor PR.Mk.10. The Meteor PR.Mk.10 is designed for high-altitude, day-only photographic-reconnaissance missions. The prototype Meteor PR.Mk.10 first flew on 29 March 1950, less than a week after the Meteor FR.Mk.9's first flight.

Similar in appearance to the Meteor FR.Mk.9, the Meteor PR.Mk.10 incorporated the best attributes of a couple different Meteor fighter aircraft marks to improve the handling of the aircraft at high altitude. As a result, the Meteor PR.Mk.10 differed from the armed Meteor FR.Mk.9 in the following areas:

- The Meteor PR.Mk.10 incorporated the longer wing of the Meteor F.Mk.3, which extended the wingspan 5 ft 10 in (1.8 m) and included rounded tips

- The Meteor PR.Mk.10 incorporated the tail assembly of the Meteor F.Mk.4, which provided better handling and control, and also had round tips. In addition the vertical stabilizer extended slightly below the aft fuselage.

- The Meteor PR.Mk.10 retained the reconnaissance nose of Meteor FR.Mk.9, but deleted the four, British Hispano Mk.5, 20 mm cannon in the nose.

- In addition to the nose camera, two F.52 cameras were installed in lower rear fuselage in a split-vertical configuration.

Delivery of the production Meteor PR.Mk.10 began in December 1950. Gloster produced a total of fifty-eight Meteor PR.Mk.10s, some of which equipped the following RAF reconnaissance squadrons in support of NATO during the Cold War:

- RAF, No. 541 Sq — Meteor PR.Mk.10 — 1951 - 1957

There are no known surviving examples of the Meteor PR.Mk.10.

Table 002, Meteor PR.Mk.10 Technical and Performance Specifications

DIMENSIONS:			
Wing Span:	43 ft 0.0 in	13.11 m	
Length:	44 ft 3.0 in	13.49 m	
Height:	13 ft 10.0 in	4.22 m	
Wheel Track:	10 ft 5.0 in	3.18 m	
Wheel Base:	13 ft 4.0 in	4.06 m	
POWERPLANT(S):			
Number of Engines / Designation:	Two (2) Rolls Royce Derwent 8 turbojets		
Maximum Power / Thrust per Engine:	3,500 lbs st	1,588 kg st	
FUEL CAPACITY:			
Internal Fuel Capacity:	504 US gal	1,909 ltrs	420 Imp gal
External Fuel Capacity:	456 US gal	1,727 ltrs	380 Imp gal
Total Fuel Capacity:	961 US gal	3,636 ltrs	800 Imp gal
WEIGHTS:			
Empty:	10,993 lbs	4,986 kg	
PERFORMANCE:			
Max Level Speed at Sea Level:	500 mph	805 kmh	434 kts
Max Level Speed at Altitude:	574 mph @ 10,000 ft	924 kmh @ 3,048 m	498 kts @ 10,000 ft
Initial Rate of Climb at Sea Level:	6,050 ft/min	1,844 m/min	
Service Ceiling:	47,000 ft	14,326 m	
Nominal Combat Radius:	477 mi	768 km	414 nm
Maximum / Ferry Range:	1,090 mi	1,754 km	947 nm

Data File for the Meteor PR.Mk.10

RB-26C/P Invader

Image 006, United States Air Force (USAF) RB-26C Invader, s/n 435581, on training mission. (Photo courtesy of the National Museum of the United States Air Force [NMUSAF])

The oldest and the only piston powered Tac Recce aircraft of the Cold War is the RB-26C Invader, a development of the WW II A-26C Invader light attack bomber. Between 1944 and 1945, 1,091 aircraft were manufactured by Douglas Aircraft Company for the US Army Air Force (USAAF). The photographic-reconnaissance variant was originally designated the FA-26C Invader, and is an unarmed, day and night, photographic-reconnaissance aircraft. In 1948 the USAF changed the designation of these aircraft to the RB-26C Invader.

The RB-26C Invader has cigar-type fuselage, rectangular in shape with a Plexiglas nose, and appears square in shape when viewed head-on. In the photographic-reconnaissance role, the RB-26C Invader carries a crew of three. The pilot and navigator sit side-by-side beneath a two-piece clamshell canopy, and the photographic-reconnaissance officer who sits in the nose of the aircraft. Each side of the canopy is hinged on the outboard side to opens up and out for easy egress in an emergency. The retractable, tricycle landing gear has a single-wheel nose gear and one wheel on each main gear. The main landing gear struts retract up into faired housings, which are an extension of the rotary engine mount fairing and cowling. The main landing gear fairings extend aft of the wing's trailing edge. One Pratt & Whitney R-2800-71 rotary engine is mounted below each wing with a large three bladed propeller. The wings are mid-mounted on the fuselage, have a slight dihedral, and a straight leading edge with a tapered trailing edge. There are four underwing hardpoints outboard of the engine for external stores. The RB-26C Invader has blunt wing tips, which are frequently obscured by tip tanks each with a capacity of 100 US gal (378 ltr/83 Imp gal). The aircraft tail unit consists of an equal-tapered horizontal stabilizer with moderate dihedral, mounted high on the aft fuselage below an unequal forward tapered vertical stabilizer. Both have blunt tips.

The RB-26C Invader differs externally from the B-26C Invader in three ways:

- The reconnaissance version employs the Plexiglas nose common on WW II bomber aircraft but with an optically flat panel just to the right of the bombsite center panel, for a K-38 camera in the forward-oblique position.
- Specially modified bomb bay doors were installed with openings for the camera lenses and photoflash cartridge dispensers. These doors allow the bomb bay doors to remain closed in flight when operating the cameras and photoflash dispensers.
- The upper and lower gun turrets were removed and the openings faired over.

Image 007, Detail of the modified RB-26 bomb bay doors; note the circular cutouts for the camera lenses and the prism shaped sensor lens protruding from the left-side door. In addition, the flash cartridge dispensers are clearly visible through the cutouts at the rear of the bomb bay doors. (Photo courtesy of the NMUSAF)

A special pallet in the bomb bay supports the installation of five cameras and the photoflash cartridge dispensers for night photography. The cameras include one K-17 or KA-2 camera with a 6 in (152 mm) focal length (fl) lens; two F-

477 day or night cameras with a 12 in (305 mm) fl lens in the split-vertical position; and two K-38 or KA-2 cameras with a 12 in (305 mm) fl lens in the vertical position. A seventh camera can be installed in the tail of the aircraft in the vertical position.

In 1960, the French AF converted fifteen RB-26C Invaders to RB-26P Invaders. These aircraft are equipped with six French manufactured cameras. The new camera suite includes one Omera 30 camera; two Omera 31 cameras; and three Sephot-Omera 11 cameras. In addition, the rectangular window on the left hand side of the nose was modified. These aircraft were designated with the letter "P" on the vertical stabilizer. Most French AF RB-26C/P Invaders were assigned to duties in Algeria, Chad and Vietnam.

The RB-26C Invader equipped the following US and NATO reconnaissance units in support of NATO during the Cold War:

- USAF, 1st TRS — RB-26C Invader — 1952 - 1955
- USAF, 30th TRS — RB-26C Invader — 1953 - 1955
- France, ERP 1/32 — RB-26C Invader — 1956 - 1957
- France, GB 2/91 — RB-26C/P Invader — 1962 - 1963

While several examples of the A-26C/B-26C Invader have survived, there is only one known example of the FA-26C/RB-26C Invader.

Table 003, RB-26C Invader Technical and Performance Specifications

DIMENSIONS:				
Wing Span:	71 ft	6.0 in	21.79 m	
Length:	51 ft	7.0 in	15.72 m	
Height:	19 ft	0.0 in	5.79 m	
Wheel Track:	19 ft	5.6 in	5.93 m	
Wheel Base:	13 ft	4.0 in	4.06 m	
Wing Area:	540.0 ft^2		50.16 m^2	
POWERPLANT(S):				
Number of Engines / Designation:	Two (2) Pratt & Whitney R-2800-71 Radial Engines			
Maximum Power / Thrust per Engine:	2,000 lbs st		1,864 kg st	
FUEL CAPACITY:				
Internal Fuel Capacity:	725 US gal		2,744 ltrs	604 Imp gal
External Fuel Capacity:	200 US gal		757 ltrs	167 Imp gal
Total Fuel Capacity:	925 US gal		3,501 ltrs	770 Imp gal
WEIGHTS:				
Maximum Take-Off:	32,000 lbs		14,515 kg	
Maximum Wing Loading:	59.3 lbs/ft^2		289.4 kg/m^2	
PERFORMANCE:				
Max Level Speed at Altitude:	359 mph @ 16,700 ft		578 kmh @ 5,090 m	312 kts @ 16,700 ft
Nominal Cruising Speed:	266 mph		428 kmh	231 kts
Service Ceiling:	28,500 ft		8,687 m	
Nominal Combat Radius:	1,400 mi		2,253 km	1,216 nm
Maximum / Ferry Range:	2,700 mi		4,345 km	2,346 nm

Data File for the RB-26C Invader

RF-80A/C Shooting Star

Image 008, USAF RF-80A Shooting Star, s/n 0-85160, of the Alabama Air National Guard (ANG), with the production nose, which includes the circular window in the nose for the forward-oblique camera. (Photo courtesy of the NMUSAF)

The RF-80A Shooting Star is the first US jet powered photographic-reconnaissance aircraft. Developed in the closing months of World War II, this single-seat, day-only, Tac Recce aircraft is an unarmed variant of the P-80A Shooting Star fighter, designed and manufactured for the USAAF by Lockheed Aircraft Corporation. The prototype RF-80A Shooting Star is a modification of the second YP-80 Shooting Star prototype and was originally designated the XF-14 (reconnaissance-photographic). The XF-14

Shooting Star was destroyed after colliding with another aircraft in flight on the night of 06 December 1944. Following WW II the USAAF changed the designation to FP-80A Shooting Star (reconnaissance-pursuit), and in 1948 the aircraft designation changed one final time to the RF-80A Shooting Star (reconnaissance-fighter).

The RF-80A Shooting Star is similar in appearance to the F-80A Shooting Star fighter aircraft. It is a single-seat, single-engine aircraft with a barrel-type fuselage, which tapers forward and aft. The fuselage houses a single, non-afterburning General Electric J33-GE-11 turbojet engine with the intakes located just forward of the wing roots below the canopy. The single-seat cockpit is covered with a moveable single-piece canopy that slides aft for pilot ingress and egress. The cockpit is located just forward of the wing's leading edge and above the engine intakes. The retractable, tricycle landing gear has a single-wheel nose gear and one wheel on each main gear. The equal-tapered wings are low mounted on the fuselage, have one underwing hardpoint and rounded tips, normally concealed by wing tip tanks each with a capacity of 165 US gal (625ltr/137 Imp gal). The unequal-tapered horizontal stabilizer is mounted high on the fuselage below the equal-tapered vertical stabilizer, both of which have rounded tips. A short tubular pitot sensor is located near the top of the vertical stabilizer.

Image 009, Field modified F-80A Shooting Star demonstrates how the aircraft nose is hinged in front to permit access to the cameras. (Photo courtesy of the NMUSAF)

To accommodate the sensor suite, the six 50-caliber guns in the nose were removed and replaced with four cameras in a modified nose with a new contour. The nose is hinged in front to open up and forward for access to the camera bay. The standard camera configuration for the production aircraft consists of one KA-22A with a 12 in (305 mm) fl lens in the forward-oblique position; and two K-17C cameras with a 6 in (152 mm) fl lens in the side-oblique positions. The side-oblique cameras are mounted one above the other with the right side-oblique camera below the left side-oblique camera. One K-38 camera with a 24 in (610 mm) fl lens in the vertical position is located in the aft camera bay.

Image 010, USAF RF-80A Shooting Star with the contoured nose of the RF-80C Shooting Star (Photo courtesy of the NMUSAF)

The first production RF-80A Shooting Star was delivered by Lockheed to the USAAF on 01 July 1946. Production of the RF-80A Shooting Star was supplemented in 1951 with the conversion of seventy Korean based F-80A Shooting Star fighters, upgraded to F-80C Shooting Star standards, then modified as RF-80C Shooting Star reconnaissance aircraft with improved camera mounts and a more contoured aircraft nose. Only the RF-80A Shooting Star variant was deployed to United States Air Force Europe (USAFE) based Tac Recce units during the Cold War.

The RF-80A Shooting Star equipped the following USAFE based Tac Recce squadrons in support of NATO during the Cold War:

- USAF, 32nd TRS   RF-80A Shooting Star   1952 - 1956

- USAF, 38th TRS RF-80A Shooting Star 1952 - 1956
- USAF, 302nd TRS RF-80A Shooting Star 1953 - 1958
- USAF, 303rd TRS RF-80A Shooting Star 1953 - 1958

The only known surviving RF-80A Shooting Star was on display at Bergstrom AFB, Austin, TX, US until the base closed in the early 1990s. The status of this aircraft is currently unknown.

Table 004, RF-80A Shooting Star Technical and Performance Specifications

DIMENSIONS:			
Wing Span:	38 ft 10.5 in	11.85 m	
Length:	34 ft 6.0 in	10.52 m	
Height:	11 ft 4.0 in	3.45 m	
Wing Area:	234.8 ft^2	21.81 m^2	
POWERPLANT(S):			
Number of Engines / Designation:	One (1) General Electric J33-GE-11 Turbojet		
Maximum Power / Thrust per Engine:	3,850 lbs st	1,746 kg st	
FUEL CAPACITY:			
Internal Fuel Capacity:	481 US gal	1,821 ltrs	401 Imp gal
External Fuel Capacity:	330 US gal	1,249 ltrs	275 Imp gal
Total Fuel Capacity:	811 US gal	3,070 ltrs	675 Imp gal
WEIGHTS:			
Empty:	7,920 lbs	3,593 kg	
Maximum Take-Off:	14,500 lbs	6,577 kg	
Maximum Wing Loading:	61.8 lbs/ft^2	301.5 kg/m^2	
PERFORMANCE:			
Max Level Speed at Sea Level:	558 mph	898 kmh	485 kts
Max Level Speed at Altitude:	508 mph @ 30,000 ft	818 kmh @ 9,144 m	441 kts @ 30,000 ft
Nominal Cruising Speed:	410 mph	660 kmh	356 kts
Initial Rate of Climb at Sea Level:	4,850 ft/min	1,478 m/min	
Service Ceiling:	45,000 ft	13,716 m	
Nominal Combat Radius:	540 mi	869 km	469 nm
Maximum / Ferry Range:	1,440 mi	2,317 km	1,251 nm

Data File for the RF-80A Shooting Star

Canberra PR.Mk.3/7

Image 011, RAF Canberra PR.Mk.7, s/n WH775, over Central Europe. The Star on the vertical stabilizer identifies the aircraft as belonging to No. 31 Squadron, stationed at RAF Base (RAFB) Laarbruch, West Germany. (Paul Wagner Collection)

For more than half a century the RAF's fleet, of twin-engine, unarmed Canberra photographic-reconnaissance aircraft have provided high-altitude, day reconnaissance support to NATO. The first Canberra reconnaissance variant, known as the Canberra PR.Mk.3 is based on the Canberra B.Mk.2 bomber. Designed and manufactured for the RAF by the English Electric Company, Ltd., the first prototype Canberra PR.Mk.3 (s/n XV181) flew on 19 March 1950.

The Canberra PR.Mk.3 has a long tubular cigar-type fuselage with a Plexiglas nose and a crew of two (pilot and navigator). Crew ingress and egress is through a small door on the right side of the fuselage directly below the canopy. The pilot is seated on the left side of a large circular bubble canopy located forward of the wing's leading edge. The canopy does not open, but in an emergency, explosive bolts jettison the canopy so the pilot can eject. The navigator is located forward and below the pilot in the prone position on a couch directly behind a clear Plexiglas nose. The retractable, tricycle landing gear has a twin-wheel nose gear and one wheel on each main gear. The Canberra PR.Mk.3 is a twin-engine aircraft, powered by two, non-afterburning Rolls Royce Avion 101 axial-flow turbojet engines, housed in wing-mounted nacelles on the inboard third of each wing. The engine intakes and exhaust extend forward and aft of the wing. The wings are mid-mounted on the fuselage with no taper between the fuselage and engine nacelles, and are equal-tapered outboard of the engine. The wings have 2° dihedral on the inboard section; 4° 21' dihedral outboard of the engine nacelles; and blunt tips. The horizontal stabilizer is mounted high on the aft fuselage with a tapered leading edge, straight trailing edge, 7° 57' dihedral, and rounded tips. The vertical stabilizer has an unequal forward taper with a blunt tip. External fuel can be carried in two tip tanks each with a capacity of 146 US gal (553 ltr/122 Imp gal).

The fuselage of the Canberra PR.Mk.3 was extended 1 ft 2 in (0.36 m) forward of the wings leading edge, and two large optically transparent windows for the cameras are installed on both sides of the lower fuselage forward of the engine intakes. The forward bomb bay is modified to increase the internal fuel capacity to 2,302 US gal (8,710 ltr/1,917 Imp gal) and the aft bomb bay is modified to carry cameras and photoflash bombs for night photography.

English Electric delivered two prototype and thirty-four production Canberra PR.Mk.3 aircraft, with the first production aircraft delivered in December 1952. The second photographic-reconnaissance variant is the Canberra PR.Mk.7 based on the Canberra B.Mk.6 aircraft. The first Canberra PR.Mk.7 (s/n WH774) flew on 28 October 1953 and deliveries began later that same year. The Canberra PR.Mk.7 has the more powerful Rolls Royce Avion 109 turbojet axial-flow engines and the internal fuel capacity was increased to 3,383 US gal (12,804 ltr/2,817 Imp gal).

The only external difference in the appearance of the Canberra PR.Mk.3 and the PR.Mk.7 is that the shock cone in the center of the engine intake for the Canberra PR.Mk.7 is significantly larger than the shock cone in the center of the engine intake for the Canberra PR.Mk.3. English Electric delivered a total of seventy-four Canberra PR.Mk.7 aircraft.

Image 012, RAF Canberra PR.Mk.7, s/n WT538, at RAFB Wyton, UK on 15 July 1984. Note the plexiglas nose, circular canopy and two camera windows on the lower fuselage. The long shock cone in the engine nacelle identifies this aircraft as Mk.7 variant. (Photo copyright by Ian Powell)

The sensor mix for the Canberra PR.Mk.3/7 aircraft includes up to seven cameras. The standard camera configuration for the main camera bay in the forward fuselage consist of up to three F.95 optical cameras mounted in the left and right side-oblique positions, and one Infrared Linescan (IRLS) sensor. Four additional cameras are installed in the aft fuselage behind the bomb bay. The aft sensor mix varies but normally includes one F.96 wide angle, long fl camera in the left oblique position; two F.96 cameras with a long fl lens in the split-vertical position; or one camera in the vertical position with a short fl lens.

In addition to the Canberra PR.Mk.3/7 aircraft, the West German AF operated three Canberra B.Mk.2 bombers, modified with cameras in the bomb bay that were used for unspecified tasks by the West German AF, Military Survey Department. In addition, The RAF's No. 1 Sq operated Canberra PR.7s in the target tug and training at RAF West Raynham role from 1972 until it was disbanded in 1991.

The following RAF reconnaissance squadrons operated the Canberra PR.Mk.3/7 aircraft in support of NATO during the Cold War:

- RAF, No.540 Sq — Canberra PR.Mk.3/7 — 1952 - 1956
- RAF, No.82 Sq — Canberra PR.Mk.3/7 — 1953 - 1956

- RAF, No.58 Sq Canberra PR.Mk.3/7 1953 - 1962
- RAF, No.69 Sq Canberra PR.Mk.3 1954 - 1958
- RAF, No.542 Sq Canberra PR.Mk.7 1954 - 1958
- RAF, No.80 Sq Canberra PR.Mk.7 1955 - 1969
- RAF, No.31 Sq Canberra PR.Mk.7 1955 - 1971
- RAF, No.527 Sq Canberra PR.Mk.7 1956 - 1956
- RAF, No.17 Sq Canberra PR.Mk.7 1956 - 1959
- RAF, No.13 Sq Canberra PR.Mk.7 1957 - 1982
- RAF, No.39 Sq Canberra PR.Mk.3/7 1957 - 1982
- RAF, No.81 Sq Canberra PR.Mk.7 1958 - 1970

There are several Canberra PR.Mk.3/7 nose, cockpit and tail sections displayed throughout GB, however, only half a dozen complete Canberra PR.Mk.3/7 aircraft are believed to survived.

Table 005, Canberra PR.Mk.7 Technical and Performance Specifications

DIMENSIONS:			
Wing Span:	63 ft 11.5 in	19.49 m	
Length:	66 ft 8.0 in	20.32 m	
Height:	15 ft 7.0 in	4.75 m	
Wheel Track:	15 ft 5.0 in	4.70 m	
Wing Area:	960.0 ft²	89.18 m²	
POWERPLANT(S):			
Number of Engines / Designation:	Two (2) Rolls Royce Avion 109 axial flow turbojets		
Maximum Power / Thrust per Engine:	7,400 lbs st	3,357 kg st	
FUEL CAPACITY:			
Internal Fuel Capacity:	3,383 US gal	12,804 ltrs	2,817 Imp gal
External Fuel Capacity:	293 US gal	1,109 ltrs	244 Imp gal
Total Fuel Capacity:	3,676 US gal	13,913 ltrs	3,061 Imp gal
WEIGHTS:			
Maximum Take-Off:	44,500 lbs	20,185 kg	
Maximum Wing Loading:	46.4 lbs/ft²	226.3 kg/m²	
PERFORMANCE:			
Max Level Speed at Altitude:	570 mph @ 40,000 ft	917 kmh @ 12,192 m	495 kts @ 40,000 ft
Service Ceiling:	48,000 ft	14,630 m	
Maximum / Ferry Range:	2,656 mi	4,274 km	2,308 nm

Data File for the Canberra PR.Mk.7

RB-45C Tornado

Image 013, Rare shot of a USAF RB-45C Tornado, s/n 8038. This particular aircraft was photographed in Korea in the early 1950's. (Photo copyright by Jimmy Lescalle)

One of the most unlikely aircraft to be assigned to a Tac Recce unit was the RB-45C Tornado. Derived from the B-45 Tornado, he RB-45C Tornado is the USAF's first jet bomber to be converted to conduct high-altitude, long-range photographic, day and night reconnaissance missions. Designed and manufactured for the USAF by North American Aviation, Inc, the XB-45 Tornado made its maiden flight on 17 March 1947, and the prototype RB-45C Tornado made its first flight in April 1950.

The RB-45C Tornado has a thick cigar-type fuselage with a solid nose. The aircraft carries a crew of four to include; a pilot and co-pilot in tandem cockpit with a non-opening teardrop-shaped greenhouse canopy located just forward of the wings leading edge; a radar navigator in the nose and a gunner in a small non-opening greenhouse canopy in the aircraft's tail. Crew ingress and egress is through a door on the lower left side of the fuselage just forward of the nose wheel. Only the pilot and co-pilot have ejection seats. In an emergency, the radar navigator exited the aircraft using the side door and the tail gunner used a side hatch near the tail of the aircraft. The RB-45C Tornado is equipped with an in-flight refueling receptacle (IFR) located behind the tandem cockpit. The retractable, tricycle landing gear has a twin-wheel nose gear and one wheel on each main gear. Power is provided by four, non-afterburning General Electric J-47-GE-13 turbojet engines, mounted horizontally in pairs in large rectangular nacelles on the inboard third of each wing. The engine nacelles extend well forward of the wing's leading edge and the exhaust nozzles extend just aft of the wing's trailing edge. The unequal-tapered wings are shoulder-mounted on the fuselage with large fuel tanks on each wing with a capacity each of 1,200 US gal (4,542 ltr/999 Imp gal) of external fuel. The unequal-tapered horizontal stabilizer has moderate dihedral and is low-mounted on the unequal-tapered vertical stabilizer. The horizontal and vertical stabilizers have blunt tips. Twin M-7, 50-caliber machine guns are located below and behind the tail gunner's position just aft of the aircraft's tail section.

Image 014, USAF RB-45C Tornado with the camera window above the radome for the forward-oblique camera (Photo courtesy of Air Systems Command Historical Office [ASCHO])

The RB-45C Tornado carries a total of twelve cameras, eleven of which are installed in the rear fuselage; four cameras in the vertical position; four cameras in the split-vertical position, and three K-17C cameras in a trimetrogon configuration mounted on a pallet behind the wings trailing edge. In addition, one camera is installed in the forward-oblique position in a modified nose above a large flat radome. The bomb bay is modified to hold additional fuel tanks and to carry twenty-five M-122 photoflash bombs for night photographic missions.

A total of thirty-three RB-45C Tornado reconnaissance aircraft were built, with the first aircraft being delivered to the USAF in June 1950. All RB-45C Tornados were initially assigned to SAC for high-altitude, deep-penetration missions. All RB-45C Tornado aircraft were transferred to other commands, including the Pacific Air Force (PACAF) for service in Korea, Tactical Air Command (TAC) and USAFE by the end of 1953.

In Britain selected RAF crews were trained to fly and operate the RB-45C Tornado and successfully conducted high-altitude reconnaissance flights over the Soviet Union and eastern European countries using RB-45C Tornados of the 19th TRS in RAF markings.

The RB-45C Tornado equipped the following USAFE based Tac Recce squadron in support of NATO during the Cold War:

- USAF, 19th TRS — RB-45C Tornado — 1953 - 1957

The only known surviving RB-45C Tornado is s/n 48-17 on display at the Strategic Air and Space Museum, Mahoney State Park, Omaha, NE, US.

Table 006, RB-45C Tornado Technical and Performance Specifications

DIMENSIONS:				
Wing Span:	89 ft	0.0 in	27.13 m	
Wing Span (over Tanks / Missiles):	96 ft	0.0 in	29.26 m	
Length:	75 ft	11.0 in	23.14 m	
Height:	25 ft	2.0 in	7.67 m	
Wing Area:	1175.0 ft^2		109.15 m^2	
POWERPLANT(S):				
Number of Engines / Designation:	Two	General Electric J47-GE-13		
Maximum Power / Thrust per Engine:	5,820 lbs st		2,640 kg st	
Number of Engines / Designation:	Two	General Electric J47-GE-15		
Maximum Power / Thrust per Engine:	6,000 lbs st		2,722 kg st	
FUEL CAPACITY:				
Internal Fuel Capacity:	7,008 US gal		26,525 ltrs	5,836 Imp gal
External Fuel Capacity:	1,125 US gal		4,258 ltrs	937 Imp gal
Total Fuel Capacity:	8,133 US gal		30,783 ltrs	6,772 Imp gal
WEIGHTS:				
Empty:	49,984 lbs		22,673 kg	
Maximum Take-Off:	112,952 lbs		51,235 kg	
Maximum Wing Loading:	96.1 lbs/ft^2		469.4 kg/m^2	
PERFORMANCE:				
Max Level Speed at Sea Level:	579 mph		932 kmh	503 kts
Max Level Speed at Altitude:	570 mph @ 4,000 ft		917 kmh @ 1,219 m	495 kts @ 4,000 ft
Nominal Cruising Speed:	506 mph		814 kmh	439 kts
Initial Rate of Climb at Sea Level:	4,340 ft/min		1,323 m/min	
Service Ceiling:	43,200 ft		13,167 m	
Nominal Combat Radius:	1,008 mi		1,622 km	876 nm
Maximum / Ferry Range:	2,426 mi		3,904 km	2,108 nm
T-O Run to 50 feet:	8,070 ft		2,460 m	

Data File for the RB-45C Tornado

SaabS29C Tunnan

Image 015, Swedish AF Saab S29C Tunnan, s/n 29974, preserved at the Västerås Flygmuseum, Västerås AB, Sweden on 08 November 2003. Note the sharp creased contour of the lower forward fuselage, which is a characteristic of the reconnaissance configuration and the circular camera window on the side of the fuselage below the cockpit. (Photo copyright by Jan Lidestrand)

The first non-aligned Western European nation to introduce a jet powered photographic-reconnaissance aircraft was Sweden. The Saab S29C Tunnan or "Flying Barrel" is the single-seat, unarmed, photographic-reconnaissance variant of the Saab J29 Tunnan fighter aircraft designed and manufactured by Saab (Saab Aktiebolag). The primary mission for the Saab J29 is day and night photographic-reconnaissance of tactical targets. The initial flight of the Saab S29C Tunnan was conducted on 03 June 1953. On 23 March 1955, a pair of Saab S29Cs Tunnan established a new world speed record of 559.6 mph (900.6 km/h/486 kts) for a 621.4 mi (1,000 km/539.9 nm) closed circuit course.

The Saab S29C Tunnan got its name from its "barrel shaped" stovepipe-type fuselage. The fuselage houses a single, afterburning De Havilland Ghost 50 turbojet engine. The single-seat cockpit is located just forward of the wing's leading edge and covered with a moveable single-piece canopy that slides aft for pilot ingress and egress. The retractable, tricycle landing gear has a single-wheel nose gear and one wheel on each main gear. The shoulder-mounted wings are sweptback at an angle of 25°, have rounded tips and a single saw tooth leading edge. There are two underwing hard points and one stall fence on each wing. External fuel is carried in two wing-mounted fuel tanks, each with a capacity of 119 US gal (450 ltr/99 Imp gal). A tubular pitot sensor is mounted on both the left and right wing tips. The horizontal stabilizer is mounted low on the vertical stabilizer, has a tapered leading edge and straight trailing edge with a rounded tip. The vertical stabilizer has a tapered leading edge and straight trailing edge with a blunt tip. The entire tail assembly is mounted above and behind the engine exhaust nozzle.

To accommodate the cameras the internal guns were removed and the lower front fuselage was enlarged and appears near flat on the bottom with square corners and flat sides. The Saab S29C Tunnan carries up to six cameras. Shutters cover the forward-oblique and vertical camera windows, with the two forward shutters opening down and forward. There are two forward-oblique cameras, one on each side of the lower fuselage. One uses panchromatic film and the other black and white Infrared (IR) film. This configuration provides simultaneous multi-sensor images of the target, aiding in the ability to detect camouflaged and concealed targets. In addition, the use of the black and white IR film extends the useful range of the sensor when imaging in hazy weather and low-light conditions. The standard sensor configuration includes four SKa 10 cameras with a 26.2 in (920 mm) fl lens (two vertical and two forward-oblique); one wide-angle SKa 15 (Williamson F.49 Mk.2) camera with a 5.9 in (150 mm) fl lens for mapping; and one SKa 5 camera with a 9.8 in (250 mm) fl lens in the vertical position. Upgrades to the Saab S29C Tunnan include an optical camera sight and modification of the camera mounts to permit the installation of the cameras in the side-oblique position.

Saab produced a total of seventy-six Saab S29C Tunnans, which equipped the following Swedish AF reconnaissance squadrons during the Cold War:

- Swedish AF, F11 Wing Saab S29C Tunnan 1953 - 1964
- Swedish AF, F21 Wing Saab S29C Tunnan 1954 - 1966

There are at least six surviving examples of the Saab S29C Tunnan on display or in storage in Sweden.

Table 007, Saab S29C Tunnan Technical and Performance Specifications

DIMENSIONS:			
Wing Span:	36 ft 1.0 in	11.00 m	
Length:	33 ft 7.0 in	10.24 m	
Height:	12 ft 4.0 in	3.76 m	
Wheel Track:	7 ft 2.0 in	2.18 m	
Wing Area:	258.0 ft²	23.97 m²	
POWERPLANT(S):			
Number of Engines / Designation:	One (1) De Havilland Ghost 50 turbojet		
Maximum Power / Thrust per Engine:	5,005 lbs st	2,270 kg st	
FUEL CAPACITY:			
Internal Fuel Capacity:	568 US gal	2,150 ltrs	473 Imp gal
External Fuel Capacity:	238 US gal	900 ltrs	198 Imp gal
Total Fuel Capacity:	806 US gal	3,050 ltrs	671 Imp gal
WEIGHTS:			
Empty:	10,362 lbs	4,700 kg	
Maximum Take-Off:	17,637 lbs	8,000 kg	
Maximum Wing Loading:	68.4 lbs/ft²	333.8 kg/m²	
PERFORMANCE:			
Max Level Speed at Altitude:	643 mph	1,035 kmh	558 kts
Nominal Cruising Speed:	497 mph	800 kmh	432 kts
Initial Rate of Climb at Sea Level:	7,875 ft/min	2,400 m/min	
Service Ceiling:	44,949 ft	13,700 m	
Maximum / Ferry Range:	932 mi	1,500 km	810 nm

Data File for the Saab J29C Tunnan

RF-84F Thunderflash

Image 016, USAF RF-84F Thunderflash, s/n 0-37554, clearly displays the extended reconnaissance nose with the multiple camera windows for forward-oblique and side-oblique cameras. The manner in which the canopy opens up and back for pilot ingress and egress is unique to the RF-84F Thunderflash. (Photo courtesy of the NMUSAF)

More NATO air forces operated the RF-84F Thunderflash than any other Tac Recce aircraft during the Cold War. Designed and manufactured for the USAF by the Republic Aviation Corporation, the RF-84F Thunderflash is the single-seat, day and night photographic-reconnaissance variant of the F-84F Thunderstreak fighter-bomber. The first pre-production YRF-84F Thunderflash was completed and flown in February 1952.

The RF-84F Thunderflash differs significantly from the F-84F Thunderstreak fighter-bomber. It has a barrel-type fuselage, which houses a single, afterburning Wright J65-W-7 Sapphire turbojet engine. The single-place cockpit is located above the engine intakes and has a modified single-piece clamshell canopy hinged aft, that lifts up and back for pilot ingress and egress. The retractable, tricycle landing gear has a single-wheel nose gear and one wheel on each main gear. The mid-mounted wings are sweptback at an angle of 40º, with 1° 30' anhedral and blunt tips. External fuel is carried in two wing-mounted fuel tanks, each with a capacity of 450 US gal (1,703 ltr/375 Imp gal). There are two stall fences on each wing and a pitot sensor on the left wing tip. The triangular shaped engine intakes are located in the wing roots. The tail assembly includes a one-piece, all moving horizontal stabilator, which is swept back and low-mounted on a swept back vertical stabilizer. Both the horizontal and vertical stabilizers have blunt tips.

To accommodate the sensor suite, the original F-84F Thunderstreak nose underwent a significant redesign. The stovepipe engine air intake was deleted and the engine intakes were moved to the wing roots. The six nose mounted 0.50-in (12.7 mm) machine guns were deleted.

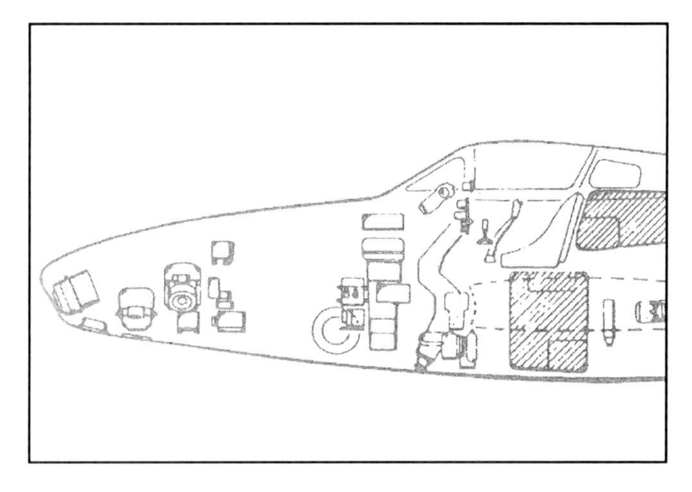

Figure 002, The RF-84F Thunderflash camera configuration includes oblique and vertical cameras. In addition, an optical periscope extended from the cockpit to the lower fuselage aft of the nose wheel well. (Courtesy of the NMUSAF)

The RF-84F Thunderflash nose was redesigned and extended 4 ft 2 in (1.27 m) to support the installation of up to six cameras. The standard camera configuration for low-level, day photographic-reconnaissance missions includes a K-22A camera with a 6 in (152 mm) fl lens in the forward-oblique position; three K-17C cameras with a 6 in (152 mm) fl lens in the trimetrogon configuration; and one (1) K-22A camera with a 12" (305 mm) fl lens or 24 in (610 mm) fl lens in the high-altitude left side-oblique position. For high-altitude day reconnaissance missions a K-38 camera with either a 24 in (610 mm) fl lens or a 36 in (914 mm) fl lens was installed in the vertical position directly behind the nose wheel well.

Image 017, Lower left side of the RF-84F Thunderflash at Bergstrom AFB, Austin, TX in 1986. The forward-oblique, vertical and three left side-oblique camera windows are all visible. (Paul Wagner Collection)

The RF-84F Thunderflash conducts low-altitude, night photographic-reconnaissance missions using a K-37 camera with a 12 in (305 mm) fl lens installed in the vertical position behind the nose wheel well and photoflash cartridges/flares for illumination. The RF-84F Thunderflash can carry up to 208 Type M-112 or 160 Type M-123 flares. Two panels on the top of the fuselage nose are hinged at the front for easy access to the cameras and film magazines.

To assist the pilot in locating the targets to be photographed, the RF-84F Thunderflash is equipped with an optical viewfinder. The window for the viewfinder is located below the cockpit, directly behind the high-altitude vertical camera position. The RF-84F Thunderflash initially retained four 0.50-in (12.7 mm) machine guns, which were relocated to the outer walls of the wing mounted engine intakes. The machine guns were not for defensive purposes, but intended to mark targets on pathfinder missions, but were eventually deleted.

A total of 715 RF-84F Thunderflash aircraft were manufactured between 1951 and 1958, and equipped following USAFE Tac Recce squadrons, and NATO air force reconnaissance units in support of NATO during the Cold War:

- Greek AF, 10 Wing, 348 Mira RF-84F Thunderflash 1953 - 1991
- USAF, 302nd TRS RF-84F Thunderflash 1954 - 1954
- USAF, 303rd TRS RF-84F Thunderflash 1954 - 1954
- USAF, 18th TRS RF-84F Thunderflash 1954 - 1957
- USAF, 17th TRS RF-84F Thunderflash 1954 - 1958
- USAF, 32nd TRS RF-84F Thunderflash 1954 - 1958
- Royal Netherlands AF, 306 Sq RF-84F Thunderflash 1954 - 1963
- USAF, 38th TRS RF-84F Thunderflash 1955 - 1958
- Belgium AF, 2nd Wing, 42 Esc RF-84F Thunderflash 1955 - 1971
- Italian AF, 3° Stormo, 18° Gruppo RF-84F Thunderflash 1955 - 1973
- Italian AF, 3° Stormo, 28° Gruppo RF-84F Thunderflash 1955 - 1973
- Italian AF, 3° Stormo, 132° Gruppo RF-84F Thunderflash 1955 - 1973
- French AF, ER33, 1/33 "Belfort" RF-84F Thunderflash 1956 - 1966
- French AF, ER33, 2/33 "Savoie" RF-84F Thunderflash 1956 - 1966
- French AF, ER33, 3/33 "Moselle" RF-84F Thunderflash 1956 - 1966
- Royal Norwegian AF, 717 Sq RF-84F Thunderflash 1956 - 1970
- Turkish AF, 183 Filo RF-84F Thunderflash 1956 - 1976
- Turkish AF, 112 Filo RF-84F Thunderflash 1956 - 1980
- Royal Danish AF, 729 Esk RF-84F Thunderflash 1957 - 1971
- West German AF, AKG 51 RF-84F Thunderflash 1958 - 1965

- West German AF, AKG 52 RF-84F Thunderflash 1959 - 1964
- Belgium AF, 2nd Wing, 1 Esc RF-84F Thunderflash 1971 - 1972

More than seventy RF-84F Thunderflash aircraft have survived and are on display, being restored or are in storage at locations in the Europe and the United States:

Table 008, RF-84F Thunderflash Technical and Performance Specifications

DIMENSIONS:			
Wing Span:	33 ft 6.0 in	10.21 m	
Length:	47 ft 6.0 in	14.48 m	
Height:	15 ft 0.0 in	4.57 m	
Wheel Base:	20 ft 4.8 in	6.22 m	
Wing Area:	325.0 ft^2	30.19 m^2	
POWERPLANT(S):			
Number of Engines / Designation:	One (1) Wright J65-W-7 Sapphire turbojet		
Maximum Power / Thrust per Engine:	7,800 lbs st	3,538 kg st	
FUEL CAPACITY:			
Internal Fuel Capacity:	575 US gal	2,176 ltrs	479 Imp gal
External Fuel Capacity:	920 US gal	3,482 ltrs	766 Imp gal
Total Fuel Capacity:	1,495 US gal	5,659 ltrs	1,245 Imp gal
WEIGHTS:			
Empty:	14,014 lbs	6,357 kg	
Maximum Take-Off:	25,900 lbs	11,748 kg	
Maximum Wing Loading:	79.7 lbs/ft^2	389.1 kg/m^2	
PERFORMANCE:			
Max Level Speed at Sea Level:	679 mph	1,093 kmh	590 kts
Max Level Speed at Altitude:	630 mph @ 5,000 ft	1,014 kmh @ 1,524 m	547 kts @ 5,000 ft
Nominal Cruising Speed:	542 mph	873 kmh	471 kts
Initial Rate of Climb at Sea Level:	5,820 ft/min	1,774 m/min	
Service Ceiling:	41,300 ft	12,588 m	
Nominal Combat Radius:	840 mi	1,352 km	730 nm
Maximum / Ferry Range:	1,801 mi	2,898 km	1,565 nm

Data File for the RF-84F Thunderflash

RT-33A Shooting Star

Image 018, Portuguese AF RT-33A Shooting Star on display on the 52nd anniversary of the Portuguese AF, at the Pole Air Museum, Sintra AB, PT in July 2004. (Photo copyright by Jorge M.A. Ruivo)

The RT-33A Shooting Star is the single-seat, unarmed, day-only, photographic-reconnaissance variant of the two-seat T-33A Shooting Star trainer, designed and manufactured by Lockheed Aircraft Corporation. Designed and manufactured for export under the Military Assistance Program (MAP), the prototype T-33A Shooting Star flew for the first time on 22 March 1948.

Like the RF-80A Shooting Star, the RT-33 shooting star has a barrel-type fuselage, which tapers forward and aft. The fuselage houses a single non-afterburning Allison J33-A-35 turbojet engine with intakes located just forward of the wing roots, below the canopy. The aircraft retains the tandem two-seat cockpit of the trainer aircraft, but replaces the instructor pilot position in the rear cockpit with radio electronics and an additional fuselage fuel tank, increasing the internal fuel load to 518 US gal (1961 ltr/431 Imp gal). The single-place cockpit is located above the engine intakes, has a one-piece clamshell canopy hinged aft for pilot ingress and egress, and is supported by a brace on the left side of the canopy immediately behind the pilot's seat, when parked with the canopy open. The retractable, tricycle landing gear has a single-wheel nose gear and one wheel on each main gear. The equal-tapered wings are low mounted on the fuselage, has one underwing hardpoint and rounded tips, which are normally concealed by wing tip tanks with a capacity each of 230 US gal (870 ltr/191 Imp gal) of external fuel. The unequal-tapered horizontal stabilizer is mounted high on the fuselage below the equal-tapered vertical stabilizer. Both the horizontal and vertical stabilizers have rounded tips.

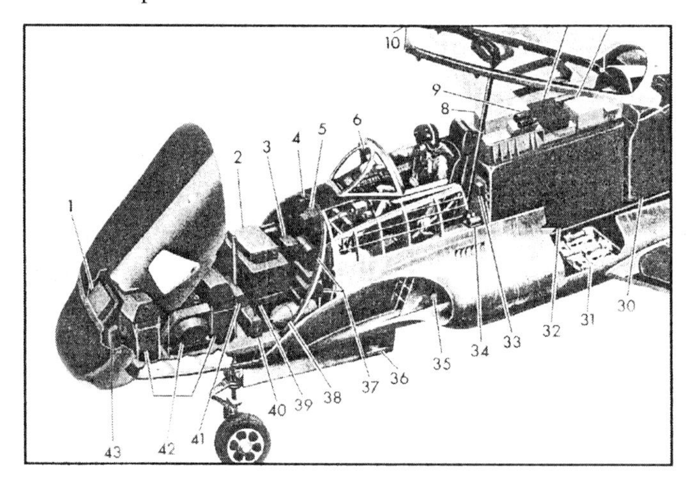

Figure 003, Sensor configuration for the RT-33 Shooting Star. Note the four cameras (annotation 42), hinged nose, large canopy and the radio electronics (annotations 8, 9, 11 and 12). (Courtesy of the NMUSAF)

The RT-33A Shooting Star is a hybrid aircraft, combining the T-33 Shooting Star airframe and the RF-80C Shooting Star nose. The twin 50-caliber machine guns in the nose were removed and replaced with four cameras in a modified nose with a new contour. The nose is hinged in front to open up and forward for access to the cameras and film magazines. The standard camera configuration for the production aircraft consists of one KA-22A with a 12 in (305 mm) fl lens in the forward-oblique position; and two K-17C cameras with a 6 in (152 mm) fl lens in the side-oblique positions.

The side-oblique cameras are mounted one above the other with the right side-oblique camera below the left side-oblique camera. One K-38 camera with a 24 in (610 mm) fl lens in the vertical position is located in the aft camera bay.

Image 019, RT-33A Shooting Star on display at Military Honor Park, Michiana Regional Airport, South Bend, IN, in September 2003. The aircraft is incorrectly painted in US national markings. (Paul Wagner Collection)

A total of ninety-five RT-33A Shooting Stars were produced and equipped the following NATO air forces reconnaissance squadrons during the Cold War:

- Belgium AF (training) RT-33A Shooting Star 1953 - 1956
- Italian AF, 36° Stormo, 636a Gruppo RT-33A Shooting Star 1953 - 1983
- Italian AF, 51° Stormo, 651a Gruppo RT-33A Shooting Star 1953 - 1983
- Turkish AF (training) RT-33A Shooting Star 1953 - 1995
- French AF (training) RT-33A Shooting Star 1955 - 1959
- Royal Netherlands AF (training) RT-33A Shooting Star 1956 - 1971
- Portuguese AF (training) RT-33A Shooting Star 1960 - 1982

At least twelve RT-33A Shooting Stars are believed to have survived. As these aircraft were built for export under the MAP, only one is available in the United States.

Table 009, RT-33A Shooting Star Technical and Performance Specifications

DIMENSIONS:			
Wing Span:	38 ft 10.5 in	11.85 m	
Length:	37 ft 8.0 in	11.48 m	
Height:	11 ft 8.0 in	3.56 m	
Wing Area:	234.8 ft²	21.81 m²	
POWERPLANT(S):			
Number of Engines / Designation:	One (1) Allison J33-A-35 turbojet		
Maximum Power / Thrust per Engine:	4,600 lbs st	2,087 kg st	
FUEL CAPACITY:			
Internal Fuel Capacity:	518 US gal	1,961 ltrs	431 Imp gal
External Fuel Capacity:	460 US gal	1,741 ltrs	383 Imp gal
Total Fuel Capacity:	978 US gal	3,702 ltrs	814 Imp gal
WEIGHTS:			
Empty:	8,365 lbs	3,794 kg	
Maximum Take-Off:	15,061 lbs	6,832 kg	
Maximum Wing Loading:	64.1 lbs/ft²	313.2 kg/m²	
PERFORMANCE:			
Max Level Speed at Sea Level:	600 mph	966 kmh	521 kts
Max Level Speed at Altitude:	543 mph @ 25,000 ft	874 kmh @ 7,620 m	472 kts @ 25,000 ft
Nominal Cruising Speed:	455 mph	732 kmh	395 kts
Initial Rate of Climb at Sea Level:	4,870 ft/min	1,484 m/min	
Service Ceiling:	48,000 ft	14,630 m	
Maximum / Ferry Range:	1,275 mi	2,052 km	1,108 nm

Data File for the RT-33A Shooting Star

RB-57A Canberra

Image 020, USAF RB-57A Canberra, s/n 21426, in the gloss black finish for night photographic-reconnaissance missions. (Photo courtesy of the NMUSAF)

Built under license by the Glenn L. Martin Company, the RB-57A Canberra is designed to conduct high and low-altitude, day and night-photographic-reconnaissance missions. The USAF equivalent of the RAF's Canberra PR.Mk.3, the RB-57A Canberra incorporated all the changes included in the license built B-57A Canberra tactical bomber. The RB-57A Canberra flew for the first time in October 1953 and delivery to the 345th Light Bomb Wing, for aircrew transition training began in 1954. The first reconnaissance unit to achieve initial operational capability (IOC) was the 363rd TRW, Shaw AFB, SC in July 1954.

With minor exceptions, the RB-57A Canberra is identical in appearance to the RAF's Canberra PR.Mk.3 described in Chapter 5. The most noticeable external difference, is the presence of a large tubular pitot sensor located on the left wing tip of the RB-57A Canberra.

Most USAF RB-57A Canberra aircraft had a glossy black finish for night reconnaissance operations. However, unlike the RAF Canberras, the USAF RB-57A Canberras had a brief career. The aircraft suffered several accidents and fatalities, some of which were attributed to trim control problems. As a result, the RB-57A Canberra fleet experienced several groundings and eventually was restricted from conducting reconnaissance operations below 3000 ft (914 m). The higher than normal accident rate and the low-level flight restrictions were contributing factors in the decision to replace the RB-57A Canberra with the RB-66B Destroyer

For the photographic-reconnaissance mission, the bomb bay of the RB-57A Canberra was modified to accommodate a suite of cameras, which could be reconfigured based on the mission profile. These included three P-2 framing cameras with a 3 in (76 mm) fl lenses in the forward-oblique, and left and right side-oblique positions; two K-37 or K-38 framing cameras in the split-vertical position in the rear fuselage with either a 12 in, 24 in or 36 in (305 mm, 610 mm or 914 mm) fl lens; and a T-11 mapping camera in the vertical position with a 6 in (152 mm) fl lens.

In August 1952, the USAF ordered sixty-seven RB-57 Canberra unarmed reconnaissance aircraft. The RB-57A Canberra equipped the following USAFE Tac Recce squadrons in support of NATO during the Cold War:

- USAF, 1st TRS RB-57A Canberra 1954 - 1958
- USAF, 30th TRS RB-57A Canberra 1955 - 1957

At least twelve RB-57A Canberra aircraft are believed to have survived and are on display, being restored or in storage in the United States.

Table 010, RB-57A Canberra Technical and Performance Specifications

DIMENSIONS:			
Wing Span:	64 ft 0.0 in	19.51 m	
Length:	65 ft 6.0 in	19.96 m	
Height:	14 ft 10.0 in	4.52 m	
Wing Area:	960.0 ft²	89.18 m²	
POWERPLANT(S):			
Number of Engines / Designation:	Two (2) Buick Built, Wright J65-W-5 Turbojets		
Maximum Power / Thrust per Engine:	7,220 lbs st	3,275 kg st	
WEIGHTS:			
Empty:	24,751 lbs	11,227 kg	
Maximum Take-Off:	48,847 lbs	22,157 kg	
Maximum Wing Loading:	50.9 lbs/ft²	248.5 kg/m²	
PERFORMANCE:			
Max Level Speed at Altitude:	609 mph @ 4,500 ft	980 kmh @ 1,372 m	529 kts @ 4,500 ft
Initial Rate of Climb at Sea Level:	7,180 ft/min	2,188 m/min	
Service Ceiling:	48,350 ft	14,737 m	
Nominal Combat Radius:	1,267 mi	2,039 km	1,101 nm
Maximum / Ferry Range:	2,568 mi	4,133 km	2,231 nm

Data File for the RB-57A Canberra

RF-100A Super Sabre

Image 021, USAF RF-100A Super Sabre, s/n 31546, photographic-reconnaissance aircraft. Note the \chin blister below the canopy and enlarged, angular lower fuselage forward of the wing leading edge. (Photo courtesy of the NMUSAF)

The RF-100A Super Sabre is the single-seat, unarmed, day-only, photographic-reconnaissance variant of the supersonic F-100A Super Sabre fighter-bomber. The RF-100A Super Sabre was a highly classified reconnaissance aircraft. As a result, few people are aware of its existence and the mission it performed. Designed and manufactured for the USAF by North American Aviation, Inc, the first RF-100A Super Sabre flew in March 1955.

The RF-100A Super Sabre was the world's first supersonic photographic-reconnaissance aircraft. In September 1954, six F-100A Super Sabres were removed from the F-100A Super Sabre production line and modified as RF-100A Super Sabre photographic-reconnaissance aircraft. Like the fighter-bomber the RF-100A Super Sabre is a single-seat aircraft. The stovepipe-type fuselage houses a single, afterburning J57-P-7 turbojet engine, and has an horizontally oriented oval shaped engine intake in the nose and a large exhaust nozzle, which protrudes aft of the vertical stabilizer. A long tubular pitot sensor is located under and extends well forward of the engine intake. The single-seat cockpit is located forward of the wings leading edge with a single-piece clamshell canopy hinged aft for pilot ingress and egress. The retractable, tricycle landing gear has a twin-wheel nose gear and one wheel on each main gear. The low-mounted wings are sweptback at an angle of 45°, with three underwing hardpoints and blunt tips. External fuel is carried in two wing-mounted fuel tanks, each with a capacity of 450 US gal (1,703 ltr/375 Imp gal). A sweptback, one-piece horizontal stabilator is low mounted at the rear of the fuselage, below the sweptback vertical stabilizer, and both have blunt tips.

Image 022, USAF RF-101A Super Sabre, s/n 31546, clearly displaying the chin blister and enlarged lower fuselage. (Photo courtesy of the NMUSAF)

To accommodate the large reconnaissance camera bodies and long lenses, the lower portion of the forward fuselage was modified to include a deeper, more angular chin fairing on both sides of the fuselage. These angular fairings are clearly visible just forward of the wing's leading edge, immediately below the aircraft canopy. The sensor configuration consist of two K-38 cameras equipped with a 36" (914 mm) fl lens, in place of the four 20 mm cannon and the associated ammunition bays in the lower forward fuselage.

The cameras are installed in the split-vertical position providing overlapping vertical coverage along the aircraft's line of flight. Sliding metal shutters cover the camera windows when they are not in use, to protect them from damage during take-off, landing and while taxing.

The RF-100A Super Sabre was never assigned to a USAFE Tac Recce unit. However, for a very brief period of time, three RF-100A Super Sabres were deployed to Germany as part of a program called "Project Slick Chick". The mission objective was to image targets over Eastern Europe. The aircraft were assigned to the 7407th Support Squadron, at Rhine Main AB, DE. However, they operated from Detachment 1, at Bitburg AB, DE, home of the 36th Fighter Wing, which operated F-100 Super Sabre fighter aircraft. It has been reported that as part of the "Project Slick Chick" program, the RF-100A Super Sabres, flew six missions over Eastern European Soviet Bloc countries imaging targets, such as cities and airfields. It was believed the RF-100A Super Sabre could cross the border, at high altitude (more than 50,000 ft/15,250 m), image the assigned targets and return to NATO airspace before being intercepted.

The RF-100A Super Sabre equipped the following USAF reconnaissance squadron in support of the United States and NATO during the Cold War:

- USAFE, 7407th Support Sq RF-100A Super Sabre 1955 - 1961

There are no surviving examples of the RF-100A Super Sabre.

Table 011, RF-101A Super Sabre Technical and Performance Specifications

DIMENSIONS:				
Wing Span:	38 ft	9.4 in	11.82 m	
Length:	47 ft	1.3 in	14.36 m	
Height:	15 ft	6.0 in	4.72 m	
Wheel Track:	12 ft	0.0 in	3.66 m	
Horizontal Stabilizer Span:	18 ft	0.0 in	5.49 m	
POWERPLANT(S):				
Number of Engines / Designation:	One (1)	Pratt & Whitney J57-P-7 Turbojet		
Maximum Power / Thrust per Engine:	14,800 lbs st		6,713 kg st	
FUEL CAPACITY:				
Internal Fuel Capacity:	1,185 US gal		4,485 ltrs	987 Imp gal
External Fuel Capacity:	744 US gal		2,816 ltrs	620 Imp gal
Total Fuel Capacity:	1,929 US gal		7,301 ltrs	1,606 Imp gal
WEIGHTS:				
Empty:	18,185 lbs		8,249 kg	
Maximum Take-Off:	32,500 lbs		14,742 kg	
PERFORMANCE:				
Max Level Speed at Altitude:	852 mph @		1,371 kmh @	740 kts @
	35,000 ft		10,668 m	35,000 ft
Landing Speed:	179 mph		288 kmh	155 kts
Service Ceiling:	44,900 ft		13,686 m	
Nominal Combat Radius:	358 mi		576 km	311 nm
Maximum / Ferry Range:	1,294 mi		2,082 km	1,124 nm
T-O Run to 50 feet:	4,500 ft		1,372 m	

Data File for the RF-100A Super Saber

Swift FR.Mk.5

Image 23, RAF Swift FR.Mk.5, s/n WK277, in the markings of No, 2 Sq, RAFB Geilenkirchen, DE on display at Newark Air Museum, Newark, UK on 03 August 2002. (Photo copyright Ian Howat)

Occasionally a new aircraft design fails to achieve the performance required for the mission it was designed to support. When this occurs, the contract is either cancelled or the government and manufacturer work together to identify a new mission for the existing airframes. This is the case with the Swift FR.Mk.5. Designed and manufactured for the RAF by the Supermarine Division of Vickers-Armstrong Ltd., the Swift F.Mk.4 was intended to be a high-altitude interceptor. However, the program was cancelled after it was learned the afterburner, a critical component for high-speed interceptors, could not be lit at high altitude. As a result, the thirty-five existing aircraft were modified for low-altitude, day photographic-reconnaissance missions and redesignated the Swift FR.Mk.5. These are the first RAF reconnaissance aircraft to be equipped with afterburning engines.

The Swift FR.Mk.5 is a single-seat, single-engine photographic-reconnaissance aircraft. The barrel-type fuselage houses an afterburning Rolls Royce Avon 114 turbojet engine. The aircraft nose is thin and tapers to a rounded point. The cockpit is located just forward of the wing's leading edge and is above the engine intakes. The engine intakes are located on fuselage sides above and forward of the wing leading edge and below the canopy, and the engine exhaust nozzle extends well aft of the vertical stabilizer. The single-seat cockpit is located above the engine intakes and with a moveable single-piece canopy that slides aft for pilot ingress and egress. The retractable, tricycle landing gear has a single-wheel nose gear and one wheel on each main gear. External fuel is carried in a bulbous, flush mounted fuel tank under the aircraft fuselage. The low-mounted wings are sweptback at an angle of 40°, with a single stall fence on the outer third of each wing, a saw-tooth leading edge and blunt tips. The sweptback horizontal stabilizer is high-mounted on the fuselage, has a moderate dihedral and blunt tips. The vertical stabilizer is sweptback with a blunt tip and positioned slightly forward and above of the horizontal stabilizer.

The nose of the Swift FR.Mk.5 is extended 1 ft 2.5 in (0.37 m) to accommodate three cameras; one in the forward-oblique position and two in the side-oblique positions.

In addition to the original thirty-five converted aircraft, a second order was placed for an addition fifty-nine aircraft, with delivery beginning in March 1956. These aircraft remained in service with the RAF until replaced by the Hunter FR.Mk.10.

Supermarine produced a total of ninety-four Swift FR.Mk.5s, which equipped the following RAF reconnaissance squadrons in support of NATO during the Cold War:

- RAF, No.2 Sq — Swift FR.Mk.5 — 1956 - 1961
- RAF, No.79 Sq — Swift FR.Mk.5 — 1956 - 1961

Only two of the ninety-four Swift FR.Mk.5 aircraft have survived.

Table 012, Swift FR.Mk.5 Technical and Performance Specifications

DIMENSIONS:								
Wing Span:	32	ft	4.0	in	9.86	m		
Length:	42	ft	5.5	in	12.94	m		
Height:	13	ft	6.0	in	4.11	m		
Wheel Track:	15	ft	2.5	in	4.64	m		
Wheel Base:	14	ft	10.0	in	4.52	m		
Wing Area:	327.7	ft^2			30.44	m^2		
POWERPLANT(S):								
Number of Engines / Designation:	One (1)	Rolls Royce Avon 114 turbojet						
Maximum Power / Thrust per Engine:	7,175	lbs st			3,255	kg st		
WEIGHTS:								
Maximum Take-Off:	21,673	lbs			9,831	kg		
Maximum Wing Loading:	66.1	lbs/ft^2			322.9	kg/m^2		
PERFORMANCE:								
Max Level Speed at Sea Level:	713	mph			1,147	kmh	619	kts
Initial Rate of Climb at Sea Level:	14,660	ft/min			4,468	m/min		
Service Ceiling:	45,800	ft			13,960	m		
Nominal Combat Radius:	630	mi			1,014	km	547	nm

Data File for the Swift FR.Mk.5

Venom FB.Mk.1R

Image 024, Venom FR.Mk.1R, s/n J-1630 in Swiss AF markings, in flight over Bern Airport on 27 July 2004. This aircraft is part of the vintage aircraft collection at the Verein Fleigermuseum, Altenrhein, Switzerland. (Photo copyright Bruno Althaus)

The Venom FB.Mk.1R is the armed, low-altitude, day-only, photographic-reconnaissance variant of the Venom FB.Mk.50 ground attack aircraft built under license in Switzerland by a Swiss consortium comprised of EFW (Federal Aircraft Factory), Pilatus and the Flug und Fahrzeugwerke.

A single-seat fighter-reconnaissance aircraft the Venom FB.Mk.1 is the only Cold War Tac Recce aircraft with a twin tail boom configuration. The elongated teardrop shaped nacelle-type fuselage houses a single afterburning Ghost 101 turbojet engine, has a short rounded nose and tapers aft as it nears the engine exhaust. The single-seat cockpit is located well forward on the fuselage, just ahead of the wing's leading edge with a single-piece moveable canopy, which slides aft for pilot ingress and egress. The retractable tricycle landing gear has a single-wheel nose gear and one wheel on each main gear. The mid-mounted taper-straight wings have a single underwing hardpoint for external stores and a single stall fence. Wing tip tanks with a capacity each of 94 US gal (356 ltr/78 Imp gal) of external fuel normally conceal the wing's blunt tips. The triangular shaped engine intakes for the fuselage-mounted engine are located in the wing roots and the engine exhaust is located at the end of the short fuselage. The tail assembly consists of a twin boom assembly extending out from the wings on either side of the fuselage. The horizontal stabilizer has a straight-straight rectangular appearance with rounded tips, which extend outboard of the vertical stabilizers, and are small and tapered-tapered with rounded tips. A short tubular pitot sensor is located at the tip of the left vertical stabilizer.

The two fuselage mounted 20 mm cannon on the right side were removed and replaced by a Eastman Kodak K-24 cameras with a 7.1 in (180 mm) fl lens. The camera is installed in the vertical position on the right side of the lower fuselage, in line with the wing's leading edge. A bump fairing is installed under the lower right fuselage housing the camera's optical window. In addition, three Vinton 360 cameras with a 3.9 in (100 mm) fl lens in the forward-oblique, vertical and side-oblique positions are installed in specially modified fixed underwing drop tanks. Normally one reconnaissance pod is installed under each wing. To assist in locating the targets the pilot has an optical periscope in the cockpit with an optical sight in the lower fuselage nose.

A total of twenty-four Venom FB.Mk.1 aircraft were modified to perform the Tac Recce mission and assigned the designation as Venom FB.Mk.1R. Delivery of the production Venom FB.Mk.1R aircraft took place between March and September 1956.

The Venom FB.Mk.1R equipped the following Swiss AF reconnaissance unit during the Cold War:

- Swiss AF, Fliegerstaffel 10 Venom FB.Mk.1R 1956 - 1969

At least six of the Venom FB.Mk.1R aircraft have survived and are in storage or on display in Europe.

In addition, the Swiss AF sold three, Venom FB.Mk.1R in June 1984. The first aircraft was sold in the UK and given the civilian registration of G-VNOM (s/n J1632); the second aircraft was also sold in the UK, relocated to New Zealand and was given the civilian registration of ZK-VNM (s/n J1634); and the third aircraft was sold in France (s/n J1636). The location and condition of the latter two aircraft are unknown.

Table 013, Venom FB.Mk.1R Technical and Performance Specifications

DIMENSIONS:				
Wing Span:	41 ft	8.0 in	12.70 m	
Length:	33 ft	0.0 in	10.06 m	
Height:	6 ft	0.0 in	1.83 m	
Wing Area:	279.8 ft²		25.99 m²	
POWERPLANT(S):				
Number of Engines / Designation:	One (1) DeHavilland Ghost 105 Turbojet			
Maximum Power / Thrust per Engine:	5,150 lbs st		2,336 kg st	
WEIGHTS:				
Maximum Take-Off:	15,310 lbs		6,945 kg	
Maximum Wing Loading:	54.7 lbs/ft²		267.2 kg/m²	
PERFORMANCE:				
Max Level Speed at Altitude:	557 mph @ 10,000 ft		896 kmh @ 3,048 m	484 kts @ 10,000 ft
Initial Rate of Climb at Sea Level:	7,230 ft/min		2,204 m/min	
Service Ceiling:	48,000 ft		14,630 m	
Maximum / Ferry Range:	1,075 mi		1,730 km	934 nm

Data File for the Venom FB.Mk.1R

RF-101A/C Voodoo

Image 025, USAFE based RF-101C Voodoo, s/n 56-0102, at RAFB Alconbury on 05 July 1969. (Photo copyright by Steve Williams)

Best known for the missions it flew during the Cuban Missile Crisis and its service in South Vietnam, the RF-101A/C Voodoo was the mainstay of USAF Tac Recce units between 1957 and 1970. Designed and manufactured by McDonnell Aircraft Corporation the RF-101A/C Voodoo is the low-level, day and night photographic-reconnaissance variant of the F-101A/C Voodoo fighter-bomber. Two F-101A Voodoo airframes, numbers 16 and 17, were removed from the production line and modified as YRF-101A Voodoo prototypes, and first flew on 10 May 1956.

The RF-101A Voodoo is a single-seat; unarmed Tac Recce aircraft designed primarily for low-altitude, day and night photographic-reconnaissance missions. The barrel-type fuselage of the RF-101A housed a pair of afterburning, Pratt & Whitney J57-PW-55 turbojet engines, but these were upgraded to the Pratt & Whitney J57-P-13 turbojets in the production RF-101C Voodoo. The triangular shaped engine intakes are located on either side of the fuselage in extended wing roots. The engine exhausts are located just aft of the wings trailing edge, below and forward of the aircraft tail assembly. The single-seat cockpit is situated well forward of the wings leading edge, with a single-piece clamshell canopy hinged aft for pilot ingress and egress. The retractable, tricycle landing gear has a twin-wheel nose gear and one wheel on each main gear. External fuel is carried in twin 450 US gal (1,703 ltr/375 imp gal) external tanks mounted on two under fuselage hard points. The mid-mounted wings are sweptback at an angle of 35°, have a single stall fence and square tips. The sweptback one-piece horizontal stabilator has square tips with a slight dihedral and is mounted high on the sweptback vertical stabilizer.

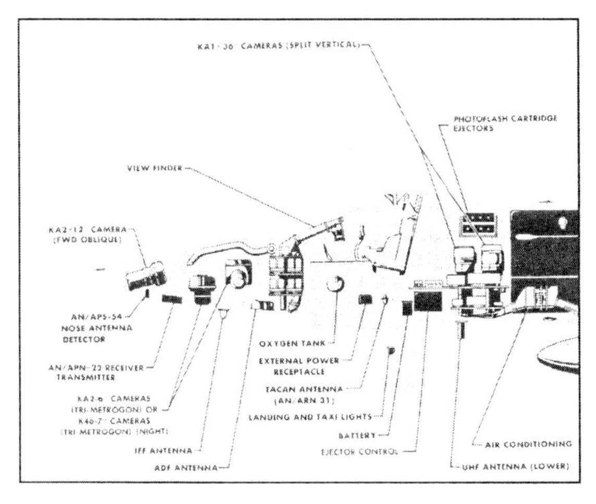

Figure 004, RF-101A Voodoo sensor detail. Note the camera locations, and the optical viewfinder and photoflash ejectors (Courtesy of the NMUSAF)

To accommodate the sensor suite, the aircraft nose was redesigned with an angular contour and lengthened by 1 ft 4 in (0.58m), to house the four cameras in the nose. The standard camera configuration for the RF-101A Voodoo includes one KA-2 camera with a 12" (305 mm) fl lens in the forward-oblique position; three KA-2 cameras with a 6 in (152 mm) fl lens installed in the trimetrogon configuration to provide simultaneous horizon-to-horizon coverage along the aircraft's line of flight; and two KA-1 high-altitude cameras with a 36" (914 mm) fl lens in the split-vertical position directly behind the cockpit. The optical window for the split-vertical cameras is covered with a retractable metal shutter for ground operations. The forward section of the aircraft nose is hinged at the top for access to the forward-oblique camera and film magazine, and hinged panels on the side and beneath the forward fuselage provided access to the trimetrogon cameras and film magazines. A short tubular pitot sensor is located on the aircraft nose immediately above the forward-oblique camera window.

Image 026, USAFE based RF-101A Voodoo at Loan Air Base, France in 1960. Note the angular nose, raised canopy with crew ladder and triangular shaped engine intakes (Photo copyright by John Dunn)

The RF-101C Voodoo is identical in appearance to the RF-101A Voodoo, but incorporates the structural changes associated with the F-101C Voodoo fighter-bomber. In addition, the RF-101C Voodoo has an upgraded sensor suite. The forward-oblique and side-oblique cameras were replaced with the newer KS-72A cameras each with a 6 in (152 mm) fl lens. The vertical camera, which was the middle camera in the trimetrogon configuration, was replaced with a KA-56 low-altitude panoramic camera with a 3 in (76 mm) fl lens, and provides single frame, horizon-to-horizon coverage along the aircraft's line of flight. The installation of this camera required modification of the lower fuselage to incorporate a prism shaped optical window, which is visible just forward of the Identification Friend and Foe (IFF) blade antenna.

To assist the pilot in locating the targets, the RF-101A/C Voodoo is equipped with a Type VF-31 viewfinder, which provides the pilot both a wide (60°) and narrow (30°) field of view (FOV). For night operation the RF-101A/C Voodoo has two photoflash cartridge ejectors located on the upper fuselage directly behind the cockpit and above the split-vertical camera position.

Image 027, RF-101A/C Voodoo with ground crew removing camera magazines following routine training mission; note hinged nose and panels for easy access to cameras and film magazines (Photo courtesy of the NMUSAF)

Image 028, USAF RF-101C Voodoo, s/n 56-0214, with prism shaped optical window just forward of the IFF antenna; the small rectangular optical window forward of the nose wheel well is for the pilot's optical viewfinder (Paul Wagner Collection))

McDonnell delivered the first production RF-101A Voodoo to the 363rd TRW, Shaw AFB, SC on 06 May 1957. A total of thirty-five RF-101A Voodoos were delivered to the USAF. Production of the RF-101A Voodoo was terminated with the introduction the RF-101C Voodoos of which 166 were built. The RF-101C Voodoo flew for the first time on 12 July 1957 and the first production RF-101C Voodoo was delivered to the USAF at the 363rd TRW, Shaw AFB, SC in September 1957.

The RF-101A/C Voodoo is "officially" known as the world's first supersonic Tac Recce aircraft. This was publicly demonstrated when four RF-101A Voodoos participated in "Operation Sun Run" in November 1957, setting several new speed records including:

- 1st Lt Gustav Klatt set an eastbound (LA-NY) coast-to-coast record of 3 hours, 7 minutes and 42 seconds, with an average speed of 781.7 mph (1,258 kmh/679 kts)

- Capt Robert Sweet set a westbound (NY-LA) coast-to-coast record of 3 hours, 36 minutes and 33 seconds, with an average speed of 677.7 mph (1,091 kmh/589 kts)

- Capt Robert Sweet set a roundtrip (LA-NY-LA) coast-to-coast record of 6 hours, 46 minutes and 36 seconds, with an average speed of 721.85 mph (1,162 kmh/627 kts)

During the Berlin Crisis of 1961, eight RF-101C Voodoos from the 66th TRW were deployed to Spangdahlem AB, DE as part of a show of force. The 66th TRW was tasked to conduct reconnaissance missions, and collect visual and image intelligence on Soviet activity in and near Berlin. The RF-101C Voodoos flew single ship reconnaissance missions to Berlin using one of the three designated air corridors, made a turn over West Berlin and flew out using one of the other two air corridors. Soviet MIG aircraft harassed the crews, attempting to force them into East German air space. These missions did not receive much publicity however, the RF-101C Voodoo was well known for reconnaissance images obtained from low-level reconnaissance mission over Cuba, and seen by millions of Americans in newspapers and on television during the 1962 Cuban Missile Crisis.

The RF-101C Voodoo equipped the following USAFE Tac Recce squadrons in support of NATO during the Cold War:

- USAFE, 17th TRS RF-101C Voodoo 1957 - 1969

- USAFE, 18th TRS RF-101C Voodoo 1957 - 1969
- USAFE, 32nd TRS RF-101C Voodoo 1958 - 1965
- USAFE, 38th TRS RF-101C Voodoo 1958 - 1966

At least eighteen RF-101C Voodoo aircraft are believed to have survived and are on display, being restored or in storage throughout the United States.

Table 014, RF-101C Voodoo Technical and Performance Specifications

DIMENSIONS:				
Wing Span:	39 ft	8.0 in	12.09 m	
Length:	69 ft	4.0 in	21.13 m	
Height:	18 ft	0.0 in	5.49 m	
Wheel Track:	19 ft	10.5 in	6.06 m	
Wing Area:	368.0 ft²		34.18 m²	
POWERPLANT(S):				
Number of Engines / Designation:	Two (2)	Pratt & Whitney J57-P-13 turbojets		
Maximum Power / Thrust per Engine:	14,880 lbs st		6,750 kg st	
FUEL CAPACITY:				
Internal Fuel Capacity:	2,250 US gal		8,516 ltrs	1,874 Imp gal
External Fuel Capacity:	900 US gal		3,407 ltrs	749 Imp gal
Total Fuel Capacity:	3,150 US gal		11,923 ltrs	2,623 Imp gal
WEIGHTS:				
Empty:	26,136 lbs		11,855 kg	
Maximum Take-Off:	51,000 lbs		23,134 kg	
Maximum Wing Loading:	138.6 lbs/ft²		676.7 kg/m²	
PERFORMANCE:				
Max Level Speed at Altitude:	1,008 mph @ 35,000 ft		1,622 kmh @ 10,668 m	875 kts @ 35,000 ft
Nominal Cruising Speed:	547 mph		880 kmh	475 kts
Initial Rate of Climb at Sea Level:	36,150 ft/min		11,019 m/min	
Service Ceiling:	50,750 ft		15,469 m	
Nominal Combat Radius:	857 mi		1,379 km	745 nm
Maximum / Ferry Range:	2,145 mi		3,452 km	1,864 nm

Data File for the RF-101C Voodoo

RB-66A/B Destroyer

Image 029, USAF RB-66B Destroyer, s/n 22830, over the Western United States. (Photo courtesy of the NMUSAF)

The last Tac Recce aircraft to be derived from a bomber aircraft was the RB-66A/B Destroyer, a variant of the B-66A/B Destroyer tactical bomber, designed and manufactured for the USAF by Douglas Aircraft Company. The primary mission of the RB-66A/B Destroyer is low-level, all-weather, night-photographic-reconnaissance. Douglas proposed the RB-66 Destroyer in response to a General Operational Requirement (GOR) issued by the USAF on 21 January 1952. The B-66 Destroyer was based on the US Navy's A3D Skywarrior, but with significant modifications to support high-speed, low-level operations. The modifications included a strengthened airframe, new engines and ejection seats for the three-man crew. The RB-66A Destroyer was the prototype for the reconnaissance variant, the first of which flew on 28 June 1954. Three RB-66A Destroyers were produced and designated preproduction aircraft. All three aircraft were delivered to the USAF in December 1954. None of the preproduction aircraft saw operational service. The production variant was the RB-66B Destroyer, which first flew in March 1955.

A twin-engine reconnaissance bomber, the RB-66B Destroyer had a long, rectangular cigar-type fuselage. The three-man crew consisting of a pilot, photo-navigator and gunner shared a crew cabin near the front of the fuselage, well forward of the wing's leading edge. The pilot sits on the left-front side of the cockpit under a greenhouse canopy. The photo-navigator and gunner sit side-by-side behind the pilot. All crewmembers face forward in separate ejection seats. Crew ingress and egress is via a hatch under the fuselage just aft of the nose wheel. The retractable, tricycle landing gear has a single-wheel nose gear and one wheel on each main gear. Immediately below the vertical stabilizer is a small radome and the M-24A-1, 20 mm gun in the remotely controlled tail turret. The high-mounted wings are sweptback at an angle of 36°, with 1.5° of anhedral and blunt tips. External fuel is carried in two wing-mounted fuel tanks, each with a capacity of 450 US gal (1,703 ltr/375 Imp gal). One non-afterburning, Allison J71-A-13 turbojet is housed under each wing in a pylon mounted engine nacelle, which extends forward of the wing's leading edge. The tail unit consists of a sweptback horizontal stabilizer with a slight dihedral and is low-mounted on a sweptback vertical stabilizer. Both the horizontal and vertical stabilizers have blunt tips.

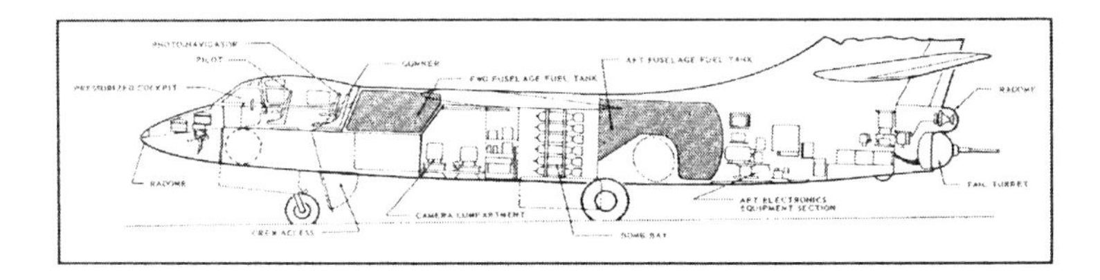

Figure 005, RB-66 Destroyer interior layout. Note the camera bays forward and aft of the main landing gear, and the photoflash bomb racks just aft of the first camera bay. (Courtesy of the NMUSAF)

The bomb bay and rear fuselage are modified to accommodate cameras, electronics and photoflash bomb racks. The standard camera configuration includes two K-47 cameras with a 7 in (178 mm) fl lens or one K-38 camera with a 12 in (305 mm) fl lens in the forward station directly below the wing and forward of the main landing gear. Two additional K-47 cameras with a 12 in (305 mm) fl lens or one T-11 camera with a 6 in (152 mm) fl lens are located in the aft station, midway between the main landing gear and aircraft tail. To provide illumination for night photography the RB-66B Destroyer carries twenty-four M120 photoflash bombs and forty M123 photoflash cartridges; or an alternate load of 140, M112 photoflash cartridges.

Douglas produced 155 RB-66B Destroyers and deliveries to the USAF began on 01 February 1956. The RB-66B Destroyer equipped the following USAFE Tac Recce squadrons in support of NATO during the Cold War:

- USAF, 19th TRS — RB-66B Destroyer — 1957 - 1967
- USAF, 30th TRS — RB-66B Destroyer — 1957 - 1976
- USAF, 1st TRS — RB-66B Destroyer — 1958 - 1966

There are four known RB-66 Destroyer survivors in the United States.

Table 015, RB-66B Destroyer Technical and Performance Specifications

Specification				
DIMENSIONS:				
Wing Span:	72 ft	6.0 in	22.10 m	
Length:	75 ft	2.0 in	22.91 m	
Height:	23 ft	7.0 in	7.19 m	
Wheel Track:	10 ft	9.5 in	3.29 m	
Wheel Base:	27 ft	7.0 in	8.41 m	
Wing Area:	780.0 ft^2		72.46 m^2	
POWERPLANT(S):				
Number of Engines / Designation:	Two (2) Allison J71-A-13 Turbojets			
Maximum Power / Thrust per Engine:	10,200 lbs st		4,627 kg st	
FUEL CAPACITY:				
Internal Fuel Capacity:	4,393 US gal		16,628 ltrs	3,658 Imp gal
External Fuel Capacity:	900 US gal		3,407 ltrs	749 Imp gal
Total Fuel Capacity:	5,293 US gal		20,034 ltrs	4,407 Imp gal
WEIGHTS:				
Empty:	43,476 lbs		19,721 kg	
Maximum Take-Off:	83,000 lbs		37,649 kg	
Maximum Wing Loading:	106.4 lbs/ft^2		519.6 kg/m^2	
PERFORMANCE:				
Max Level Speed at Altitude:	548 mph @ 6,000 ft		882 kmh @ 1,829 m	476 kts @ 6,000 ft
Nominal Cruising Speed:	496 mph		798 kmh	431 kts
Initial Rate of Climb at Sea Level:	4,840 ft/min		1,475 m/min	
Service Ceiling:	38,900 ft		11,857 m	
Nominal Combat Radius:	927 mi		1,492 km	805 nm
Maximum / Ferry Range:	2,426 mi		3,904 km	2,108 nm

Data File for the RB-66B Destroyer

Saab S32C Lansen

Image 030, Swedish AF Saab S32C Lansen during the late 1970s. Note the crew ladder on the right side of the tandem cockpit and the bulbous, flush mounted external fuel tank under the fuselage. (Photo copyright by Tor Karlsson)

Developed as a replacement for the Saab 29 Tunnan, the Saab 32 Lansen was Sweden's first two-seat jet aircraft and the first equipped with a built-in search radar. Like its predecessor, the Saab S32C Lansen is an unarmed, day and night photographic-reconnaissance aircraft, designed and manufactured by SAAB (Saab Aktiebolag). The Saab S32C Lansen made its first flight on 26 March 1957.

The Saab S32C Lansen has a barrel-type fuselage, which tapers to a rounded radome in the nose and houses an afterburning, Rolls Royce Avon RM5A turbojet engine. The engine intakes are mounted below the cockpit, just forward and above the wing's leading edge. The pilot and navigator are housed in tandem two-place cockpit, under a single-piece clamshell canopy hinged on the left for crew ingress and egress. The cockpit is located just forward of the wing's leading edge, above the engine intakes. In addition, a second windscreen is located between the pilot and navigator's cockpit to protect the navigator if the canopy is inadvertently jettisoned. The retractable, tricycle landing gear has a single-wheel nose gear and one wheel on each main gear. Additional fuel is carried externally in a 159 US gal (600 ltr/132 imp gal) bulbous and flush-mounted fuel tank under the fuselage just aft of the wing's leading edge. The low-mounted wings are sweptback at an angle of 39°, have three underwing hardpoints, a single stall fence on the outer third of the wing, blunt tips and a tubular pitot sensor on the right wingtip. The sweptback and tapered horizontal stabilizer has rounded tips and is mounted high on the fuselage. The upper portion of the rear fuselage presents a flat surface created by an angular fairing from just behind the wings trailing edge and extends above the horizontal stabilizer. The sweptback and tapered vertical stabilizer has a squared tip.

The PS-432/A search radar and a battery of up to six cameras are installed in place of the four internally mounted 20 mm cannon of the Saab A32A Lansen. Due to the limited space in the gun bays, the nose contour was modified with chin blisters on either side of the upper fuselage just forward of the canopy to house the camera bodies. The original Saab S32C Lansen camera

Image 031, Swedish AF Saab S32C Lansen at Stockholm, SE in June 1975. Note the chin blister on the nose for the camera body, the open canopy hinged on the left side and the windscreen between the pilot and navigator. (Photo copyright by Tor Karlsson)

configuration consisted of two SKa 17 (F.97 Mk.2) cameras with a 5.1 in (130 mm) fl lens; and two SKa 18 (F.89 Mk.3) cameras with a 36.2 in (920 mm) fl lens. Both cameras were designed for night photography. In 1962 the cameras were upgraded to include one SKa 15 (Williamson F.49 Mk.2) camera with a 5.9 in (150mm) fl lens; three SKa 16 (Vinten) cameras with a 3.9 in (100mm) fl lens; and two SKa 23s (Modified Fairchild K47) cameras with a 23.6 in (600mm) lens. In addition, the Saab S32C Lansen carries twelve M62 flash bombs for night photography.

Saab produced a total of forty-four Saab S32C Lansens between 1958 and 1960, which equipped the following Swedish AF reconnaissance unit during the Cold War:

- Swedish AF, F11 Wing   Saab S32C Lansen   1958 - 1978

There is at least one surviving example of the Saab S32C Lansen on display or in storage at Nylcoping AB, SE. The current status of that aircraft is unknown.

Table 016, Saab S32C Lansen Technical and Performance Specifications

DIMENSIONS:								
Wing Span:	42	ft	7.8	in	13.00	m		
Length:	48	ft	0.8	in	14.65	m		
Height:	16	ft	3.0	in	4.95	m		
Wing Area:	403.0	ft²			37.44	m²		
POWERPLANT(S):								
Number of Engines / Designation:	One (1)	Rolls Royce Avon RM5A turbojet						
Maximum Power / Thrust per Engine:	10,362	lbs st			4,700	kg st		
FUEL CAPACITY:								
Internal Fuel Capacity:	925	US gal			3,500	ltrs	770	Imp gal
External Fuel Capacity:	159	US gal			600	ltrs	132	Imp gal
Total Fuel Capacity:	1,083	US gal			4,100	ltrs	902	Imp gal
WEIGHTS:								
Empty:	16,250	lbs			7,371	kg		
Maximum Take-Off:	28,660	lbs			13,000	kg		
Maximum Wing Loading:	71.1	lbs/ft²			347.3	kg/m²		
PERFORMANCE:								
Max Level Speed at Altitude:	692	mph @			1,114	kmh @	601	kts @
	49,200	ft			14,996	m	49,200	ft
Nominal Cruising Speed:	528	mph			850	kmh	459	kts
Initial Rate of Climb at Sea Level:	11,810	ft/min			3,600	m/min		
Service Ceiling:	49,212	ft			15,000	m		
Maximum / Ferry Range:	1,400	mi			2,253	km	1,216	nm

Data File for the J32C Lansen

Fiat G91R

Image 032, Italian AF Fiat G91R1 assigned to 2° Stormo, 103rd Gruppo at Treviso AB, San Angelo, IT in May 1985. Note the smoke from the engine start using a starter cartridge, one of which can be seen sitting on the right wing. (Photo copyright by Giuseppe Tonelotto)

The Fiat G91R was developed in response to NATO's requirement for a light tactical combat aircraft capable of operating from semi-prepared grass strips. A single-seat, multi-mission aircraft, the primary mission of the Fiat G91R is ground attack, but the Fiat G91R has a secondary mission of low-level day-only photographic-reconnaissance and was assigned to ground attack, Tac Recce and advanced training squadrons. Designed and manufactured for the Italian AF by Fiat (Societa per Azioni Fiat), the prototype Fiat G91R first flew on 09 August 1956.

Similar in appearance to the F-86 Sabre fighter, the Fiat G91R has a barrel-type fuselage, which houses a single, afterburning Bristol Siddeley Orpheus 803 turbojet engine with a large engine intake directly below an extended nose. The single-seat cockpit is located forward of the wing's leading edge, with a single-piece clamshell canopy hinged aft for pilot ingress and egress. The retractable, tricycle landing gear has a single-wheel nose gear and one wheel on each main gear. Depending on the model, the internal armament of the Fiat G91R consists of either two 30 mm cannon or four 0.50-in (12.7 mm) machine guns. The low-mounted wings are sweptback at an angle of 37° 13", with 1° 30' of dihedral and blunt tips. There are two underwing hard points on each wing for external stores and fuel, and a single stall fence above the outboard hard point. External fuel is carried in two wing-mounted fuel tanks, each with a capacity of 137 US gal (518 ltr/114 imp gal). In addition, a tubular pitot sensor is mounted near the wing tip and can be located on either the left or right wing. The sweptback horizontal stabilizer is high mounted on the aft fuselage, directly below the sweptback vertical stabilizer. Both the horizontal and vertical stabilizers have blunt tips.

Image 033, German AF Fiat G-91R3 easily identified by the two, 30mm cannon. Note the circular window for the forward-oblique camera and the two square windows for the left side-oblique and vertical camera positions just above the engine intake. (Photo copyright by Luis Rosa)

For the Tac Recce mission, the G91R carries up to three Vinten, 70 mm cameras. The cameras are mounted in the vertical, forward, and left and right side-oblique positions. Hinged panels on either side of the fuselage nose provide access to the cameras. The forward-oblique nose camera window is flat and circular; the vertical and side-oblique camera windows are flat and square.

In 1957 the Fiat G91R competed with other allied aircraft to become NATO's primary tactical strike aircraft, outperforming three French contenders. Several countries evaluated the Fiat G91R, including the USAF, which purchased eight for trials. However, only Italy and West Germany placed production orders.

The first variant, the G91R1, carried four 0.50-in (12.7 mm) machine guns installed in pairs on each side of the lower fuselage directly below the cockpit. The G91R1 first flew in 1959. The second variant designed and built for the West German AF was the Fiat G91R3. It differed from the Fiat G91R1 in that the internal armament consisted of two 30 mm cannon. In addition, the G91R3 included a Doppler radar, and position and homing indicator equipment. The Fiat G91R3 was produced under license in West Germany, for the West German AF by the Flugzeug Union Süd (Messerschmitt-Dornier-Heinkel). The first German built Fiat G91R3 flew on 20 July 1961; the aircraft became operational in 1962.

The final variant was the Fiat G91R4, which retained the capabilities of the Fiat G91R3, and the four 0.50-in (12.7 mm) machine guns of the Fiat G91R1. Production of the Fiat G91R totaled, ninety-eight G91R1s; 344 G91R3s (including twelve assembled by and 282 manufactured by Flugzeug Union Süd), and fifty G91R4s. In 1976 the Portuguese AF acquired ex-German AF Fiat G91Rs for use in the ground attack mission.

The Fiat G91R equipped units of the following NATO air forces during the Cold War:

- Italian AF, 2° Stormo, 14° Gruppo — Fiat G91R/1 — 1959 - 1993
- Italian AF, 2° Stormo, 103° Gruppo — Fiat G91R/1 — 1959 - 1993
- West German AF, WS 50 — Fiat G91R/3 — 1960 - 1992
- Portuguese AF, BA 6, ESq 301 — Fiat G91R/3 — 1976 - 1993

More than fifty-five Fiat G91R aircraft have survived and are on display, being restored or in storage throughout the Europe.

Table 017, Fiat G91R3 Technical and Performance Specifications

Wing Span:	28	ft	1.0	in	8.56	m		
Length:	33	ft	9.3	in	10.29	m		
Height:	13	ft	1.3	in	3.99	m		
Wheel Track:	8	ft	11.0	in	2.72	m		
Wheel Base:	10	ft	4.5	in	3.16	m		
Wing Area:	176.7	ft^2			16.42	m^2		
POWERPLANT(S):								
Number of Engines / Designation:	One (1)	Bristol Siddeley Orpheus 803 turbojet						
Maximum Power / Thrust per Engine:	5,000	lbs st			2,268	kg st		
FUEL CAPACITY:								
Internal Fuel Capacity:	425	US gal			1,609	ltrs	354	Imp gal
External Fuel Capacity:	274	US gal			1,036	ltrs	228	Imp gal
Total Fuel Capacity:	699	US gal			2,645	ltrs	582	Imp gal
WEIGHTS:								
Empty:	7,275	lbs			3,300	kg		
Maximum Take-Off:	12,500	lbs			5,670	kg		
Maximum Wing Loading:	70.7	lbs/ft^2			345.4	kg/m^2		
PERFORMANCE:								
Max Level Speed at Sea Level:	668	mph			1,075	kmh	580	kts
Max Level Speed at Altitude:	675	mph @			1,085	kmh @	586	kts @
	4,988	ft			1,520	m	4,988	ft
Nominal Cruising Speed:	404	mph			650	kmh	351	kts
Initial Rate of Climb at Sea Level:	6,003	ft/min			1,830	m/min		
Service Ceiling:	42,978	ft			13,100	m		
Nominal Combat Radius:	391	mi			630	km	340	nm
Maximum / Ferry Range:	1,150	mi			1,850	km	999	nm

Data File for the Fiat G91R

Hunter FR.Mk.10

Image 034, RAF Hunter FR.Mk.10. The lightning bolts on the nose identify the aircraft as belonging to No. 4 Sq, which was station in West Germany during the 1960s. (Photo copyright by Vic Flintham)

In 1957 Hawker Aircraft Ltd designed and manufactured the Hunter FR.Mk.10 for the RAF in response to the Ministry of Defense (MOD) Specification 164. A single-seat, fighter-reconnaissance variant of the Hunter F.Mk.6 interceptor, it was Hawker's second attempt to develop a reconnaissance variant of the Hunter aircraft. Designed for low-level, day-only photographic-reconnaissance, the aircraft modifications were based on Hawker's experience with the Hunter FR.Mk.4, a privately funded development effort by Hawker Aircraft Ltd. The prototype Hunter FR.Mk.10 first flew on 07 November 1958.

The Hunter FR.Mk.10 has a barrel-type fuselage, which houses a single, afterburning Rolls Royce Avon RA-28 turbojet engine. The triangular shaped engine intakes are located in the wing roots and the single exhaust extends aft of the tail plane. Due to the manner the wing stub was integrated into the fuselage, when viewed from above the Hunter FR.Mk.10 has an hourglass appearance. The Hunter series aircraft have two unique identification features. The first is the presence of a raised dorsal spine running from the canopy to the vertical stabilizer. The second is the installation of link collector pods on either side of the lower fuselage behind the four 30 mm Aden cannons in the nose. The pilot is seated in a single-seat cockpit, located well forward of the wing's leading edge with a single-piece moveable canopy which slides aft for pilot ingress and egress. The retractable, tricycle landing gear has a single-wheel nose gear and one wheel on each main gear. The mid-mounted wings are sweptback at an angle of 40°, have a single saw-tooth leading edge and blunt tips. There are two underwing hardpoints on each wing and a tubular pitot sensor on the left wingtip. External fuel is carried in two wing-mounted fuel tanks, each with a capacity of 276 US gal (1,045 ltr/230 imp gal). The sweptback horizontal stabilizer is low-mounted on the sweptback vertical stabilizer and both have blunt tips.

To accommodate the sensor suite, the aircraft nose was modified and lengthened by 10.5 in (0.3 m). In addition, the interceptor's ranging radar was removed and replaced by three cameras; one in the forward-oblique position and two in the side-oblique positions.

Delivery of the thirty-three production Hunter FR.MK.10s to the RAF began in 1960. The Hunter FR.Mk.10 equipped the following RAF reconnaissance squadrons in support of NATO during the Cold War:

- RAF, No.2 Sq Hunter FR.Mk.10 1960 - 1970
- RAF, No.4 Sq Hunter FR.Mk.10 1960 - 1970

Only three, Hunter FR.Mk.10s have survived in the UK.

Table 018, Hunter FR.Mk.10 Technical and Performance Specifications

DIMENSIONS:			
Wing Span:	33 ft 8.0 in	10.26 m	
Length:	46 ft 1.0 in	14.05 m	
Height:	13 ft 2.0 in	4.01 m	
Wheel Track:	14 ft 9.0 in	4.50 m	
Wing Area:	349.0 ft^2	32.42 m^2	
POWERPLANT(S):			
Number of Engines / Designation:	One (1) Rolls Royce Avon RA-28 turbojet		
Maximum Power / Thrust per Engine:	10,000 lbs st	4,536 kg st	
FUEL CAPACITY:			
Internal Fuel Capacity:	471 US gal	1,783 ltrs	392 Imp gal
External Fuel Capacity:	552 US gal	2,089 ltrs	460 Imp gal
Total Fuel Capacity:	1,023 US gal	3,872 ltrs	852 Imp gal
WEIGHTS:			
Empty:	13,100 lbs	5,942 kg	
Maximum Take-Off:	24,000 lbs	10,886 kg	
Maximum Wing Loading:	68.8 lbs/ft^2	335.8 kg/m^2	
PERFORMANCE:			
Max Level Speed at Sea Level:	710 mph	1,143 kmh	617 kts
Max Level Speed at Altitude:	715 mph @ 36,000 ft	1,151 kmh @ 10,973 m	621 kts @ 36,000 ft
Initial Rate of Climb at Sea Level:	15,600 ft/min	4,755 m/min	
Service Ceiling:	55,000 ft	16,764 m	
Nominal Combat Radius:	350 mi	563 km	304 nm
Maximum / Ferry Range:	1,843 mi	2,965 km	1,601 nm

Data File for the Hunter FR.Mk.10

Canberra PR. Mk.9

Image 035, RAF Canberra PR.Mk.9, s/n XH234, of No. 39 Sq, RAFB Wyton, UK over West Germany in the 1970s. (Paul Wagner Collection)

The Canberra PR.Mk.9 is the final photographic-reconnaissance variant of the Canberra series of aircraft. Based on the Canberra B(I).Mk.8 bomber, the Canberra PR.Mk.9 is a two-seat, unarmed, day-only, photographic-reconnaissance aircraft designed and manufactured for the RAF by Short Brothers and Harland. The prototype Canberra PR.Mk.9 (s/n WH 793) was a converted Canberra PR.Mk.7 airframe and first flew on 08 July 1955.

Like the previous marks, the Canberra PR.Mk.9 has a crew of two (pilot and navigator) and a sensor mix similar to the Canberra PR.Mk.3/7. There are two significant differences between the Canberra PR.Mk.9 and the earlier Canberra PR.MK.3/7.

First, the fixed bubble canopy of the Canberra PR.Mk.3/7 is replaced by the elongated clamshell canopy of the Canberra B(I).Mk.8. The canopy is offset to the left side of the fuselage, and hinged aft for pilot ingress and egress.

The crew access door on the right side of the fuselage was eliminated and the aircraft nose was modified. The modifications include replacing the Plexiglas nose with a solid nose packed with avionics equipment and an optical periscope sight. A prism shaped viewfinder is located beneath the forward section of the nose. The new nose is hinged on the right side and swings open for navigator ingress and egress. There is a small rectangular window on each side of the fuselage, near the top, just aft of the hinged nose. The navigator's "couch" is replaced with an ejection seat.

Image 036, RAF Canberra PR.Mk.9 at RAFB Fairford on 19 July 2003. Note the elongated, fighter style canopy and crew ladder; the open, hinged nose revealing the navigator avionics panel and optical viewfinder. The prism shaped viewfinder window below the hinged nose section. (Photo copyright by Stephen Boreham)

The sensor mix of the Canberra PR.Mk.9 is similar to the Canberra PR.Mk.3/7, however there are notable external differences. Three of the four large camera windows located on the lower forward lower fuselage are eliminated, leaving only one on the right side. Three small round cameras windows are installed in the forward lower fuselage, one in the side-oblique position on each side of the lower fuselage just forward of the canopy, and one in the forward-oblique position in the nose.

The first production Canberra PR.Mk.9 was delivered to the RAF in early 1960. A total of twenty-three Canberra PR.Mk.9s were produced for the RAF and equipped the following RAF reconnaissance squadrons assigned to support NATO during the Cold War:

- RAF, No.58 Sq — Canberra PR.Mk.9 — 1960 - 1970
- RAF, No.13 Sq — Canberra PR.Mk.9 — 1962 - 1981
- RAF, No. 39 Sq/1st PRU — Canberra PR.Mk.9 — 1962 - Present

A limited number of Canberra PR.Mk.9 aircraft remain in active service more than 45 years after entering service with the RAF. However, at least two are on displays at museums in the United Kingdom and Chile:

Table 019, Canberra PR.Mk.9 Technical and Performance Specifications

DIMENSIONS:				
Wing Span:	67 ft	10.0 in	20.68 m	
Length:	66 ft	8.0 in	20.32 m	
Height:	15 ft	8.0 in	4.78 m	
Wheel Track:	15 ft	5.0 in	4.70 m	
Wing Area:	960.0 ft²		89.18 m²	
POWERPLANT(S):				
Number of Engines / Designation:	Two (2) Rolls Royce Avion 206 turbojets			
Maximum Power / Thrust per Engine:	11,250 lbs st		5,103 kg st	
FUEL CAPACITY:				
Internal Fuel Capacity:	3,321 US gal		12,568 ltrs	2,765 Imp gal
External Fuel Capacity:	586 US gal		2,218 ltrs	488 Imp gal
Total Fuel Capacity:	3,907 US gal		14,786 ltrs	3,253 Imp gal
WEIGHTS:				
Empty:	23,173 lbs		10,511 kg	
Maximum Take-Off:	56,250 lbs		25,515 kg	
Maximum Wing Loading:	58.6 lbs/ft²		286.1 kg/m²	
PERFORMANCE:				
Max Level Speed at Sea Level:	514 mph		827 kmh	446 kts
Max Level Speed at Altitude:	545 mph @ 40,025 ft		876 kmh @ 12,200 m	473 kts @ 40,025 ft
Initial Rate of Climb at Sea Level:	3,397 ft/min		1,035 m/min	
Nominal Combat Radius:	805 mi		1,295 km	699 nm
Maximum / Ferry Range:	3,629 mi		5,840 km	3,153 nm
T-O Run to 50 feet:	6,005 ft		1,830 m	
Landing Run with Aux Braking:	3,905 ft		1,190 m	

Data File for the Canberra PR.Mk.9

Saab J29OF Tunnan

Image 037, Austrian AF Saab J29ÖF Tunnan in the markings of Fliegerregiment 3, Fliegerhorst Vogler near Linz, Austria. Note the flush mounted removable reconnaissance pod on the left side with square windows for the left side-oblique cameras. (Photo copyright by Diego Bigolin)

In July 1961 the Austrian AF entered the jet age when an initial batch of fifteen Saab modified J29B Tunnan fighter and attack aircraft were delivered with designation Saab J29ÖF Tunnan. In the autumn of 1961 a second batch of fifteen aircraft were delivered. Unlike the first batch of Saab J29ÖF Tunnan aircraft, the second batch was modified to perform three missions: fighter, attack and day-photographic-reconnaissance.

Externally, the Austrian AF Saab J29ÖF Tunnan is similar in appearance to the Swedish AF Saab S29C Tunnan. However, the camera installation for the Saab J29ÖE differed significantly from the earlier Swedish AF installation, making it easy to distinguish between the two variants. Unlike the Saab S29C Tunnan, which houses the reconnaissance cameras internally in place of the four machine guns, the cameras for the Saab J29ÖF Tunnan are housed in an flush mounted reconnaissance pod installed under the left side of the fuselage. When installed, the pod requires the removal of two of the machine guns, allowing the Saab J29ÖF Tunnan to retain the two machine guns in the lower right fuselage for ground attack missions and self-defense. The sensor configuration for the Saab J29ÖF Tunnan includes three Vinten cameras, installed in the forward and side-oblique positions with metal shutters covering the camera windows during take-off, landing and while taxing.

Saab produced a total of thirty Saab J29ÖF Tunnans, fifteen of which equipped the following Austrian AF fighter-reconnaissance unit during the Cold War:

- Austrian AF, Fliegerregiment 3 — Saab J29F Tunnan — 1961 - 1972

There is one confirmed example of the Saab J29ÖF Tunnan with a reconnaissance pod installed on display at Graz-Thalerhof AB, AT.

Table 020, Saab J29F Tunnan Technical and Performance Specifications

DIMENSIONS:				
Wing Span:	36 ft	1.0 in	11.00 m	
Length:	33 ft	7.0 in	10.24 m	
Height:	12 ft	4.0 in	3.76 m	
Wheel Track:	7 ft	2.0 in	2.18 m	
Wing Area:	260.0 ft²		24.15 m²	
POWERPLANT(S):				
Number of Engines / Designation:	One (1)	De Havilland Ghost 50 turbojet		
Maximum Power / Thrust per Engine:	5,005 lbs st		2,270 kg st	
FUEL CAPACITY:				
Internal Fuel Capacity:	568 US gal		2,150 ltrs	473 Imp gal
External Fuel Capacity:	238 US gal		900 ltrs	198 Imp gal
Total Fuel Capacity:	806 US gal		3,050 ltrs	671 Imp gal
WEIGHTS:				
Empty:	10,680 lbs		4,844 kg	
Maximum Take-Off:	17,020 lbs		7,720 kg	
Maximum Wing Loading:	65.5 lbs/ft²		319.6 kg/m²	
PERFORMANCE:				
Max Level Speed at Altitude:	659 mph		1,061 kmh	572 kts
Nominal Cruising Speed:	497 mph		800 kmh	432 kts
Initial Rate of Climb at Sea Level:	11,810 ft/min		3,600 m/min	
Service Ceiling:	50,850 ft		15,499 m	
Maximum / Ferry Range:	684 mi		1,101 km	594 nm

Data File for the Saab J29OF Tunnan

Fiat G91T

Image 038, Fiat G91T1, s/n 3427, of the West German AF over West Germany in the 1970s. (Paul Wagner Collection)

The Fiat G91T is the two-seat advanced trainer variant of the Fiat G91R. Like the Fiat

G91R, the Fiat G91T retains both the strike and day-photographic-reconnaissance capabilities. Designed and manufactured for the Italian AF by Fiat (Societa per Azioni Fiat), the prototype Fiat G91T first flew on 31 May 1960.

With the exception of the tandem cockpits, the Fiat G91T is nearly identical to Fiat G91R. However, to accommodate the second cockpit, the fuselage

Image 039, Portuguese AF Fiat G91T at Cambrai AB, FR on 15 June 1986 with open tandem canopies, crew ladders and G91R reconnaissance nose. (Photo copyright by Ian Powell)

of the Fiat G91T was extended 4 ft 6 in (1.38 m) and the aircraft height was increased by 1 ft 6 in (0.46 m). An instructor pilot occupies the second cockpit immediately behind and slightly above the student pilot. The two-place tandem cockpit is located just forward of the wing's leading edge, with individual aft-hinged clamshell canopies. The Fiat G91T has one 0.50-in (12.7 mm) machine gun installed on each side of the lower fuselage, deleting the upper gun to make additional room for the second cockpit. However, the Fiat G91T retains the reconnaissance nose and camera configuration of the single seat Fiat G91R.

Production of the Fiat G91T totaled seventy-six Fiat G91T/1s; and forty-four Fiat G91T/3s. The Fiat G91T equipped the following NATO air force units in support of NATO during the Cold War:

- West German AF, WS 50 Fiat G91T/1 1962 - 1992
- Italian AF, 2° Stormo, 602° Gruppo Fiat G91T/1 1963 - 1991
- Italian AF, 8° Stormo, 608° Gruppo Fiat G91T/1 1963 - 1991
- Italian AF, 32° Stormo, 632° Gruppo Fiat G91T/1 1963 - 1991
- Portuguese AF, BA 6, ESq 301 Fiat G91T/1 1976 - 1993

Several Fiat G91T advanced trainers have survived and can be viewed throughout Europe.

Table 021, Fiat G91T1 Technical and Performance Specifications

DIMENSIONS:						
Wing Span:	28 ft	1.0 in	8.56 m			
Length:	38 ft	3.5 in	11.67 m			
Height:	14 ft	7.3 in	4.45 m			
Wheel Track:	9 ft	3.0 in	2.82 m			
Wheel Base:	11 ft	6.3 in	3.51 m			
Wing Area:	176.7 ft²		16.42 m²			
POWERPLANT(S):						
Number of Engines / Designation:	One (1)	Bristol Siddeley Orpheus 803 turbojet				
Maximum Power / Thrust per Engine:	5,000 lbs st		2,268 kg st			
FUEL CAPACITY:						
Internal Fuel Capacity:	555 US gal		2,100 ltrs		462 Imp gal	
External Fuel Capacity:	274 US gal		1,036 ltrs		228 Imp gal	
Total Fuel Capacity:	829 US gal		3,136 ltrs		690 Imp gal	
WEIGHTS:						
Empty:	8,250 lbs		3,742 kg			
Maximum Take-Off:	13,340 lbs		6,051 kg			
Maximum Wing Loading:	75.5 lbs/ft²		368.6 kg/m²			
PERFORMANCE:						
Max Level Speed at Altitude:	640 mph @ 4,920 ft		1,030 kmh @ 1,500 m		556 kts @ 4,920 ft	
Nominal Cruising Speed:	404 mph		650 kmh		351 kts	
Service Ceiling:	40,025 ft		12,200 m			
Nominal Combat Radius:	391 mi		630 km		340 nm	
Maximum / Ferry Range:	1,150 mi		1,850 km		999 nm	

Data File for the Fiat G91T

Mirage IIIR/RD/RS and 5BR

Image 040, French AF Mirage III in flight over Western Europe during the 1970s. The aircraft designation "33-NO" indicates the aircraft is assigned to the 2nd ER (Escadron de Reconnaissance) of the 33rd Wing, Strasbourg, FR. The bird on the tail is the 2nd squadron emblem. (Paul Wagner Collection)

The Mirage IIIR is the first of a family of single-seat, unarmed, day and night Tac Recce aircraft designed and manufactured for the French AF by Dassault (Avions Marcel Dassault). Based on the Mirage IIIE airframe, the Mirage IIIR is equipped with the Mirage IIIC avionics, has no radar and a modified reconnaissance nose. The prototype Mirage IIIR first flew on 31 October 1961.

A waisted-type fuselage houses an after-burning SNECMA Antar 9C turbo-jet engine. The engine intakes are mounted on the sides of the fuselage just

Image 041, Belgium AF Mirage 5BR from the 42nd Sq, Florennes AB, BE, with the original reconnaissance nose configuration common with the Mirage IIIR. (Paul Wagner Collection)

aft and below the cockpit, and include a moveable semi-conical compression cone in the intake. The single-seat cockpit is located forward of the engine intakes, with a single-piece clamshell canopy hinged aft for pilot ingress and egress. The retractable, tricycle landing gear has a single-wheel nose gear and one wheel on each main gear. One static port is located on the right side of the upper right fuselage just forward of the canopy. The low-mounted, delta wings are sweptback at an angle of 60° 34", have 1° anhedral and squared tips. There is one underwing hardpoint for external fuel or stores and a short, small stall fence above the underwing hardpoint on each wing. External fuel is carried in two wing-mounted fuel tanks, each with a capacity of 450 US gal (1,703 ltr/375 imp gal). There is no horizontal stabilizer and the sweptback vertical stabilizer has a square tip.

The modified nose can carry up five Omera Type 31 cameras. For low-level missions, the standard camera configuration includes one camera each in the forward-oblique, and right and left-side-oblique positions; and one to two cameras in the vertical position. Later models of the Mirage IIIR replaced the vertical camera with a panoramic camera. An updated version known as the Mirage IIIRD includes an improved Doppler navigation system in a fairing under the forward fuselage and the capability to carry a reconnaissance pod on the aircraft's centerline position with SAT's Cyclope IRLS sensor. With the exception of the forward-oblique camera, all cameras are installed on a hatch on the bottom of the fuselage, hinged at the rear for easy access to the cameras and film magazines. An optical site for the pilot's periscope is located just aft of the forward-oblique camera position on the bottom of the

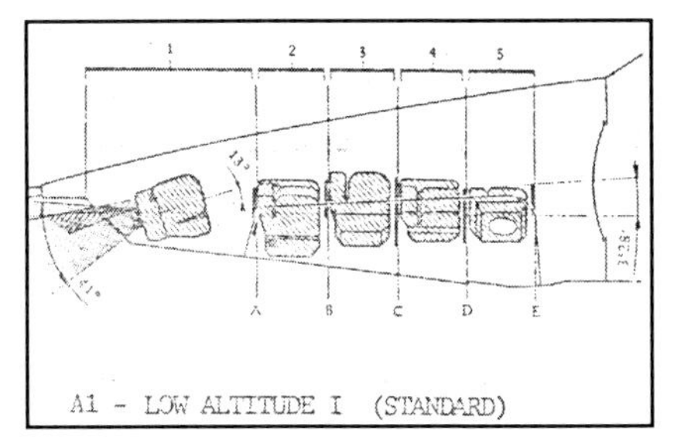

Figure 006, Low-altitude sensor configuration includes a forward oblique camera in station 1: a vertical or panoramic camera in station 2; a vertical camera in station 3; and side oblique cameras in stations 4 and 5. (Paul Wagner Collection)

fuselage. A long tubular pitot sensor located above the forward-oblique camera position extends well forward of the nose cone.

Other variants for NATO and non-aligned air forces in central Europe include the Mirage IIIRS for Swiss AF; and Mirage 5BR for the Belgium AF. Both aircraft are identical in appearance to the Mirage IIIR and did not include the Doppler system and fairing under the forward fuselage of the Mirage IIIRD. Unlike the Mirage IIIR, the Mirage IIIRS only carries four cameras in the reconnaissance nose. Following the Cold War, the Mirage IIIRS went through an upgrade program, which included new avionics and the addition of fixed canards just aft of and above the engine intakes.

Image 042, French AF Mirage IIIRD from ER 3/33, Strasbourg, FR over Western Europe. Note the fairing for the Doppler Navigation System under the fuselage. (Paul Wagner Collection)

The Mirage 5BR is the single-seat, photographic-reconnaissance version of the Mirage 5BA ground attack aircraft, which is also derived from the Mirage IIIE. The Mirage 5BR has the same camera configuration as the Mirage III, but uses the Vinten Type 360 cameras instead of the Omera Type 31 cameras. Like the Mirage IIIR, later upgrades to the Mirage 5BR replaced the forward vertical camera with a panoramic camera and added an IRLS sensor.

Image 043, Swiss AF Mirage IIIRS of Fliegerstaffel 10 on final approach. The camera windows are clearly visible, as is the viewfinder sight between the twin probes under the fuselage. (Photo copyright by Ian Powell)

The first production Mirage IIIR flew 01 February 1963. The Mirage IIIR entered service with the French AF in 1963. The first prototype Mirage 5BR flew on 06 March 1970. A total of 117 Mirage III/5 Tac Recce variants were manufactured. These included fifty-two Mirage IIIRs; twenty Mirage IIIRDs; eighteen Mirage IIIRSs; and twenty-seven Mirage 5BRs.

Image 044, Belgium AF Mirage 5BR at RAFB Finningley in September 1986. This aircraft has the modified reconnaissance nose common with later models of the Mirage IIIR/RD, this includes the prism shaped optical window used with a panoramic camera (Photo copyright by Trevor Thornton))

The Mirage IIIR and its variants equipped reconnaissance units of the following NATO and Western European non-aligned air forces during the Cold War:

- French AF, ER33, 3/33 "Moselle" Mirage IIIR 1963 - 1967
- French AF, ER33, 1/33 "Belfort" Mirage IIIR 1963 - 1983
- French AF, ER33, 2/33 "Savoie" Mirage IIIR 1963 - 1983
- Swiss AF, Fliegerstaffel 10 Mirage IIIRS 1965 - 1998
- French AF, ER33, 3/33 "Moselle" Mirage IIIRD 1967 - 1990
- Belgium AF, 2nd Wing, 42 Esc Mirage 5BR 1970 – 1994

At least fifteen, Mirage III and Mirage 5 series aircraft have survived and can be viewed throughout Europe.

Table 022, Mirage IIIR Technical and Performance Specifications

DIMENSIONS:			
Wing Span:	27 ft 0.0 in	8.23 m	
Length:	50 ft 10.3 in	15.50 m	
Height:	13 ft 11.5 in	4.25 m	
Wheel Track:	10 ft 4.0 in	3.15 m	
Wheel Base:	16 ft 0.0 in	4.88 m	
Wing Area:	375.0 ft^2	34.84 m^2	
POWERPLANT(S):			
Number of Engines / Designation:	One (1) SNECMA Antar 09C turbojet		
Maximum Power / Thrust per Engine:	13,670 lbs st	6,201 kg st	
FUEL CAPACITY:			
Internal Fuel Capacity:	940 US gal	3,558 ltrs	783 Imp gal
External Fuel Capacity:	1,242 US gal	4,701 ltrs	1,034 Imp gal
Total Fuel Capacity:	2,182 US gal	8,259 ltrs	1,817 Imp gal
WEIGHTS:			
Empty:	14,550 lbs	6,600 kg	
Maximum Take-Off:	30,200 lbs	13,699 kg	
Maximum Wing Loading:	80.5 lbs/ft^2	393.2 kg/m^2	
PERFORMANCE:			
Max Level Speed at Sea Level:	870 mph	1,400 kmh	756 kts
Max Level Speed at Altitude:	1,460 mph @ 39,375 ft	2,350 kmh @ 12,002 m	1,268 kts @ 39,375 ft
Initial Rate of Climb at Sea Level:	16,400 ft/min	5,000 m/min	
Service Ceiling:	55,775 ft	17,000 m	
Nominal Combat Radius:	808 mi	1,300 km	702 nm
Maximum / Ferry Range:	2,485 mi	3,999 km	2,159 nm

Data File for the Mirage IIIR/RD/RS/5BR

RF-104G/CF-104G Starfighter

Image 045, Italian AF RF-104G Starfighter with an Oude Delft Orpheus reconnaissance pod. on final approach at Verona AB, IT in August 1992. The number "3" identifies the aircraft as belonging to the 3° Stormo (Wing) CBR (Caccia Bombardieri Ricognotori); and the "Flying Witch" on the engine intake indicates the aircraft is assigned to the 28° Gruppo (Sq). (Photo copyright by Daniele Faccioli)

The F-104G Starfighter was designed in response to NATO's requirements for a fighter-bomber aircraft. The RF-104 Starfighter is the single-seat, day and night Tac Recce variant designed by Lockheed Aircraft Corporation and manufactured in the United States and Europe. Of the 189 RF-104G Starfighters, 149 or 78% were manufactured under license in NATO by European manufacturers including SABCA in Belgium; Fokker in the Netherlands; Fiat in Italy; and Messerschmitt in West Germany. The first flight of the F-104G Starfighter took place on 05 October 1960. In addition,

Canadair produced 200 Starfighters for the Canadian Armed Forces (CAF) under the designation CF-104G Starfighter.

The RF-104G/CF-104G Starfighter resembles a manned rocket. This single-seat supersonic aircraft has a long thin barrel-type fuselage with a sharply pointed nose cone, which houses a single afterburning, General Electric J79-GE-11A turbojet engine. The engine intakes are mid-mounted on the sides of the fuselage well aft of the cockpit, and include a moveable semi-conical compression cone in the intake. The single-seat cockpit is located well forward of the engine intakes, with a single-piece clamshell canopy hinged on the left side for pilot ingress and egress. The retractable, tricycle landing gear has a single-wheel nose gear and one wheel on each main gear. A long tubular pitot sensor located on the end of the nose cone. One static port is located on the left side of the upper right fuselage just below the canopy. The unequal-tapered wings are extremely short with a very thin cord, have very sharp leading and trailing edges, and squared tips. The wings are mid-mounted on the fuselage well aft of the engine intakes, with one underwing hardpoint for external fuel or stores. The RF-104G Starfighter normally carries wing tip tanks with a capacity each of 170 US gal (643 ltr/142 Imp gal) of external fuel. The vertical stabilizer has an unequal-taper, a blunt tip and extends aft and above the engine exhaust. The one-piece, all moving horizontal stabilator has an equal-tapered leading and trailing edge with square tips and is mounted at the top of the vertical stabilizer.

Image 046, Italian AF RF-104G Starfighter of 3° Stormo CBR, 28° Gruppo at Verona AB, IT on 04 January 1990. Note the camera fairing immediately behind the nose (Photo copyright by Giuseppe Tonelotto)

Image 047, Oude Delft Orpheus reconnaissance pod on the centerline position of an Italian AF RF-4G Starfighter. (Paul Wagner collection)

The RF-104G Starfighter was purchased by the NATO nations to replace the RF-84F Thunderflash and produced in two variants. Early versions of the RF-104G Starfighter had a modified fuselage to permit the 20 mm cannon and its 725 round magazine to be removed and replaced in the field with a camera pallet and bulged sensor window fairing. The sensor pallet and window fairing are installed on a hinged panel immediately behind the nose wheel, and include three, Old Delft T46M, or three KS-67A, 70 mm cameras in the vertical and side-oblique positions in the faring or bump immediately behind the nose wheel gear doors.

Later models of the RF-104G Starfighters deleted the internal camera configuration and were modified to accept and interface with a reconnaissance pod installed on the aircraft's centerline position.

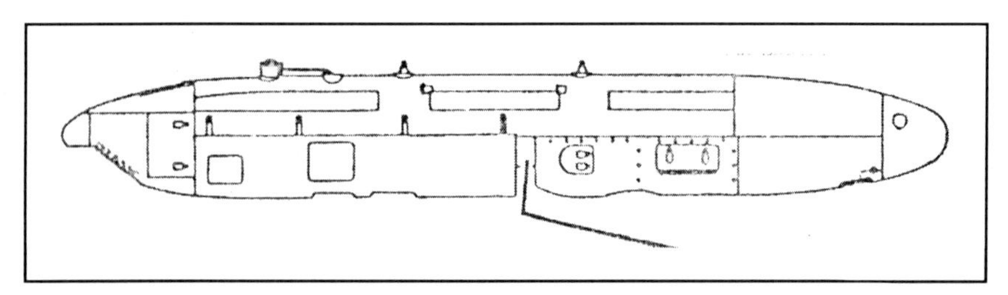

Figure 007, Oude Delft Orpheus reconnaissance pod used on Dutch and Italian RF-104C Freedom Fighters (Paul Wagner collection)

- The Royal Netherlands and West German AF RF-104G Starfighters used the low-altitude Oude Delft Orpheus reconnaissance pod equipped with five TA-8M cameras (one forward-oblique and two side-oblique positions; and two in either the high oblique or split-vertical positions) and one Oude Delft IRLS-5 sensor.

- The Italian AF used the low-altitude Oude Delft Orpheus reconnaissance pod equipped with a Fairchild 70 mm panoramic camera and three TA-8M cameras (one forward-oblique and two side-oblique positions), and one Oude Delft IRLS-5 sensor.

The Canadian Armed Forces selected the CF-104G Starfighter primarily as the delivery platform for nuclear weapons. However, the mission eventually changed to tactical strike aircraft with a secondary role of day only photographic-reconnaissance. The CF-104G was also equipped with a removable probe and drogue in-fight refueling system. In the reconnaissance role, the CF-104G Starfighter carries a Vinten Vicom, low-altitude reconnaissance pod with four Vinten 70 mm cameras in the forward-oblique, right and left side-oblique, and vertical positions. The first flight of the CF-104G took place on 28 March 1961.

Image 048, CAF CF-104G Starfighter equipped with the Vinten reconnaissance pod, from CAF Base, DE on display at RAFB Upper Heyford, UK in June 1971. (Photo copyright by Ian Howat)

The RF-104G/CF-104G Starfighter equipped reconnaissance units of the following NATO air forces during the Cold War:

• Royal Norwegian AF, 332 Sq	RF-104G Starfighter	1963 - 1966
• West German AF, AKG 52	RF-104G Starfighter	1963 - 1971
• Royal Netherlands AF, 306 Sq	RF-104G Starfighter	1963 - 1984
• West German AF, AKG 51	RF-104G Starfighter	1964 - 1971
• Canadian Armed Forces, 439 Sq	CF-104G Starfighter	1965 - 1973

- Italian AF, 3° Stormo, 28° Gruppo   RF-104G Starfighter   1971 - 1997
- Italian AF, 3° Stormo, 132° Gruppo   RF-104G Starfighter   1971 - 1997

At least four RF-104G Starfighter aircraft are on display in Europe, but none of the aircraft include the internal camera suite or have the reconnaissance pod mounted on the aircraft centerline.

Table 023, RF-104G Starfighter Technical and Performance Specifications

DIMENSIONS:								
Wing Span:	21	ft	11.0	in	6.68	m		
Length:	56	ft	8.0	in	17.27	m		
Height:	13	ft	6.0	in	4.11	m		
Wheel Track:	8	ft	10.8	in	2.71	m		
Wheel Base:	15	ft	0.5	in	4.58	m		
Wing Area:	196.1	ft²			18.22	m²		
POWERPLANT(S):								
Number of Engines / Designation:	One (1)	General Electric J79-GE-11A Turbojet						
Maximum Power / Thrust per Engine:	15,600	lbs st			7,076	kg st		
FUEL CAPACITY:								
Internal Fuel Capacity:	1,018	US gal			3,853	ltrs	848	Imp gal
External Fuel Capacity:	730	US gal			2,763	ltrs	608	Imp gal
Total Fuel Capacity:	1,748	US gal			6,616	ltrs	1,456	Imp gal
WEIGHTS:								
Empty:	13,996	lbs			6,349	kg		
Maximum Take-Off:	29,038	lbs			13,172	kg		
Maximum Wing Loading:	148.1	lbs/ft²			723.1	kg/m²		
PERFORMANCE:								
Max Level Speed at Sea Level:	461	mph			741	kmh	400	kts
Max Level Speed at Altitude:	1,456	mph @			2,343	kmh @	1,264	kts @
	50,000	ft			15,240	m	50,000	ft
Nominal Cruising Speed:	510	mph			821	kmh	443	kts
Initial Rate of Climb at Sea Level:	48,000	ft/min			14,630	m/min		
Service Ceiling:	58,000	ft			17,678	m		
Nominal Combat Radius:	745	mi			1,199	km	647	nm
Maximum / Ferry Range:	2,180	mi			3,508	km	1,894	nm

Data File for the RF-014G/CF-104G Starfighter

Saab S35E/RF-35 Draken

Image 049, Danish AF Saab RF-35 Draken assigned to Eskadrille (Esk) 729 stationed at Karup AB, DK on 24 August 1993. Note the tailskid and roller wheel under the engine exhaust. (Photo copyright by Joop de Groot)

The Saab S35E/RF-35 Draken is the low-level, day and night reconnaissance variant of the Saab J35 Lansen interceptor designed and manufactured by Saab (Saab Aktiebolag). Two different reconnaissance models were manufactured. The Saab S35E Draken is the unarmed, Swedish AF reconnaissance variant; and the RF-35 Draken is the armed, Royal Danish AF reconnaissance variant. The first flight of the Saab S35E Draken took place 27 June 1963.

A single-seat, single-engine aircraft the S35E/RF-35 Draken has a barrel-type fuselage which houses an afterburning Rolls Royce Avon 300 turbojet engine. The oval shaped engine intakes are located in the extended wing's leading edge below the canopy, and the engine nozzle exhaust extends aft of the vertical stabilizer. The single-seat cockpit is located above the engine intakes, with a single-piece clamshell canopy hinged on the left side for pilot ingress and egress. The retractable, tricycle landing gear has a single-wheel nose gear and one wheel on each main gear. A tubular pitot sensor located on the extended nose just above the forward-oblique camera position. There are two hardpoints under the fuselage for external fuel tanks. A tailskid with a roller wheel is located beneath the engine exhaust to protect the tail during take-off and landing. The S35E/RF-35 Draken has unique double delta wing mounted low on the fuselage with square tips. The broad and thick inner wing is swept up to 80° and provides space for the engine intakes, main under carriage, fuel and cameras. The outer wing is swept 60° and designed for low-speed operations. There are three hardpoints under each wing for external fuel and stores. The wing's trailing edge provides both elevator and aileron functions. The aircraft has a large sweptback vertical stabilizer, with a square tip, but no horizontal stabilizer.

The nose of the Saab S35E Draken is modified to accommodate a suite of four Omera Segid cameras. A modified nose with an angular contour is mounted on rails to slide out for easy access to the cameras and film magazines. The standard camera configuration includes one SKa 1 in the forward-oblique position; and three SKa 24 cameras with a 4.7 in (120 mm) fl lens; one each in the vertical, left side-oblique and right side-oblique positions. In addition, the Swedish AF Saab S35E carries one SKa 24 cameras in each wing in place of the Aden 20 mm cannon. These cameras produce vertical coverage by shooting through an optical periscope lens just inside and forward of the of the outer wing section.

The reconnaissance nose of the Saab RF-35 Draken is similar to the reconnaissance nose of the Saab S35E Draken. The primary difference is the RF-35 Draken has two right side-oblique camera positions. The Saab RF-35 Draken retains the wing cannon and has no cameras installed in the wings.

The pilot of the Saab S35E/RF-35 Draken uses an optical periscope sight to locate the targets to be imaged. The window for the optical sight is located behind the vertical camera position window, immediately below the cockpit.

In 1970 the Saab S35E/RF-35 Draken was upgraded to accept both the Edgerton, Graiier and Germeshausen (EG&G) "Blue Baron" night photography reconnaissance pod employing Vinten SKa 34 night cameras, and the

Vinten "Red Baron" IR reconnaissance pod. The S35E Draken production aircraft made its first flight on 13 May 1965.

Saab produced a total of sixty Saab S35E/RF-35 Drakens, which served in the following NATO and non-allied Western European air force reconnaissance units during the Cold War:

• Swedish AF, F11 Wing, 1 Div	Saab S35E Draken	1964 - 1979
• Swedish AF, F21 Wing, 1 Div	Saab S35E Draken	1966 - 1979
• Swedish AF, F11 Wing, 2 Div	Saab S35E Draken	1966 - 1979
• Royal Danish AF, Esk 729	RF-35 Draken	1970 - 1993

There is only one reported Saab S35E Draken survivor and six RF-35 Draken survivors on display in Sweden, Denmark and Norway.

Table 024, S35E Draken Technical and Performance Specifications

DIMENSIONS:			
Wing Span: [80° sweep]	36 ft 11.0 in	11.25 m	
Length:	50 ft 4.0 in	15.34 m	
Height:	12 ft 9.0 in	3.89 m	
Wheel Track:	8 ft 10.5 in	2.71 m	
Wheel Base:	13 ft 1.0 in	3.99 m	
Wing Area:	529.6 ft²	49.20 m²	
POWERPLANT(S):			
Number of Engines / Designation:	One (1) Rolls Royce Avon 300 turbojet		
Maximum Power / Thrust per Engine:	17,636 lbs st	8,000 kg st	
FUEL CAPACITY:			
Internal Fuel Capacity:	1,057 US gal	4,000 ltrs	880 Imp gal
External Fuel Capacity:	936 US gal	3,544 ltrs	780 Imp gal
Total Fuel Capacity:	1,993 US gal	7,544 ltrs	1,660 Imp gal
WEIGHTS:			
Empty:	25,132 lbs	11,400 kg	
Maximum Take-Off:	35,274 lbs	16,000 kg	
Maximum Wing Loading:	66.6 lbs/ft²	325.2 kg/m²	
PERFORMANCE:			
Max Level Speed at Altitude:	1,320 mph @ 36,006 ft	2,125 kmh @ 10,975 m	1,147 kts @ 36,006 ft
Initial Rate of Climb at Sea Level:	34,450 ft/min	10,500 m/min	
Service Ceiling:	65,617 ft	20,000 m	
Nominal Combat Radius:	623 mi	1,003 km	541 nm
Maximum / Ferry Range:	2,020 mi	3,250 km	1,755 nm

Data File for the Saab S35E/RF-35 Draken

RF-101G/H Voodoo

Image 050, USAF RF-101H Voodoo of the Kentucky ANG. (Photo courtesy of the NMUSAF)

In 1965, as part of a modernization effort for the US Air National Guard (ANG), Lockheed Aircraft Service Company of Ontario, CA began modifying twenty-nine, F-101A and thirty-one, F-101C Voodoo fighter-bomber aircraft. These aircraft were reconfigured as unarmed day and night reconnaissance aircraft, designated the RF-101G/H respectively.

These aircraft differed in appearance from the RF-101A/C in that they had a different shaped nose than their earlier processors. Externally, the RF-101G and H models Voodoos are identical. Structurally however, the RF-101H has the strengthened airframe of the F-101C Voodoo aircraft. The standard camera configuration for the RF-101G/H Voodoo is one KS-87

Image 051, USAF RF-101H Voodoo with the nose cone slid forward for access to the forward oblique camera and the side panels raised for access to the remaining cameras (Photo courtesy of the NMUSAF)

camera with a 6 in (150 mm) fl lens in the forward-oblique position; two KS-87 cameras with a 6 in (150 mm) fl lens in the left and right side-oblique positions; and one KA-56, panoramic camera with a 3 in (76 mm) fl lens. The aircraft nose slides out on rails for access to the forward-oblique camera and film magazine. Top hinged panels on the sides of the forward fuselage provided easy access to the panoramic and side-oblique cameras and film magazines. In addition, like the RF-101A/C Voodoos, two KA-1 high-altitude cameras with a 36" (914 mm) fl lens in the split-vertical position are located behind the cockpit and accessed by panels on the side of the aircraft that are hinged at the bottom.

In 1965 the ANG took delivery of these aircraft; with the RF-101G Voodoos being delivered to the Kentucky ANG and the RF-101H Voodoos being delivered to the Nevada ANG.

The RF-101G/H Voodoo equipped the following USAF Tac Recce squadrons during the Cold War:

• USAF, Kentucky ANG	RF-101G Voodoo	1965 - 1971
• USAF, Nevada ANG	RF-101H Voodoo	1965 - 1971

- USAF, Arkansas ANG RF-101G Voodoo 1971 - 1975
- USAF, Kentucky ANG RF-101H Voodoo 1971 - 1976

Only two examples of the RF-101G/H Voodoos have survived and can be seen in the United States.

Table 025, RF-101H Voodoos Technical and Performance Specifications

DIMENSIONS:								
Wing Span:	39	ft	8.0	in	12.09	m		
Length:	69	ft	4.0	in	21.13	m		
Height:	18	ft	0.0	in	5.49	m		
Wheel Track:	19	ft	10.5	in	6.06	m		
Wing Area:	368.0	ft^2			34.18	m^2		
POWERPLANT(S):								
Number of Engines / Designation:	Two (2)	Pratt & Whitney J57-P-13 turbojets						
Maximum Power / Thrust per Engine:	15,000	lbs st			6,804	kg st		
FUEL CAPACITY:								
Internal Fuel Capacity:	2,250	US gal			8,516	ltrs	1,874	Imp gal
External Fuel Capacity:	900	US gal			3,407	ltrs	749	Imp gal
Total Fuel Capacity:	3,150	US gal			11,923	ltrs	2,623	Imp gal
WEIGHTS:								
Empty:	26,136	lbs			11,855	kg		
Maximum Take-Off:	51,000	lbs			23,134	kg		
Maximum Wing Loading:	138.6	lbs/ft^2			676.7	kg/m^2		
PERFORMANCE:								
Max Level Speed at Altitude:	1,008	mph @			1,622	kmh @	875	kts @
	35,000	ft			10,668	m	35,000	ft
Nominal Cruising Speed:	547	mph			880	kmh	475	kts
Initial Rate of Climb at Sea Level:	36,150	ft/min			11,019	m/min		
Service Ceiling:	50,750	ft			15,469	m		
Nominal Combat Radius:	857	mi			1,379	km	745	nm
Maximum / Ferry Range:	2,145	mi			3,452	km	1,864	nm

Data File for the RF-101H Voodoo

RF-4C/CR.12 and RF-4E Phantom II

Image 052, USAF RF-4C Phantom II from the 10th Tactical Reconnaissance Wing (TRW), RAFB Alconbury, UK in July 1973. (Photo copyright by Steve Williams)

Introduced during the Vietnam conflict, the RF-4 Phantom II was the USAF's only twin-seat, all-weather Tac Recce aircraft. The most versatile Tac Recce aircraft of the Cold War, it was capable of carrying a variety of optical, thermal, radar and electronic sensors. During the Cold War, USAFE and NATO tasked the RF-4C/E Phantom II to conduct high-altitude, long-range surveillance, area mapping and area cover missions for the army, and daily low-level photographic-reconnaissance training missions in a variety of weather conditions, day and night. Designed and manufactured by McDonnell Aircraft Corporation, the first pre-production YRF-4C Phantom II flew on 09 August 1963, and the first production RF-4C Phantom II flew on 18 May 1964.

Derived from the F-4C Phantom II fighter-bomber, the RF-4C/E Phantom II has a large barrel-type fuselage with twin, afterburning General Electric J79-GE-15 turbofan engines. The engine intakes are elongated and rectangular in shape with the outboard side presenting a slightly curved profile with rounded corners. The engine intakes are mounted vertically on each side of the fuselage well forward of the wing's leading edge, immediately below the aft canopy. The twin-engine exhaust nozzles are located below and forward of the all-moving horizontal stabilator. The pilot and weapons systems officer (WSO) are located in a tandem cockpit forward of the wing's leading edge, with individual, aft hinged clamshell canopies for crew ingress and egress. A short tubular pitot sensor is mounted on the extended nose cone above the forward-oblique camera window. The retractable, tricycle landing gear has a twin-wheel nose gear and one wheel on each main gear. An arrestor hook, reminiscent of the F-4 Phantom's naval heritage is mounted on the lower fuselage behind the engine exhaust nozzles. The aft tail cone at the base of the vertical stabilizer houses the aircraft drag chute. The RF-4C/E Phantom II has an in-flight refueling receptacle on the top of the fuselage aft of the tandem canopy. However, the Spanish AF RF-4C Phantom II, designated the CR.12 Phantom II, is equipped with a modified probe-and-drogue in-flight refueling receptacle on the right side of the fuselage, which extends out and alongside the tandem crew canopies. There is one centerline hardpoint under the fuselage for external fuel and stores. The low-mounted wings are sweptback at a 45° angle, with a single saw-tooth leading edge and square tips. The outer wing panels have a pronounced 12° dihedral and fold up to reduce the aircraft's footprint when parked. There are two hardpoints under each wing for external fuel and stores. Normally the RF-4C/E Phantom II carries one external fuel tank on the outboard hardpoint of each wing, each with a capacity of 370 US gal (1,400 ltr/308 Imp gal). The vertical stabilizer has an unequal-tapered appearance with a square tip; and the one-piece, all moving horizontal stabilator is low-mounted on the rear fuselage with square tips and 23° anhedral.

An unarmed Tac Recce aircraft, the nose of the RF-4C/E Phantom II is extended 4 ft 7.5 in (1.41 m) and the contour changed to accommodate the reconnaissance sensors. The sensor configuration for low-level, day and night includes one KS-72 or later KS-87 camera with a 3" (76 mm) fl lens in the forward-oblique position with a 23.5° depression angle; two KS-87 cameras with either a 3" (76 mm) or 6" (150 mm) fl lens in the side-oblique positions with depression angles of either 30° or 37.5°; one KA-56 panoramic camera with a 3" (76 mm) fl lens and a 180° FOV; and one IRLS sensor. The Spanish AF CR.12 Phantom IIs and the German AF RF-4E Phantom IIs use the KS-72 camera in place of the KS-87. This camera has a similar form and fit, and uses the same film as the KS-87.

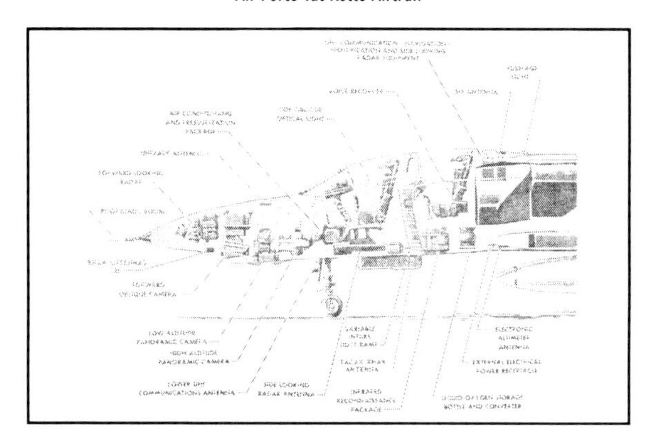

Figure 008, RF-4C Phantom II sensor layout (Paul Wagner Collection)

To aid in locating and imaging targets along the aircraft's line of flight, the pilot has an optical viewfinder, on the top right side of pilot's console. This is integrated into a periscope, which ends at the viewing window on the right side of the lower fuselage, just forward of the nose wheel well. Selected later models replaced the viewfinder with a CRT that was used for other sensors such as the AN/AVQ-26 Pave Tac pod.

Image 053, Spanish AF CR.12 Phantom II of the Ala 12 (Wing) and the 123rd Escudaron (Squadron) at Torrejon AB, Spain; note the in-flight refueling probe on the upper fuselage (Photo copyright by Roberto Yanez)

Like the Mirage III/5 series of Tac Recce aircraft, there are two (2) different nose contours. Early versions of the RF-4C Phantom II have a prism shaped optical window for use with the low-altitude panoramic cameras. Later models of the RF-4C Phantom II and the RF-4E Phantom II have a revised nose contour with a flat panel optical window for the panoramic cameras. Two hatches on the bottom of the fuselage nose provide access to the cameras and film magazines.

Image 054, Underside of RF-4C Phantom II nose showing the window for the optical viewfinder in the upper left hand corner, adjacent to the optical window for the split-vertical cameras. (Paul Wagner Collection)

RF-4C/E Phantom II reconnaissance nose contour. (Image 055) Note the prism shaped optical window for the panoramic camera on the early version of the RF-4C Phantom II on the left and (Image 056) the flat panel optical window which wraps up the side of the nose on the updated RF-4C Phantom IIs and the German RF-4E Phantom IIs. (Paul Wagner Collection)

For night-photographic-reconnaissance missions, the aircraft is equipped with thermal imaging sensors and photoflash cartridges. The original thermal sensor was the AN/AAS-18 IRLS sensor. The IRLS is located just aft of the nose wheel well, below the WSO's cockpit and is accessed by a hinged cover under the fuselage. By the 1980s the USAF replaced the AN/AAS-18 with the more capable and higher resolution AN/AAD-5 IRLS sensor. The AN/AAD-5 has two operating modes, a narrow FOV which images 30° either side of the aircraft's line of flight and with an equivalent fl of 3.94 in (100 mm); and a wide FOV, which images 60° either side of the aircraft's line of flight and has an equivalent fl of 1.31 in (33.3 mm). The German AF RF-4E Phantom IIs and the Spanish AF CR.12 Phantom IIs are equipped with the AN/AAS-18 IRLS sensor.

Photoflash cartridges provide illumination for optical cameras at night. These cartridges are ejected from a photoflash dispenser located on upper fuselage, on both sides of and just below the leading edge of the vertical stabilizer. The RF-4C/E Phantom II carries 104, M-112 photoflash cartridges for night photography below 4,000 ft (1,220 m) above ground level (AGL); or 40 M-123 cartridges for night photography at altitudes between 4,000 ft (1,220 m) and 8,500 ft (2,590 m) AGL.

Image 057 RF-4C/E Phantom II with camera doors open and film canisters being downloaded (Photo courtesy of the Department of Defense Visual Information Center [DVIC])

Image 058, AN/AVQ-26 Pave Tack Laser Designator Pod. (Paul Wagner Collection)

In an attempt to add a near-real-time capability to the RF-4C Phantom II in the low-level Tac Recce role, selected aircraft of the 1st TRS at Royal Air

Force Base (RAFB) Alconbury, UK were modified to carry the AN/AVQ-26 Pave Tack Laser Designator Pod. Developed as targeting system for the F-111 Ardvark, the system provides a steerable, video IR imaging capability to locate and track tactical targets without having to over fly the target area. Unlike conventional cameras, the Pave Tack sensor lens can be rotated 180° (horizon-to-horizon) in the vertical and 360° horizontally to allow the sensor to track the target as the aircraft approaches and departs the target area. In addition, the sensor has the ability to zoom in on a target, which reduces the FOV but increases the level of detail available to the WSO and Image Analyst. In addition, the data is recorded on videotape and immediately available for playback and analysis with the mission imagery. Another key feature of the system is the images can be viewed as either negative images (hot is white) or as positive images (hot is black), which is a more natural presentation for the WSO and Image Analyst. The Pave Tack Pod is installed on the aircraft centerline position, but is not jettisonable in flight. While the capabilities of the Pave Tack system and the image quality are very good, the pod creates an excessive amount of drag and significantly reduces the amount of external fuel that could be carried on a mission, reducing the aircraft's range and limiting its ability to perform aggressive, defensive maneuvers in a combat environment.

Mapping, medium-altitude and high-altitude photographic-reconnaissance missions, require the installation of longer focal length lenses and/or specialized cameras. For example, the KS-87 framing cameras can be reconfigured with an 18 in (457 mm) fl lens and used in either the split-vertical or side-oblique positions. Specialized cameras include the T-11/KC-1B mapping camera with a 6 in (150 mm) fl lens, which can be installed in place of the KS-87. The primary benefit of the KC-1B/T-11 mapping camera is it covers nearly four times the area of

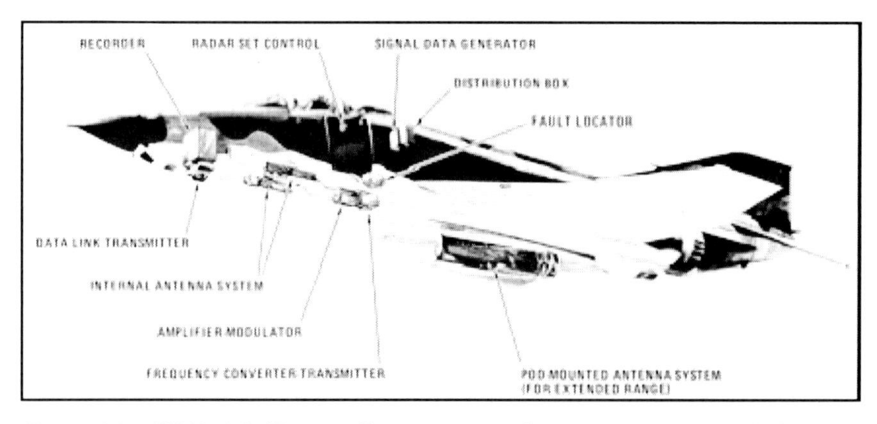

Figure 009, UPD-8 SAR surveillance sensor configuration as it is installed on an RF-4C Phantom II. (Courtesy Lockheed Martin)

KS-87 camera using the same size lens. This is possible, because the KC-1B/T-11 film format has a square, large film format [8.5 in (228 mm) on a side] versus the KS-87, which also uses a square film format but is only 4.5 in (114 mm). For medium-altitude to high-altitude reconnaissance missions, the RF-4C Phantom II can replace the KA-56 low-altitude panoramic camera with either the KA-55 medium-altitude panoramic camera with a 12 in (305 mm) fl lens or the KA-91 high-altitude panoramic camera with an 18 in (457 mm) fl lens.

For long-range surveillance missions, selected USAFE and German AF RF-4C/E Phantom II aircraft were modified to carry synthetic aperture radar (SAR) surveillance sensors. Unlike conventional radar systems, the SAR sensors carried on the RF-4C/E Phantom II aircraft create images by transmitting and receiving radar energy perpendicular the aircraft's line of flight, using the aircraft's forward motion to create the Doppler video phase history required to form a radar image. Because these systems transmit and receive radar energy from the side, they are also referred to as Side Looking Airborne Radars (SLAR) systems. The first SAR sensor employed on the RF-4C Phantom II was the AN/APQ-102 mapping radar set. This system was a coarse resolution system with an image resolution greater than 50 ft (15 m) in range and azimuth. The radar antennas were installed in the sides of the lower fuselage directly below the pilot's cockpit. In the mid-1970s the USAF replaced the AN/APQ-102 radar mapping set with a higher resolution mapping radar. The new radar mapping set, the AN/APD-10, also referred to as the UPD-4 SAR, has six operating modes, and is capable of collecting SAR image data on stationary and moving targets out to 30 nm (55.5 km) and with a resolution of 12.5 ft (3.8 m) to 15 ft (4.6 m). A subse,t of the UPD-4 equipped aircraft were upgraded in the 1980s with an extended range antenna in a non-jettisonable centerline pod and a real time data link in the nose of the aircraft in place of the cameras. This enhanced SAR imaged system is designated the UPD-8 SAR system. The extended range antenna adds two additional modes and extends the imaging range of the SAR system to 50 nm (92.5 km). However the image scale and resolution are reduced at the extended ranges. In addition, the data link provides the capability to down link in real-time the unprocessed video phase history data collected by the radar for any of the radar's modes of operation. The down linked video phase history data can be processed and exploited by Imagery Analyst before the aircraft returns to base. The effective data link range is limited to the direct line of sight between the airborne data link antenna and the receive antenna on the ground. In addition, heavy rain and thunderstorms do impact the quality and range of the data link signal.

The German AF used the AN/APD-11, also referred to as the UPD-6 SAR system. The UPD-6 has a near range resolution of approximately 50 ft (15 m) and an imaging range out to 50 nm (92.5 km). However the image scale and resolution are reduced at the extended ranges. Like the UPD-8 SAR system, the UPD-6 has six operating modes and requires the use of a pod mounted extended range antenna. The Spanish AF CR.12 Phantom IIs are not equipped with a SAR imaging system.

Image 059, USAF RF-4C Phantom II with the UPD-8 system installed. The extended range antenna is in the centerline tank and the data link antenna is located in the circular radome under the aircraft nose. (Photo courtesy Lockheed Martin)

In addition to the imaging sensors, selected USAF RF-4C Phantom IIs were equipped with the AN/ALQ-125 Tactical Electronic Reconnaissance (TEREC) system. The TEREC system provides the RF-4C Phantom II the capability to do precision direction finding, passive ranging and threat emitter identification. This was accomplished using a pair of side looking interferometer arrays installed on each side of the lower fuselage in the same location as the SAR antennas. In addition the TEREC system includes on board threat displays, data recording and a real-time data link to ground processors.

A total of 668 RF-4C/E Phantom IIs were build by the McDonnell Aircraft Corporation. The RF-4C/E Phantom II equipped reconnaissance units of the following USAFE based Tac Recce squadrons and NATO air forces reconnaissance squadrons during the Cold War:

- USAFE, 32nd TRS — RF-4C Phantom II — 1965 - 1975
- USAFE, 1st TRS — RF-4C Phantom II — 1965 - 1987
- USAFE, 38th TRS — RF-4C Phantom II — 1966 - 1991
- USAFE, 17th TRS — RF-4C Phantom II — 1969 - 1979
- USAFE, 18th TRS — RF-4C Phantom II — 1969 - 1970
- West German AF, AKG 51 — RF-4E Phantom II — 1970 - 2000
- West German AF, AKG 52 — RF-4E Phantom II — 1970 - 2000

- Greek AF, 110 Pterix, 348 Mira "Matia" RF-4E Phantom II 1976 - Present
- Turkish AF, 1 AJU, 113 Filo 'Isik' RF-4E Phantom II 1977 - Present
- Turkish AF, 7 AJU, 173 Filo 'Safak' RF-4E Phantom II 1977 - Present
- Spanish AF, Grupo 12, Esc 123 CR.12 Phantom II 1978 - 2004

More than 30 RF-4C/CR.12 and RF-4E Phantom II aircraft are on display or being restored throughout Europe and the United States.

Table 026, RF-4C Phantom II Technical and Performance Specifications

DIMENSIONS:			
Wing Span:	38 ft 4.9 in	11.71 m	
Length:	62 ft 10.5 in	19.16 m	
Height:	16 ft 5.0 in	5.00 m	
Wheel Track:	17 ft 10.5 in	5.45 m	
Wheel Base:	24 ft 9.0 in	7.54 m	
Wing Area:	530.0 ft^2	49.23 m^2	
POWERPLANT(S):			
Number of Engines / Designation:	Two (2) General Electric J79-GE-15 Turbofans		
Maximum Power / Thrust per Engine:	17,900 lbs st	8,119 kg st	
FUEL CAPACITY:			
Internal Fuel Capacity:	1,889 US gal	7,150 ltrs	1,573 Imp gal
External Fuel Capacity:	1,340 US gal	5,072 ltrs	1,116 Imp gal
Total Fuel Capacity:	3,229 US gal	12,222 ltrs	2,689 Imp gal
WEIGHTS:			
Empty:	28,292 lbs	12,833 kg	
Maximum Take-Off:	58,000 lbs	26,309 kg	
Maximum Wing Loading:	109.4 lbs/ft^2	534.4 kg/m^2	
PERFORMANCE:			
Max Level Speed at Sea Level:	910 mph	1,464 kmh	790 kts
Max Level Speed at Altitude:	1,485 mph @ 40,000 ft	2,390 kmh @ 12,192 m	1,290 kts @ 40,000 ft
Nominal Cruising Speed:	585 mph	941 kmh	508 kts
Initial Rate of Climb at Sea Level:	40,800 ft/min	12,436 m/min	
Service Ceiling:	59,400 ft	18,105 m	
Nominal Combat Radius:	526 mi	846 km	457 nm
Maximum / Ferry Range:	1,750 mi	2,816 km	1,521 nm

Data File for the RF-4C Phantom II

Table 027, RF-4E Phantom II Technical and Performance Specifications

DIMENSIONS:			
Wing Span:	38 ft 4.9 in	11.71 m	
Length:	63 ft 10.9 in	19.48 m	
Height:	16 ft 5.0 in	5.00 m	
Wheel Track:	17 ft 10.5 in	5.45 m	
Wheel Base:	24 ft 9.0 in	7.54 m	
Wing Area:	530.0 ft^2	49.23 m^2	
POWERPLANT(S):			
Number of Engines / Designation:	Two (2) General Electric J79-GE-15 Turbofans		
Maximum Power / Thrust per Engine:	17,900 lbs st	8,119 kg st	
FUEL CAPACITY:			
Internal Fuel Capacity:	1,889 US gal	7,150 ltrs	1,573 Imp gal
External Fuel Capacity:	1,340 US gal	5,072 ltrs	1,116 Imp gal
Total Fuel Capacity:	3,229 US gal	12,222 ltrs	2,689 Imp gal
WEIGHTS:			
Empty:	30,400 lbs	13,789 kg	
Maximum Take-Off:	61,000 lbs	27,670 kg	
Maximum Wing Loading:	115.1 lbs/ft^2	562.0 kg/m^2	
PERFORMANCE:			
Max Level Speed at Sea Level:	910 mph	1,464 kmh	790 kts
Max Level Speed at Altitude:	1,485 mph @ 40,000 ft	2,390 kmh @ 12,192 m	1,290 kts @ 40,000 ft
Nominal Cruising Speed:	585 mph	941 kmh	508 kts
Initial Rate of Climb at Sea Level:	61,400 ft/min	18,715 m/min	
Service Ceiling:	62,250 ft	18,974 m	
Nominal Combat Radius:	526 mi	846 km	457 nm
Maximum / Ferry Range:	1,885 mi	3,034 km	1,638 nm

Data File for the RF-4E Phantom II

Saab Sk60C

Image 060, Swedish AF Saab Sk60C landing at Tampere, Finland on 17 May 2005. Note the extended nose and the IR seeker head below the faired over prism shaped optical window. (Photo copyright by Ville Jalonen)

The Saab Sk60C is a light attack aircraft modified to conduct the secondary mission of day and night photographic-reconnaissance. The Sk60 series of aircraft are upgraded variants of the Saab 105 trainer, designed and manufactured for the Swedish AF by Saab (Saab Aktiebolag). The first production Saab SK60C flew on 18 January 1967.

The Saab Sk60c is a twin-engine, two-seat light attack aircraft with a short, thick barrel-shaped fuselage. The twin, non-afterburning General Electric J85-GE-17B turbojets are mounted on each side of the fuselage, immediately below the wing. The engine intakes are below and extend slightly forward of the wing's leading edge, and the engines exhaust nozzles extend to midway between the wing's trailing edge and horizontal stabilizer. The crew shares a single side-by-side cockpit arrangement, with a one-piece clamshell canopy hinged aft for crew ingress and egress. However, only a single pilot in the left seat is assigned to fly attack missions. The retractable, tricycle landing gear has a single-wheel nose gear and one wheel on each main gear. The high-mounted wings are sweptback at a modest angle of 12° 48', are flush with the top of the fuselage, with a pronounced 6° anhedral and blunt tips. There are two stall fences and three under wing hard points for external stores on each wing. The Saab SK60C can carry one fuel tank on each wing, each with a capacity of 143 US gal (541 ltr/119 Imp gal). A tubular pitot sensor is located on the right wing tip. The vertical stabilizer is swept back, and the horizontal stabilizer, mounted at the top of the vertical stabilizer, has an unequal-tapered appearance and blunt tips. For improved handling, there are two ventral fins, canted outboard, mounted below the aft fuselage.

Image 061, Swedish AF Saab SK60C on display at Deblin, PL on 26 August 1995. Note the optically transparent prism window for the KB-18 panoramic camera in the nose and the IR seeker head below the window. (Photo copyright by Piotr Biskupski)

The nose of the Saab SK60C is extended by 1 ft 8 in (0.5 m) with a modified contour to accommodate a KB-18 panoramic camera and IR seeker. Unlike other panoramic cameras, the KB-18 is installed in the forward-oblique position, as evidenced by the prism shaped optical window in the nose of the Sk60C aircraft. The IR seeker is installed behind the camera and the seeker head is located below the KB-18 camera. For night photography, a photoflash pod can be carried on a wing pylon.

Most of the Sk60C aircraft were converted back to the ground attack and liaison role. These aircraft have had their cameras removed and the camera window replaced with a fairing. Saab produced a total of twenty-nine SK60Cs, which equipped the following Swedish AF reconnaissance unit during the Cold War:

- Swedish AF, F21 Wing Saab SK60C 1967 - 1994

There are no known Saab Sk60C aircraft on display at this time.

Table 028, Saab SK60C Technical and Performance Specifications

DIMENSIONS:				
Wing Span:	31 ft	2.0 in	9.50 m	
Length:	36 ft	1.0 in	11.00 m	
Height:	8 ft	10.0 in	2.69 m	
Wheel Track:	6 ft	6.8 in	2.00 m	
Wheel Base:	12 ft	9.5 in	3.90 m	
Wing Area:	175.0 ft^2		16.26 m^2	
POWERPLANT(S):				
Number of Engines / Designation:	Two (2) General Electric J85-GE-17B turbojets			
Maximum Power / Thrust per Engine:	2,850 lbs st		1,293 kg st	
FUEL CAPACITY:				
Internal Fuel Capacity:	528 US gal		2,000 ltrs	440 Imp gal
External Fuel Capacity:	106 US gal		400 ltrs	88 Imp gal
Total Fuel Capacity:	634 US gal		2,400 ltrs	528 Imp gal
WEIGHTS:				
Empty:	5,534 lbs		2,510 kg	
Maximum Take-Off:	9,920 lbs		4,500 kg	
Maximum Wing Loading:	56.7 lbs/ft^2		276.8 kg/m^2	
PERFORMANCE:				
Max Level Speed at Sea Level:	603 mph		970 kmh	524 kts
Max Level Speed at Altitude:	544 mph @ 32,810 ft		875 kmh @ 10,000 m	472 kts @ 32,810 ft
Nominal Cruising Speed:	438 mph		705 kmh	380 kts
Initial Rate of Climb at Sea Level:	11,155 ft/min		3,400 m/min	
Service Ceiling:	42,650 ft		13,000 m	
Nominal Combat Radius:	618 mi		995 km	537 nm
Maximum / Ferry Range:	1,678 mi		2,700 km	1,458 nm

Data File for the Saab SK60C

RF-5A/CF-5A/CR.9 Freedom Fighter

Image 062, Spanish AF CR.9 Freedom Fighter, s/n 1062, on display in Madrid, ES on 23 August 2003. Originally assigned to Ala 21 at Moron AB, Spain, this aircraft carries the markings of the Ala 23 at Talevera AB, Spain where it was used for advanced training and redesignated the AR.9. (Photo copyright by Carlos Pulido Romera)

The RF-5A Freedom Fighter is a single-seat, armed, photographic-reconnaissance variant of the F-5A Freedom Fighter strike-fighter, designed and manufactured by Northrop Corporation for export to foreign countries under the MAP. The first flight of the F-5A Freedom Fighter took place on 19 May 1964. The Canadian version, designated the CF-5A Freedom Fighter was produced under license by Canadair and made its first flight on

Image 063, CAF CF-5A Freedom Fighter, s/n CL-219 at London CAFB in June 1983 with the canopy, cannon, and camera access panels open. (Photo copyright by Den Pascoe)

06 May 1968. The RF-5A Freedom Fighters operated by the Spanish AF are designated the CR.9 Freedom Fighter, but are frequently and incorrectly referred to as the SRF-5A Freedom Fighter.

Viewed from above, the long, slender barrel-type fuselage houses twin, afterburning General Electric J85-GE-13 turbojet engines. When viewed from above the fuselage has an hourglass shape. Semi-circular engine intakes are located forward and above the wings leading edge, just behind the canopy. The twin-engine exhaust nozzles are side-by-side and extend aft of the vertical stabilizer. The single-seat cockpit has a one-piece clamshell canopy hinged aft for pilot ingress and egress. Twin M-39, 20 mm cannons are mounted in the aircraft nose just forward of the cockpit. A tubular pitot sensor is mounted on the nose above the forward-oblique camera. The retractable, tricycle landing gear has single nose wheel and one wheel on each main gear. The uneven-tapered wings are low-mounted on the fuselage. The wings are sweptback at an angle of 24° and have square tips. A 50 gal (189 ltr/42 Imp gal) external fuel tank is normally carried on each wing tip. There is one hardpoint under the fuselage and two underwing hardpoints on each wing for external fuel and stores. The equal-tapered vertical stabilizer has a square tip and the one-piece, uneven-tapered horizontal stabilator is low-mounted on the fuselage, with a slight anhedral and square tips.

The RF-5A Freedom Fighter has a modified nose contour which retains the 20 mm cannon, and added four, KS-92, 70 mm cameras in the forward-oblique, vertical and side-oblique positions.

The RF-5A Freedom Fighter was also built under license in Canada by Canadair LTD for the Canadian Armed Forces with the designation CF-5A Freedom Fighter. Identical in appearance to the RF-5A Freedom Fighter, these aircraft are equipped with a "Quick Change" nose that houses three Vinten Model 547 cameras and can be fitted with an in-flight refueling probe receptacle on the right side of the fuselage just forward of the canopy. The forward section of the nose is hinged to tilt down and forward for access to the cameras and film magazines. The Spanish AF variant is designated the CR.9 Freedom Fighter and was used for both Tac Recce and advanced training until 1995.

The RF-5A/CF-5A/CR.9 Freedom Fighters equipped units of the following NATO air forces during the Cold War:

- Royal Norwegian AF, 717 Sq — RF-5A Freedom Fighter — 1966 - 1987
- Greek AF, 110 Pterix, 348 Mira — RF-5A Freedom Fighter — 1968 - 1993
- Canadian Armed Forces, 433 Sq — CF-5A Freedom Fighter — 1968 - 1995
- Canadian Armed Forces, 434 Sq — CF-5A Freedom Fighter — 1968 - 1995
- Spanish AF, Ala 21, Esc 211 — CR.9 Freedom Fighter — 1969 - 1982
- Spanish AF, Esc 464 — CR.9 Freedom Fighter — 1969 - 1982
- Turkish AF, 112 Filo — RF-5A Freedom Fighter — 1972 - 1994
- Turkish AF, 184 Filo — RF-5A Freedom Fighter — 1976 - 1994
- Spanish AF, Ala 21, Esc 212 — CR.9 Freedom Fighter — 1982 - 1992
- Spanish AF, Ala 23 — CR.9 Freedom Fighter — 1992 - 2001

At least ten RF-5A/CF-5A/CR.9 Freedom Fighters are on display, being restored or in storage in Europe and North America.

Table 029, RF-5A Freedom Fighter Technical and Performance Specifications

DIMENSIONS:			
Wing Span:	25 ft 3.0 in	7.70 m	
Length:	47 ft 2.0 in	14.38 m	
Height:	13 ft 2.0 in	4.01 m	
Wheel Track:	11 ft 0.0 in	3.35 m	
Wheel Base:	15 ft 4.0 in	4.67 m	
Wing Area:	170.0 ft^2	15.79 m^2	
POWERPLANT(S):			
Number of Engines / Designation:	Two (2) General Electric J85-GE-13 turbojets		
Maximum Power / Thrust per Engine:	4,080 lbs st	1,851 kg st	
FUEL CAPACITY:			
Internal Fuel Capacity:	583 US gal	2,207 ltrs	485 Imp gal
External Fuel Capacity:	450 US gal	1,703 ltrs	375 Imp gal
Total Fuel Capacity:	1,033 US gal	3,910 ltrs	860 Imp gal
WEIGHTS:			
Empty:	8,085 lbs	3,667 kg	
Maximum Take-Off:	20,677 lbs	9,379 kg	
Maximum Wing Loading:	121.6 lbs/ft^2	593.9 kg/m^2	
PERFORMANCE:			
Max Level Speed at Altitude:	924 mph @ 36,000 ft	1,487 kmh @ 10,973 m	802 kts @ 36,000 ft
Nominal Cruising Speed:	640 mph	1,030 kmh	556 kts
Initial Rate of Climb at Sea Level:	28,700 ft/min	8,748 m/min	
Service Ceiling:	50,000 ft	15,240 m	
Nominal Combat Radius:	558 mi	898 km	485 nm
Maximum / Ferry Range:	1,400 mi	2,253 km	1,216 nm

Data File for the RF-5A/CF-5A Freedom Fighter

Harrier GR.Mk.1/3

Image 064, RAF Harrier GR.Mk.1, s/n XV804 assigned to No. 233 Sq, and Operational Conversion Unit (OCU). The aircraft is seen taxing at RAF Finningley on 20 September 1975. (Photo copyright by Mick Bajcar)

The Harrier GR.Mk.1/3 is a single-seat, ground attack aircraft with a secondary mission of day and night photographic-reconnaissance, designed and manufactured for the RAF by Hawker Siddeley Aviation Ltd. The Harrier is the result of the P.1127 program, which began in 1957 a private venture between Hawker Siddeley and the Bristol Engine Company, to develop a Vertical/ Short Take-Off and Landing (V/STOL) aircraft. Nine years later, the first pre-production, Harrier GR.Mk.1 flew on 31 August 1966. This was followed with the maiden flight of the first production Harrier GR.Mk.1 on 28 December 1967.

The barrel-type fuselage houses a single, non-afterburning Rolls Royce Pegasus 103 vectored thrust turbofan engine with four rotatable two-vane exhaust nozzles. Two nozzles are located on each side of the fuselage, the first pair is located just forward and below the wings leading edge, the second further aft under the wing and just forward of the wing flaps. The semi-circular engine intakes are located on the fuselage sides, below and well forward of the wing's leading edge, just aft of the cockpit. The early Harrier GR.Mk.1s had a sharply pointed nose with a short pitot tube sensor at the tip. The single-seat cockpit has a moveable canopy that slides aft for pilot ingress and egress. A unique characteristic of the Harrier GR.Mk.1/3 is the bicycle main landing gear. Each main gear has a single wheel that retracts forward into the fuselage. The shoulder-mounted wings are sweptback at an angle of 34°, with 12° anhedral and curved tips. There is one outrigger landing gear with a small, single wheel on each wing tip, which extend aft of the wing's trailing edge when retracted. There are two hardpoints under the fuselage, and two under-wing hardpoints on each wing for external fuel and stores. The Harrier GR.Mk.1/3 can carry two external fuel tanks, each with a capacity of up to 228 US gal (863 ltr/190 Imp gal). The vertical stabilizer is sweptback with a blunt tip and the sweptback one-piece horizontal stabilator is high-mounted on the fuselage, with 10° anhedral and blunt tips. For improved maneuverability, there is one ventral fin below the aft fuselage. The conical fairing extending aft of the tail assembly houses the VHF antenna.

Image 065, RAF Harrier GR.Mk.3 from No. 4 Sq on display at RAFB Finningley, GB in September 1988, note the IR seeker head and the optical teardrop shaped window for the F.95 camera (Photo copyright by Trevor Thornton)

For the Tac Recce mission Hawker Siddeley installed a single F.95 camera in the nose of the Harrier GR.Mk.1/3, in the left side-oblique position. In addition, the Harrier GR.Mk.1/3 can carry a reconnaissance pod on the right-side fuselage pylon with five cameras installed in a fan configuration consisting of the one in the forward-oblique position; two each in the left and right, side-oblique positions.

Image 066, RAF Harrier GR.Mk.3 of No. 4 Squadron assigned to RAF Germany on display at Zweibrucken AB, GE. Note the Harrier Recce Pod on the aircraft centerline.

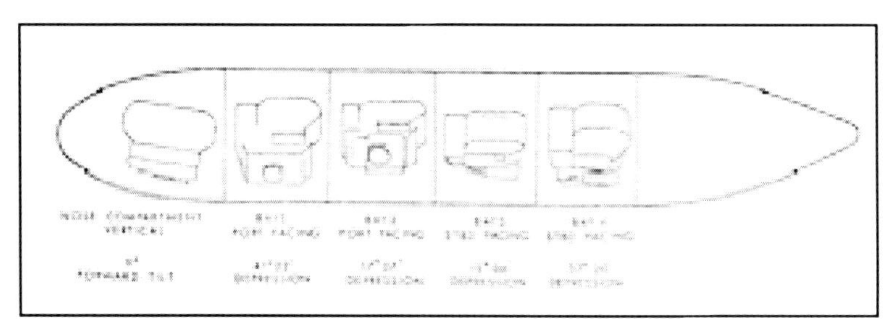

Figure 010, the Harrier Recce Pod on the right carried five optical cameras. (Paul Wagner Collection)

The upgraded Harrier GR.Mk.3 differs externally from the early Harrier GR.Mk.1s in the following areas:

- The Harrier GR.Mk.3 nose is longer with a modified nose contour to accommodate the electronics and IR seeker head for the Laser Ranging and Marked Target Seeking (LRMTS) system
- The tubular pitot sensor is relocated to a vertical fairing above the IR seeker head in the nose
- A Radar Warning Receiver (RWR) system is added to the Harrier GR.Mk.3 and the vertical stabilizer height increased 8 in (0.2 m) to accommodate the antenna, which is installed in a rectangular fairing near the top of the vertical fins leading edge

By late 1975 all Harrier GR.Mk.1s were upgraded to the Harrier GR.Mk.3 standard and configuration. Hawker Siddeley produced a total of seventy-eight Harrier GR.Mk.1s and thirty-six new-built Harrier GR.Mk.3s. Deliveries of the Harrier GR.Mk.1 began in May 1969. Only one RAF Squadron was assigned the secondary mission of Tac Recce and only 50% of the assigned aircraft were equipped to perform the Tac Recce mission.

The Harrier GR.Mk.1/3 equipped the following RAF squadron assigned the secondary mission of Tac Recce in support of NATO during the Cold War:

- RAF, No.4 Sq		Harrier GR.Mk.1/3		1970 - 1990

At least eighteen Harrier GR.Mk.1/3 aircraft are on display, being restored or in storage throughout Europe.

Table 030, Harrier GR.Mk.3 Technical and Performance Specifications

DIMENSIONS:			
Wing Span:	25 ft 3.0 in	7.70 m	
Length:	45 ft 2.8 in	13.79 m	
Height:	11 ft 11.0 in	3.63 m	
Wheel Track (outriggers):	22 ft 2.0 in	6.76 m	
Wheel Base:	11 ft 4.0 in	3.45 m	
Wing Area:	201.0 ft²	18.67 m²	
POWERPLANT(S):			
Number of Engines / Designation:	One (1) Rolls Royce Pegasus 103 vectored thrust turbofan		
Maximum Power / Thrust per Engine:	21,500 lbs st	9,752 kg st	
FUEL CAPACITY:			
Internal Fuel Capacity:	757 US gal	2,864 ltrs	630 Imp gal
External Fuel Capacity:	793 US gal	3,000 ltrs	660 Imp gal
Total Fuel Capacity:	1,549 US gal	5,864 ltrs	1,290 Imp gal
WEIGHTS:			
Empty:	12,300 lbs	5,579 kg	
Maximum Take-Off:	25,200 lbs	11,430 kg	
Maximum Wing Loading:	125.4 lbs/ft²	612.2 kg/m²	
PERFORMANCE:			
Max Level Speed at Sea Level:	730 mph	1,175 kmh	634 kts
Max Level Speed at Altitude:	737 mph @ 1,000 ft	1,186 kmh @ 305 m	640 kts @ 1,000 ft
Initial Rate of Climb at Sea Level:	29,003 ft/min	8,840 m/min	
Service Ceiling:	55,000 ft	16,764 m	
Nominal Combat Radius:	414 mi	667 km	360 nm
Maximum / Ferry Range:	2,129 mi	3,425 km	1,849 nm

Data File for the Harrier GR.Mk.3

Saab 105ÖE

Image 067, Austrian AF Saab 105ÖE on final approach at Graz AB, AT on 11 May 2004. (Photo copyright by Werner Horvath)

The Saab 105ÖE is the export version of the Swedish AF Saab 105 two-seat jet trainer designed and manufactured by Saab (Saab Aktiebolag). Modified to accept the Austrian AF photographic-reconnaissance pod, the primary mission for the Saab 105ÖE is ground attack, with a secondary mission of low-level, day and night photographic-reconnaissance.

The Saab 105ÖE is a twin-engine, two-seat light attack aircraft with a short, thick barrel-type fuselage with a rounded nose. The twin, non-afterburning General Electric J85-GE-17B turbojets are mounted on each side of the fuselage, immediately below the wing. The engine intakes are below and extend slightly forward of the wing's leading edge, and the engines and exhaust nozzles midway between the wing's trailing edge and horizontal stabilizer. The crew shares a single side-by-side cockpit arrangement, with a one-piece clamshell canopy hinged at the rear for crew access. A "towel rack" or long range (LORAN) navigation system antenna runs along the top of the fuselage between two large blade antennas. The retractable tricycle landing gear has a single nose wheel gear and one wheel on each main gear. The high-mounted wings are flush with the top of the fuselage, sweptback at modest angle of 12° 48', with a pronounced 6° anhedral and blunt tips. There are two stall fences and three under wing hard points for external stores on each wing. The Saab 105ÖE can carry one fuel tank on each wing, each with a capacity of 143 US gal (541 ltr/119 Imp gal). A tubular pitot sensor is located on the right wing tip. The vertical stabilizer is swept back, and the horizontal stabilizer, mounted at the top of the vertical stabilizer has an unequal-tapered appearance and blunt tips. For improved handling, there are two ventral fins, canted outboard, mounted below the aft fuselage.

The Austria AF photographic-reconnaissance pod is installed on a wing hardpoint and includes three Vinton 360 cameras with a 3.9 in (100 mm) fl lens in the forward-oblique, vertical and side-oblique positions, and two IR cameras.

Saab produced and delivered forty Saab 105ÖE aircraft to the Austrian AF between 1970 and 1972, which equipped the following Austrian AF reconnaissance unit in Western Europe during the Cold War:

- Austrian AF, Fliegerregiment 3 Saab 105ÖE 1970 - Present

There are no known Saab 105ÖE aircraft on display at this time.

Table 031, Saab 105ÖE Technical and Performance Specifications

DIMENSIONS:			
Wing Span:	31 ft 2.0 in	9.50 m	
Length:	34 ft 5.4 in	10.50 m	
Height:	8 ft 10.0 in	2.69 m	
Wheel Track:	6 ft 6.8 in	2.00 m	
Wheel Base:	12 ft 9.5 in	3.90 m	
Wing Area:	175.0 ft²	16.26 m²	
POWERPLANT(S):			
Number of Engines / Designation:	Two (2) General Electric J85-GE-17B turbojets		
Maximum Power / Thrust per Engine:	2,850 lbs st	1,293 kg st	
FUEL CAPACITY:			
Internal Fuel Capacity:	528 US gal	2,000 ltrs	440 Imp gal
External Fuel Capacity:	106 US gal	400 ltrs	88 Imp gal
Total Fuel Capacity:	634 US gal	2,400 ltrs	528 Imp gal
WEIGHTS:			
Empty:	5,534 lbs	2,510 kg	
Maximum Take-Off:	9,920 lbs	4,500 kg	
Maximum Wing Loading:	56.7 lbs/ft²	276.8 kg/m²	
PERFORMANCE:			
Max Level Speed at Sea Level:	603 mph	970 kmh	524 kts
Max Level Speed at Altitude:	544 mph @ 32,810 ft	875 kmh @ 10,000 m	472 kts @ 32,810 ft
Nominal Cruising Speed:	438 mph	705 kmh	380 kts
Initial Rate of Climb at Sea Level:	11,155 ft/min	3,400 m/min	
Service Ceiling:	42,650 ft	13,000 m	
Nominal Combat Radius:	618 mi	995 km	537 nm
Maximum / Ferry Range:	1,678 mi	2,700 km	1,458 nm

Data File for the Saab 105

RF-101B Voodoo

Image 068, USAF RF-101B, s/n 63-453, of the 192nd TRS of The Nevada ANG, Reno, Nevada. Note the rectangular sensor "canoe" below the aircraft nose. (Photo copyright by John P. Stewart)

The RF-101B Voodoo was part of an on-going effort to modernize the USAF ANG during the Vietnam conflict. Between September 1971 and January 1972, Ling-Temco-Vought Corporation of Greenville, SC converted twenty-two Canadian manufactured CF-101B Voodoos to conduct low-altitude, day and night tactical reconnaissance missions. The RF-101B Voodoo is the single-seat Tac Recce variant of the two-seat F-101B Voodoo fighter-bomber.

The barrel-type fuselage houses a pair of afterburning, Pratt & Whitney J57-PW-55 Turbojets. The triangular shaped engine intakes are located on either side of the fuselage in extended wing roots. The engine exhausts are located just aft of the wings trailing edge, below and before the aircraft tail assembly. The pilot is housed in forward section of the tandem twin-cockpit, which is situated well forward of the wings leading edge, with a one-piece clamshell canopy, hinged aft for pilot ingress and egress. The canopy is supported by a short brace between the front and rear cockpit when the aircraft is parked with the canopy open. The retractable tricycle landing gear has a twin wheel nose gear and one wheel on each main gear. A tubular pitot sensor extends forward from the nose of the aircraft, and a static port is located on the left side of the fuselage nose just forward of the canopy. External fuel is carried in two wing-mounted fuel tanks, each with a capacity of 450 US gal (1,703 ltr/375 imp gal). The mid-mounted wings are sweptback at an angle of 35°, have a single stall fence and square tips. The sweptback one-piece horizontal stabilator has square tips with a slight dihedral and is high-mounted on the sweptback vertical stabilizer.

Image 069, USAF RF-101B Voodoo on display at Reno IAP, Reno, NV, note the forward and vertical sensor windows for the television cameras, the prism shaped window for the panoramic camera and the two circular windows for the side-oblique cameras (Paul Wagner Collection)

This conversion from fighter to reconnaissance aircraft eliminated the second crew position and resulted in the installation of a rectangular canoe under the aircraft's nose, which houses an array of five cameras. The sensor configuration includes two AXQ-2 television cameras in the forward-oblique and vertical positions; one KA-56, panoramic camera with a 3 in (76 mm) fl lens; and KS-87 cameras with either a 3 in (76 mm) or a 6 in (152 mm) fl lens in the left and right side-oblique positions. To assist the pilot in locating the targets the RF-101 Voodoo is equipped with an optical viewfinder, probably the Type VF-31 viewfinder used on the RF-101A/C Voodoo, which provides the pilot both a wide (60°) and narrow (30°) field of view.

The RF-101B Voodoos were delivered to the Air National Guard in 1971 and 1972 and equipped the following USAF reconnaissance squadrons during the Cold War:

- USAF, 192nd TRS, Nevada ANG RF-101B Voodoo 1971 - 1975

The only surviving RF-101B Voodoo is the Gate Guard at the Reno IAP, Reno, NV.

Table 032, RF-101B Voodoo Technical and Performance Specifications

DIMENSIONS:			
Wing Span:	39 ft 8.0 in	12.09 m	
Length:	71 ft 1.0 in	21.67 m	
Height:	18 ft 0.0 in	5.49 m	
Wheel Track:	19 ft 10.5 in	6.06 m	
Wing Area:	368.0 ft²	34.18 m²	
POWERPLANT(S):			
Number of Engines / Designation:	Two (2) Pratt & Whitney J57-PW-55 Turbojets		
Maximum Power / Thrust per Engine:	14,990 lbs st	6,799 kg st	
FUEL CAPACITY:			
Internal Fuel Capacity:	2,250 US gal	8,516 ltrs	1,874 Imp gal
External Fuel Capacity:	900 US gal	3,407 ltrs	749 Imp gal
Total Fuel Capacity:	3,150 US gal	11,923 ltrs	2,623 Imp gal
WEIGHTS:			
Empty:	28,000 lbs	12,701 kg	
Maximum Take-Off:	46,673 lbs	21,171 kg	
Maximum Wing Loading:	126.8 lbs/ft²	619.3 kg/m²	
PERFORMANCE:			
Max Level Speed at Altitude:	1,220 mph @ 40,000 ft	1,963 kmh @ 12,192 m	1,059 kts @ 40,000 ft
Nominal Cruising Speed:	545 mph	877 kmh	473 kts
Initial Rate of Climb at Sea Level:	17,000 ft/min	5,182 m/min	
Service Ceiling:	52,100 ft	15,880 m	
Maximum / Ferry Range:	1,724 mi	2,774 km	1,498 nm

Data File for the RF-101B Voodoo

Phantom FGR.Mk.2

Image 070, RAF Phantom FGR.Mk.2 of No 41 Sq assigned to RAFB Coningsby, UK on display at Leck AB, DE in 1972 or 1973. Note the EMI reconnaissance pod on the centerline position under the fuselage. (Photo copyright by Willie Metz)

The Phantom FGR.Mk.2 (F-4M Phantom II) is a two-seat fighter, ground attack and reconnaissance aircraft designed and manufactured for the RAF by the McDonnell Aircraft Corporation. The first of two pre-production YF-4M Phantoms (s/n XT852 and s/n XT853) first flew on 17 February 1967.

The Phantom FGR.Mk.2 has a large barrel-type fuselage with twin, after-burning Rolls Royce RB-168-25R Mk 202/203 Sprey turbofan engines. The engine intakes are elongated and rectangular in shape with the outboard side presenting a slightly curved profile with rounded corners. The engine intakes are mounted vertically on the side of the fuselage well forward of the wing's leading edge, immediately below the aft canopy. The twin-engine exhaust nozzles are located below and forward of the all-moving horizontal stabilator. The pilot and weapons systems officer (WSO), are seated in a tandem cockpit forward of the wing's leading edge, with individual, aft hinged clamshell canopies for crew ingress and egress. A short tubular pitot sensor is mounted on the aircraft nose. The retractable, tricycle landing gear has a twin-wheel nose gear and one wheel on each main gear. An arrestor-hook, reminiscent of the F-4 Phantom's naval heritage is mounted on the lower fuselage behind the engine exhaust nozzles. The aft tail cone at the base of the vertical stabilizer houses the aircraft drag chute. The RF-4C/E Phantom II has an in-flight refueling receptacle on the top of the fuselage aft of the tandem canopy. There is one centerline hardpoint under the fuselage for external fuel and stores. The low-mounted wings are sweptback at an angle of 45° angle, with a single saw-tooth leading edge and square tips. The outer wing panels have a pronounced 12° dihedral and fold up to reduce the aircraft's footprint when parked. There are two hardpoints under each wing for external fuel and stores. Normally the Phantom FGR.Mk.2 carries one external fuel tank on the outboard hardpoint of each wing, each with a capacity of 370 US gal (1,400 ltr/308 Imp gal). The vertical stabilizer has an unequal-tapered appearance with a square tip; and the one-piece, all moving horizontal stabilator is low-mounted on the rear fuselage with square tips and 23° anhedral.

Image 071, Close-up view of the EMI reconnaissance pod. Note the flat underside of the pod and the two air scoops located on the lower sides directly behind the pod's nose cone. (Photo copyright by Willie Metz)

In the reconnaissance role the Phantom FGR.Mk.2 carries a pressurized reconnaissance pod on the aircraft's centerline position. The reconnaissance pod developed by EMI and produced by Hawker Siddeley is about the same size as a 600 US gal (2,271 ltr/500 Imp gal) centerline external fuel tank, but has a flat bottom and one air scoop on each side of the pod's lower nose section. The sensor suite normally consists of F.95 and F.135 cameras in the for ward-oblique, vertical and side-oblique positions; a Texas Instruments RS-700 IRLS sensor; and an EMI P391 Q-Band SLAR sensor. For night photography, four F.135 cameras can be installed in the pod and electronic flash equipment is carried in a separate pod on the wing. Metal shutters protect the sensor windows when the pod is not in operation.

The pressurized EMI reconnaissance pod was expensive, and difficult to operate and maintain. In addition, the reconnaissance pod had to be pressurized before flight, and depressurized after landing, before the access panels could be opened to load and unload the film magazines. This process delayed the delivery of mission film to the photographic processing and interpretation facility by as much as thirty minutes. As a result, the Phantom FGR.Mk.2 had a brief career as a Tac Recce aircraft, only serving in the Tac Recce role for a little more than a year. It has been reported that some of the equipment used in the EMI reconnaissance pod was later used in the Jaguar Reconnaissance Pod (JRP).

The first production Phantom FGR.Mk.2 was delivered to the RAF at RAFB Yeovilton, UK on 18 July 1968. A total of 116 Phantom FGR.Mk.2s were produced and delivered to the RAF by 29 October 1969, some of which equipped the following RAF reconnaissance squadrons assigned to support NATO during the Cold War:

- RAF, No.2 Sq — Phantom FGR.Mk.2 — 1971 - 1976
- RAF, No.41 Sq — Phantom FGR.Mk.2 — 1972 - 1977

There are at least seven examples of the Phantom FGR.Mk.2 on display throughout the United Kingdom, however none of the aircraft are displayed with the EMI Reconnaissance Pod.

Table 033, Phantom FGR.Mk.2 Technical and Performance Specifications

DIMENSIONS:								
Wing Span:	38	ft	4.9	in	11.71	m		
Length:	57	ft	7.0	in	17.55	m		
Height:	16	ft	1.0	in	4.90	m		
Wheel Track:	17	ft	10.5	in	5.45	m		
Wheel Base:	24	ft	9.0	in	7.54	m		
Wing Area:	530.0	ft^2			49.23	m^2		
POWERPLANT(S):								
Number of Engines / Designation:	Two (2)	Rolls Royce RB-168-25R Mk 202/203 Sprey turbofans						
Maximum Power / Thrust per Engine:	20,515	lbs st			9,306	kg st		
FUEL CAPACITY:								
Internal Fuel Capacity:	1,977	US gal			7,483	ltrs	1,646	Imp gal
External Fuel Capacity:	1,340	US gal			5,072	ltrs	1,116	Imp gal
Total Fuel Capacity:	3,317	US gal			12,555	ltrs	2,762	Imp gal
WEIGHTS:								
Empty:	31,000	lbs			14,062	kg		
Maximum Take-Off:	56,000	lbs			25,402	kg		
Maximum Wing Loading:	105.7	lbs/ft^2			515.9	kg/m^2		
PERFORMANCE:								
Max Level Speed at Altitude:	1,386	mph @			2,230	kmh @	1,204	kts @
	40,000	ft			12,192	m	40,000	ft
Nominal Cruising Speed:	585	mph			941	kmh	508	kts
Initial Rate of Climb at Sea Level:	32,000	ft/min			9,754	m/min		
Service Ceiling:	60,800	ft			18,532	m		
Nominal Combat Radius:	1,000	mi			1,609	km	869	nm
Maximum / Ferry Range:	1,750	mi			2,816	km	1,521	nm

Data File for the Phantom FGR.Mk.2

Fiat G91Y

Image 072, Italian AF Fiat G91Y, s/n MM6541 at RAFB Alconbury, UK. (Photo copyright by Steve Williams)

Designed and manufactured by Fiat (Societa per Azioni Fiat) in response to a 1965 Italian AF requirement for improved capabilities, the Fiat G91Y is a Fiat G91R on "steroids". The redesigned Fiat G91Y, has twin engines versus one, 63% more power, extended range, increased payload and improved reliability. The Fiat G91Y is approximately 10% larger than the earlier Fiat G91R. To accommodate the new engines, the fuselage is 4 ft 6 in (1.38 m) longer and wider, increasing the wingspan by 1 ft 6 in (0.46 m). The Fiat G91Y flew for the first time on 27 December 1966.

Similar in appearance to the older Fiat G91R, the barrel-type fuselage of the Fiat G91Y, houses twin, afterburning, General Electric J85-GE-18A turbojet engines with a large engine intake directly below an extended nose. The single-seat cockpit is located forward of the wing's leading edge, with an aft hinged clamshell canopy for pilot ingress and egress. The retractable, tricycle landing gear has a single nose wheel and one wheel on each main gear. The Fiat G91Y retains the twin 30 mm cannon of the G9R/3. The low-mounted wings are sweptback at an angle 37° 40' 38" and have blunt tips. There are two underwing hard points on each wing for external stores and fuel and a single stall fence above the outboard hard point. External fuel is carried in two wing-mounted fuel tanks, each with a capacity of 137 US gal (518 ltr/114 imp gal). In addition, a tubular pitot sensor is mounted on the left wing tip. The sweptback horizontal stabilizer is high-mounted on the aft fuselage, directly below the sweptback vertical stabilizer. Both the horizontal and vertical stabilizers have blunt tips. There are two ventral fins, canted outboard under the aft fuselage below the vertical stabilizer.

The Fiat G91Y nose has a redesigned angular contour with a prism shaped window in the forward-oblique position to accommodate a panoramic lens. The side-oblique camera windows are flat with a trapezoid shape. The vertical camera window has a flat, square window. For the Tac Recce mission, the G91Y is configured with one panoramic camera in the forward-oblique position, and up to three, TA/7M2, 70mm cameras in the vertical, and left and right side-oblique positions. Hinged panels on either side of the fuselage nose provide access to the cameras and film magazines.

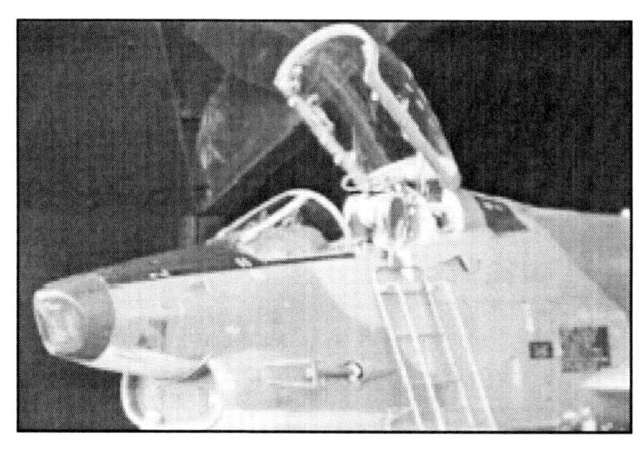

Image 072, Italian AF Fiat G91Y, s/n MM6541 at RAFB Alconbury, GB (Photo copyright by Steve Williams)

The Fiat G91Y equipped the following Italian AF reconnaissance squadrons in support of NATO during the Cold War:

- Italian AF, 8° Stormo, 101° Gruppo   Fiat G91Y   1971 - 1995
- Italian AF, 32° Stormo, 13° Gruppo   Fiat G91Y   1971 - 1995

There are at least seven examples of the Fiat G91Y on display throughout Europe.

Table 034, Fiat G91Y Technical and Performance Specifications

DIMENSIONS:			
Wing Span:	29 ft 6.5 in	9.00 m	
Length:	38 ft 3.5 in	11.67 m	
Height:	14 ft 6.5 in	4.43 m	
Wheel Track:	9 ft 8.0 in	2.95 m	
Wheel Base:	11 ft 8.0 in	3.56 m	
Wing Area:	195.2 ft²	18.13 m²	
POWERPLANT(S):			
Number of Engines / Designation:	Two (2) General Electric J85-GE-13A turbojets		
Maximum Power / Thrust per Engine:	4,080 lbs st	1,851 kg st	
FUEL CAPACITY:			
Internal Fuel Capacity:	844 US gal	3,195 ltrs	703 Imp gal
External Fuel Capacity:	274 US gal	1,036 ltrs	228 Imp gal
Total Fuel Capacity:	1,118 US gal	4,232 ltrs	931 Imp gal
WEIGHTS:			
Empty:	8,398 lbs	3,809 kg	
Maximum Take-Off:	19,180 lbs	8,700 kg	
Maximum Wing Loading:	98.3 lbs/ft²	479.9 kg/m²	
PERFORMANCE:			
Max Level Speed at Altitude:	690 mph @ 30,000 ft	1,110 kmh @ 9,145 m	599 kts @ 30,000 ft
Initial Rate of Climb at Sea Level:	17,323 ft/min	5,280 m/min	
Service Ceiling:	41,010 ft	12,500 m	
Nominal Combat Radius:	373 mi	600 km	324 nm
Maximum / Ferry Range:	2,175 mi	3,500 km	1,890 nm

Data File for the Fiat G91Y

Harrier T.Mk.2/4

Image 074, RAF Harrier T.Mk.2 with the tandem canopy and relocated camera. (Photo copyright by Ian Howat)

The Harrier T.Mk.2/4 is the two-seat, operational trainer variant of the Harrier GR.Mk.1/3 ground attack and reconnaissance aircraft. The prototype Harrier T.Mk.2 made its first flight on 24 April 1969.

Externally the Harrier T.Mk.2/4 differed significantly from the Harrier GR.Mk.1/3. The forward fuselage is extended 3 ft 11 in (1.2 m) to accommodate a tandem two-place tandem cockpit with a one-piece, clamshell canopy hinged on the right side for crew ingress and egress. Like the Swedish AF Saab S32C Lansen, the tandem cockpit incorporated a second windscreen is incorporated between the forward and aft cockpit to protect the instructor pilot in the event canopy is jettisoned. The F.95 left side-oblique camera is relocated from the left side of the nose to the left side of the fuselage below the aft cockpit, in front of the left engine intake, with a square camera window instead of the earlier teardrop shaped camera window. And the tail boom is extended 2 ft 9 in (0.8 m) to counterbalance the extended nose.

Image 075, RAF Harrier T.Mk.4; note the open canopy with the second windscreen, the square camera window forward of the engine intake and the extended nose with the IR seeker head. (Photo copyright by Michael Schmidt)

The Harrier T.Mk.2 is the trainer variant of the Harrier GR.Mk.1. The Harrier T.Mk.4 is the trainer variant of the Harrier GR.Mk.3 and incorporates the upgrades from the Harrier GR.Mk.3 to include:

- Lengthened nosecone with the electronics and IR seeker head for the Laser Ranging and Marked Target Seeking (LRMTS) system

- The Radar Warning Receiver (RWR) and a rectangular antenna fairing located near the top of the vertical fin's leading edge

- The relocated tubular pitot sensor above the IR seeker head

The Harrier T.Mk.2/4 retains the operational capabilities of the Harrier GR.Mk.1/3 but are used primarily in OCU (Operational Conversion Units). However, one Harrier T.Mk.2/4 is assigned to each operational unit.

The Harrier T.Mk.2/4 equipped the following RAF reconnaissance squadron in support of NATO during the Cold War:

- RAF, No.4 Sq Harrier T.Mk.2 1971 - 1990

There are five Harrier T.Mk.2/4 aircraft on display throughout the United Kingdom.

Table 035, Harrier T.Mk.4 Technical and Performance Specifications

DIMENSIONS:			
Wing Span:	25 ft 3.0 in	7.70 m	
Length:	57 ft 5.0 in	17.50 m	
Height:	13 ft 8.0 in	4.17 m	
Wheel Track:	22 ft 2.0 in	6.76 m	
Wheel Base:	11 ft 4.0 in	3.45 m	
Wing Area:	201.1 ft²	18.68 m²	
Horizontal Stabilizer Span:	13 ft 11.0 in	4.24 m	
Vertical Stabilizer Area:	5.3 ft²	0.49 m²	
POWERPLANT(S):			
Number of Engines / Designation:	One	Rolls-Royce Pegaasus Mk.103 Vectored Thrust Turbofan	
Maximum Power / Thrust per Engine:	21,500 lbs st	9,752 kg st	
FUEL CAPACITY:			
Internal Fuel Capacity:	757 US gal	2,865 ltrs	630 Imp gal
External Fuel Capacity:	396 US gal	1,499 ltrs	330 Imp gal
Total Fuel Capacity:	1,153 US gal	4,364 ltrs	960 Imp gal
WEIGHTS:			
Empty:	15,100 lbs	6,849 kg	
Maximum Take-Off:	26,200 lbs	11,884 kg	
Maximum Wing Loading:	130.3 lbs/ft²	636.2 kg/m²	
PERFORMANCE:			
Max Level Speed at Sea Level:	730 mph	1,175 kmh	634 kts
Max Level Speed at Altitude:	737 mph @ 1,000 ft	1,186 kmh @ 305 m	640 kts @ 1,000 ft
Nominal Cruising Speed:	29,003 ft/min	46,674 kmh	25,186 kts
Service Ceiling:	51,200 ft	15,606 m	
Nominal Combat Radius:	414 mi	666 km	360 nm
Maximum / Ferry Range:	2,129 mi	3,426 km	1,850 nm

Data File for the Harrier T.Mk.4

Jaguar GR.Mk.1A/3A

Image 076, RAF Jaguar GR.Mk.3A, s/n XZ104, of No. 41 Sq landing at RAFB Coltishall, UK in October 1996. (Photo copyright by Keith Blincow)

The Jaguar GR.Mk.1A/3A is single-seat, ground attack and reconnaissance aircraft designed and manufactured for the RAF by Société Européenne de Production de L'avion E.C.A.T. (SEPECAT). Designed as a replacement for the Phantom FGR.Mk.2, its primary mission is ground attack with a secondary capability for low-level, day and night Tac Recce. The Jaguar program was an international program initiated by the British and French Ministries of Defense in May 1965 to design and produce a new strike fighter. The first flight of an RAF Jaguar took place on 12 October 1969.

The Jaguar has a barrel-type fuselage, which is rectangular in appearance when viewed head on and has a waisted shape when viewed from above. The fuselage houses twin, afterburning Rolls Royce Turbomeca Adour Mk.104 turbofan engines. The square engine intakes are located on the fuselage sides, below and well forward of the wing's leading edge, just aft of the cockpit. The engines twin-exhaust nozzles are located below the vertical stabilizer, just forward of the horizontal stabilator. The Jaguar GR.Mk.1/3 has a tubular pitot sensor above the clear prism-shaped nose of the laser designator's optical sighting system. Twin static ports are located on the upper fuselage nose, forward of the canopy. The single-seat cockpit has a one-piece clamshell canopy hinged aft for pilot ingress and egress. A thick dorsal spine extends from the rear of the canopy to the base of the vertical stabilizer. The Jaguar GR.Mk.1/3 has twin, 30 mm Aden cannon in the lower fuselage aft of the cockpit. The retractable tricycle landing gear has a single nose wheel and twin wheels on each main gear. The shoulder-mounted wings are sweptback at an angle of 40°, have 3° anhedral, with blunt tips and two underwing and one over-wing hardpoint on each wing. External fuel is carried in two wing-mounted fuel tanks, each with a capacity of 317 US gal (1,200 ltr/264 imp gal). The vertical stabilizer is sweptback 43° with blunt tips; and the one-piece horizontal stabilator is mid-mounted on the fuselage, sweptback 40° with a pronounced 10° anhedral and square tips. For improved high-speed maneuverability, there is one ventral fin, canted outboard, below the aft portion of each engine.

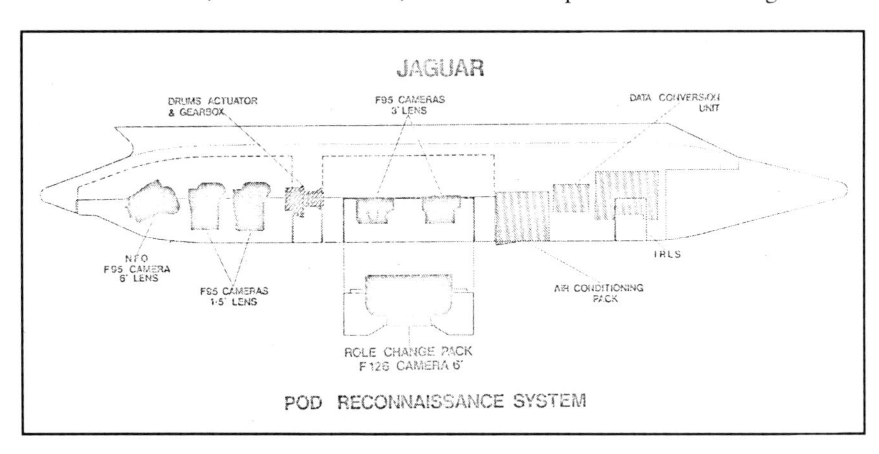

Figure 011, Jaguar Reconnaissance Pod (JRP) showing sensor configuration and layout. (Paul Wagner Collection)

The Jaguar GR.Mk.1A/3A is equipped with the Jaguar Reconnaissance Pod (JRP) for the Tac Recce mission, which provides horizon-to-horizon coverage at low and medium-altitude. The JRP sensor suite includes one Vinten F.95 Mk.7 camera in the forward-oblique position; four Vinten F.95 Mk.10 cameras in the side-oblique positions; and one Linescan Type 401 IRLS sensor. The Jaguar GR.Mk.1A/3A carries flare dispensers for low-level night-reconnaissance missions.

The Jaguar GR.Mk.1A/3A equipped the following RAF reconnaissance squadrons in support of NATO during the Cold War:

- RAF, No.31 Sq — Jaguar GR.Mk.1A — 1975 - 1984
- RAF, No.2 Sq — Jaguar GR.Mk.1A — 1976 - 1990
- RAF, No.41 Sq — Jaguar GR.Mk.1A/3A — 1977 - Present

There is at least one example of the Jaguar GR.Mk.1A on display in the UK at the Royal Air Force Museum, RAFB Duxford, UK

Table 036, Jaguar GR.Mk.1A Technical and Performance Specifications

DIMENSIONS:								
Wing Span:	28	ft	6.0	in	8.69	m		
Length:	55	ft	2.5	in	16.83	m		
Height:	16	ft	0.5	in	4.89	m		
Wheel Track:	7	ft	11.0	in	2.41	m		
Wheel Base:	18	ft	8.0	in	5.69	m		
Wing Area:	260.2	ft²			24.17	m²		
POWERPLANT(S):								
Number of Engines / Designation:	Two (2)	Rolls Royce Turbomeca Adour Mk.104 turbofans						
Maximum Power / Thrust per Engine:	8,040	lbs st			3,647	kg st		
FUEL CAPACITY:								
Internal Fuel Capacity:	1,110	US gal			4,200	ltrs	924	Imp gal
External Fuel Capacity:	951	US gal			3,600	ltrs	792	Imp gal
Total Fuel Capacity:	2,061	US gal			7,800	ltrs	1,716	Imp gal
WEIGHTS:								
Empty:	15,432	lbs			7,000	kg		
Maximum Take-Off:	34,612	lbs			15,700	kg		
Maximum Wing Loading:	133.0	lbs/ft²			649.5	kg/m²		
PERFORMANCE:								
Max Level Speed at Sea Level:	840	mph			1,352	kmh	729	kts
Max Level Speed at Altitude:	1,056	mph @			1,699	kmh @	917	kts @
	36,000	ft			10,973	m	36,000	ft
Service Ceiling:	44,600	ft			13,594	m		
Nominal Combat Radius:	875	mi			1,408	km	760	nm
Maximum / Ferry Range:	2,190	mi			3,524	km	1,903	nm

Data File for the Jaguar GR.Mk.1A

Saab SF37 Viggen

Image 077, Swedish AF Saab SF37 Viggen at RAFB Fairford, UK in July 1995. (Photo copyright by Alastair McBean)

Designed to replace the Saab S32E Draken, the Saab SF37 Viggen is the single-seat, armed, day and night, Tac Recce variant of the Saab AJ37 Viggen attack aircraft designed and manufactured by Saab (Saab Aktiebolag). The Saab SF37 Viggen prototype made its first flight on 21 May 1973.

The Saab SF37 Viggen has a barrel-type fuselage, which houses a single, afterburning Volvo Flygmotor RM8A turbojet engine. The semi-circular engine intakes are located on the sides of the fuselage, below the single-place cockpit. The engine exhaust nozzle is located below and behind the vertical stabilizer. A short tubular pitot sensor is extends from the aircraft nose above the forward-oblique camera position. The single-seat cockpit has a one-piece clamshell canopy hinged aft for pilot ingress and egress. A thick dorsal spine extends from the rear of the canopy to the base of the vertical stabilizer.

Swedish AF Saab SF37 Viggen with the hatches open (right-Image 079) for access to the cameras. Note the rectangular forward-oblique window, the circular windows for the vertical and side oblique cameras, and the large rectangular window forward of the nose wheel well for the split-vertical cameras. The small circular window on the right side of the nose is for the pilot's optical site (left-Image 078). (Photos are copyright by Tom Houquet [left] and Robert Lundin [right]

There is one hardpoint under each engine intake and one centerline hardpoint under the fuselage. Additional fuel is carried in a centerline fuel tank under the aircraft fuselage. The retractable tricycle landing gear has a twin nose wheel and unique tandem twin wheels on each main gear. Mounted above the engine intakes are delta shaped canards with square tips for improved high-speed maneuverability. The double-delta wings are low-mounted on the fuselage; have a single-saw tooth leading edge, square tips and two underwing hardpoints on each wing. The aircraft has no horizontal stabilizer, only a vertical stabilizer with an uneven-tapered leading and trailing edge and a square tip. There is a single ventral fin, centered under the fuselage, immediately behind the main lading gear.

The nose of the Saab SF37 Viggen is modified to accommodate a suite of seven sensors including; one SKa 24 cameras with a 2.2 in (57 mm) fl lens in the vertical position; three SKa 24 cameras with a 4.7 in (120 mm) fl lens in the forward-oblique, and left and right side-oblique positions; two SKa 31 cameras with a 23.6 in (600 mm) fl lens in the split-vertical position; and a VKa 702 IRLS sensor. For night missions, the SF37 Viggen carries Vinten's "Red Baron" IR reconnaissance pod on the forward port station beneath the aircraft fuselage. The pod is equipped with three SKa 34 cameras with a 3 in (76 mm) fl lens (which use IR sensitive film) and electronic IR flashers at the rear of the pod. A second pod can be carried on the forward starboard station with additional electronic IR flashes. In addition, the Saab SF37 Viggen can also carry a forward-looking LOROP camera pod. The pilot has an optical sight to aid in locating the targets to be imaged. The sight consists of a periscope and optics with a circular viewing window under the lower right side of the fuselage nose.

Saab produced a total of twenty-eight Saab SF37 Virgins, which equipped the following Swedish AF reconnaissance units during the Cold War:

- Swedish AF, F13 Wing Saab SF37 Viggen 1976 - 1993
- Swedish AF, F17 Wing Saab SF37 Viggen 1977 - 1993
- Swedish AF, F21 Wing Saab SF37 Viggen 1979 - Present

There are no known Saab SF37 Viggen aircraft on display at this time.

Table 037, Saab SF37 Viggen Technical and Performance Specifications

DIMENSIONS:								
Wing Span:	34	ft	9.3	in	10.60	m		
Length:	53	ft	5.8	in	16.30	m		
Height:	19	ft	4.5	in	5.91	m		
Wheel Track:	15	ft	7.5	in	4.76	m		
Wheel Base:	18	ft	8.5	in	5.70	m		
Wing Area:	495.1	ft^2			45.99	m^2		
POWERPLANT(S):								
Number of Engines / Designation:	One (1)	Volvo Flygmotor RM8A turbojet						
Maximum Power / Thrust per Engine:	26,015	lbs st			11,800	kg st		
FUEL CAPACITY:								
Internal Fuel Capacity:	1,057	US gal			4,000	ltrs	880	Imp gal
External Fuel Capacity:	1,321	US gal			5,000	ltrs	1,100	Imp gal
Total Fuel Capacity:	2,378	US gal			9,000	ltrs	1,980	Imp gal
WEIGHTS:								
Maximum Take-Off:	45,084	lbs			20,450	kg		
Maximum Wing Loading:	91.1	lbs/ft^2			444.6	kg/m^2		
PERFORMANCE:								
Max Level Speed at Sea Level:	912	mph			1,468	kmh	792	kts
Max Level Speed at Altitude:	1,320	mph			2,124	kmh	1,146	kts
Service Ceiling:	59,055	ft			18,000	m		
Nominal Combat Radius:	622	mi			1,000	km	540	nm
Maximum / Ferry Range:	1,243	mi			2,000	km	1,080	nm

Data File for the SF37 Viggen

Mirage IVP

Image 080, French AF Mirage IVP assigned to EB 91, 1/91 "Gascogne" at Dijon, FR on 27 June 2004. (Photo copyright by Nicolas Laroudie)

Like the Mirage IVA, the Mirage IVP is a two-seat, long-range, strategic bomber, but with a secondary capability of strategic, day and night reconnaissance. Designed and manufactured for the French AF by Dassault (Avions Marcel Dassault), the prototype Mirage IVA first flew on 17 June 1959. Beginning in the early 1980s, eighteen Mirage IVA aircraft were modified to improve their penetration capabilities. These modifications included the installation of dual SAGEM Uliss inertial navigation systems (INS); Thomson-CSF ARCANA pulse-Doppler radar with a high-resolution ground-mapping mode; improved Thomson-CSF Serval radar warning receivers (RWR) and electronic countermeasures (ECM) equipment; and a centerline pod to carry the Aerospatiale ASMP supersonic nuclear missile.

These aircraft were redesignated the Mirage IVP, and the first flight of a Mirage IVP took place on 12 October 1982.

The Mirage IVP has a large waisted-type fuselage, which houses twin after-burning SNECMA Antar 9K turbojet engines. The engine intakes are located on the fuselage sides just aft and below the cockpit, and include a moveable semi-conical compression cone in the intake. The two-man crew (pilot and navigator) is housed in separate tandem cockpits with individual clamshell canopies, hinged aft for crew ingress and egress. The forward canopy has a center support structure that runs from the front to the back of the canopy. The rear canopy only has a small rectangular window on either side of the canopy hood. The retractable, tricycle landing gear has a twin-wheel nose gear and twin-axle main gear with two wheels on each axle. Two static ports are located on the lower fuselage just aft of the aircraft nose. An in-flight refueling probe receptacle extends forward from the aircraft nose. A small, slightly swept vertical fin, extends above and below the tip of the aircraft nose. The mid-mounted, delta wings are swept back at an angle of 60°, with two underwing hardpoints and blunt tips. External fuel is carried in two fuel tanks mounted on the inboard hardpoint, each with a capacity of 660 US gal (2,498 ltr/550 Imp gal). There is one underwing hardpoint for external fuel on each wing. The Mirage IVP has no horizontal stabilizer, only a sweptback vertical stabilizer with a square tip.

Twelve Mirage IVP aircraft were modified to carry the CT-52 reconnaissance sensor pod. The sensor pod is installed in place of the AN-22 nuclear free fall bomb, which was recessed under the aft portion of the

Image 081, CT-52 Reconnaissance Pod on a Mirage IVP. Note optical windows for vertical and oblique cameras. (Photo copyright by Chris Muir)

Mirage IVP fuselage. The sensor pod is configurable, but the normal sensor configuration includes three Omera 35 low-altitude cameras; three Omera 36 high-altitude cameras; and one Wildt mapping camera. For low-altitude operations, a SAT Super Cyclone IRLS sensor can be installed in place of one of the Omera 36 cameras.

The Mirage IVP was delivered to the French AF in 1983 and equipped the following French AF strategic bomber squadrons in support of NATO during the Cold War:

- French AF, CIFAS 328 — Mirage IVP — 1983 - 1991
- French AF, EB 91, 2/91 "Bretagne" — Mirage IVP — 1986 - 1996
- French AF, EB 91, 1/91 "Gascogne" — Mirage IVP — 1986 - Present

There are no known Mirage IVP aircraft on display at this time.

Table 038, Mirage IVP Technical and Performance Specifications

DIMENSIONS:				
Wing Span:	38 ft	10.5 in	11.85 m	
Length:	77 ft	1.0 in	23.50 m	
Height:	17 ft	8.5 in	5.40 m	
Wing Area:	839.6 ft²		77.99 m²	
POWERPLANT(S):				
Number of Engines / Designation:	Two (2) SNECMA Atar 09K turbojet			
Maximum Power / Thrust per Engine:	15,432 lbs st		7,000 kg st	
FUEL CAPACITY:				
Internal Fuel Capacity:	3,699 US gal		14,000 ltrs	3,080 Imp gal
External Fuel Capacity:	1,320 US gal		4,996 ltrs	1,099 Imp gal
Total Fuel Capacity:	5,019 US gal		18,996 ltrs	4,179 Imp gal
WEIGHTS:				
Empty:	31,967 lbs		14,500 kg	
Maximum Take-Off:	73,800 lbs		33,476 kg	
Maximum Wing Loading:	87.9 lbs/ft²		429.2 kg/m²	
PERFORMANCE:				
Max Level Speed at Altitude:	1,454 mph @ 40,600 ft		2,340 kmh @ 12,375 m	1,263 kts @ 40,600 ft
Nominal Cruising Speed:	690 mph		1,110 kmh	599 kts
Service Ceiling:	65,000 ft		19,812 m	
Nominal Combat Radius:	770 mi		1,239 km	669 nm
Maximum / Ferry Range:	2,845 mi		4,578 km	2,472 nm

Data File for the Mirage IVP

Mirage F1CR

Image 082, French AF Mirage F1CR landing at Florennes AB, BE on 16 March 2004. The aircraft designation "33-NE" identifies the aircraft is assigned to the 2nd ER (Escadron de Reconnaissance) of the 33rd Wing. The bird on the tail is the 2nd ER emblem. (Photo copyright by Dirk Jan de Ridder)

Designed and manufactured by Dassault (Avions Marcel Dassault) the Mirage F1CR was intended to replace the French AF Mirage IIIR/RD. The Mirage F1CR is a single-seat, all weather, day and night, armed, Tac Recce variant of the Mirage F1C interceptor. The first prototype Mirage F1CR flew on 20 November 1981.

The barrel-type fuselage houses a single, axial-flow turbo jet with a modulated afterburner. The curved engine intakes are located on the sides of the fuselage, below and well forward of the wing's leading edge and just aft of the cockpit. Each intake has a moveable semi-conical, compression cone to control the shock wave generated at supersonic speeds. A fixed refueling probe receptacle may be installed just forward and to the right of the canopy, and is angled forward at approximately 45°. A short tubular pitot sensor extends from the aircraft nose, and a single static port is located on the right side of the fuselage nose, forward of the cockpit.

The Mirage F1CR cockpit is covered with a one-piece clamshell canopy hinged aft for pilot ingress and egress. The retractable, tricycle landing gear has a twin-wheel nose gear and two wheels on each main gear. The shoulder-mounted wings are sweptback at an angle of 47° 30' with an uneven single saw tooth leading edge, 5° anhedral and square tips. There are two underwing hardpoints on each wing and one wingtip missile shoe. External fuel is carried in two fuel tanks mounted on the inboard hardpoint, each with a capacity of 317 US gal (1,200 ltr/264 Imp gal) and one under fuselage fuel tank with a capacity of 581 US gal (2,199 ltr/484 Imp gal). The vertical stabilizer is sweptback with a blunt tip and the sweptback one-piece horizontal stabilator is mid-mounted on the fuselage with square tips. Two ventral fins, canted outboard, are mounted below the aft fuselage for improved high-speed maneuverability. A bullet shaped fairing at the base of the vertical fin houses the aircraft's drag chute. For self-defense, the Mirage F1CR retains the left internal gun. In addition, the F1CR is capable of carrying bombs and rocket launchers on the wing hardpoints for ground attack missions.

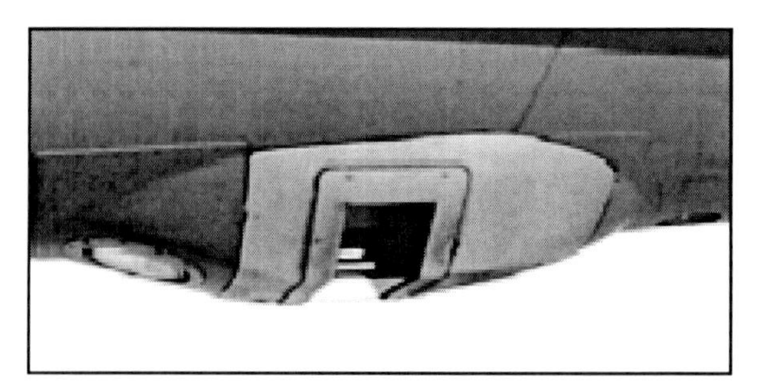

Image 083, French AF Mirage F1CR Internal sensors include a panoramic camera identified by the blister fairing and prism window (center) and a vertical camera identified by the round window in front of the blister fairing (right). The landing light is in the retracted position on the backside of the blister fairing (left). (Paul Wagner Collection)

The forward fuselage of the Mirage F1CR lower fuselage contour was modified with the addition of a bump fairing to house a panoramic camera. The Omera 40 panoramic camera provides 180° (horizon-to-horizon) coverage. In addition, the Mirage F1CR carries an Omera 35 vertical cameras just forward of the bump fairing and the Super Cyclope IRLS sensor in place of the right gun. The Super Cyclopes IRLS provides a sweep angle of 60° along either side of the aircraft's line of flight. The Mirage F1CR is also capable of carrying the Omera LOROP (Long Range Optical) camera reconnaissance pod and the Thompson-CSF SLAR (Side Looking Radar) system. Photoflash cartridges can be installed in the fuselage for night reconnaissance operations.

A total of sixty-four Mirage F1CR aircraft were produced and deliveries to the French AF began in March 1983. The Mirage F1CR equipped the following French AF reconnaissance squadrons in support of NATO during the Cold War:

- French AF, ER33, 1/33 "Belfort" Mirage F1CR 1983 - Present
- French AF, ER33, 2/33 "Savoie" Mirage F1CR 1983 - Present

There are no known Mirage F1CR aircraft on display at this time.

Table 039, Mirage F1CR Technical and Performance Specifications

DIMENSIONS:			
Wing Span:	27 ft 6.7 in	8.40 m	
Length:	49 ft 2.6 in	15.00 m	
Height:	14 ft 9.2 in	4.50 m	
Wheel Track:	8 ft 2.4 in	2.50 m	
Wheel Base:	16 ft 4.8 in	5.00 m	
Wing Area:	269.1 ft²	25.00 m²	
POWERPLANT(S):			
Number of Engines / Designation:	One (1) SNECMA Antar 09K50 turbojet		
Maximum Power / Thrust per Engine:	15,873 lbs st	7,200 kg st	
FUEL CAPACITY:			
Internal Fuel Capacity:	1,136 US gal	4,300 ltrs	946 Imp gal
External Fuel Capacity:	1,215 US gal	4,599 ltrs	1,012 Imp gal
Total Fuel Capacity:	2,351 US gal	8,899 ltrs	1,958 Imp gal
WEIGHTS:			
Empty:	16,314 lbs	7,400 kg	
Maximum Take-Off:	35,715 lbs	16,200 kg	
Maximum Wing Loading:	132.7 lbs/ft²	648.1 kg/m²	
PERFORMANCE:			
Max Level Speed at Sea Level:	914 mph	1,470 kmh	793 kts
Max Level Speed at Altitude:	1,451 mph @ 39,370 ft	2,335 kmh @ 12,000 m	1,260 kts @ 39,370 ft
Nominal Cruising Speed:	550 mph	885 kmh	478 kts
Initial Rate of Climb at Sea Level:	41,930 ft/min	12,780 m/min	
Service Ceiling:	65,600 ft	19,995 m	
Nominal Combat Radius:	864 mi	1,390 km	751 nm
Maximum / Ferry Range:	1,492 mi	2,400 km	1,296 nm

Data File for the Mirage F1CR

TR-1A

Image 084, TR-1A Dragon Lady in flight. Note the large "Super Pod" on the left wing and the wing-tip fairing used to protect the wingtip during landing. (Photo courtesy of the DVIC)

The most unlikely aircraft to be identified as a "Tac Recce" asset is the TR-1A "Dragon Lady". The TR-1A has the same airframe as the U-2R high-altitude reconnaissance aircraft. The aircraft was redesignated "TR-1" for "Tactical Reconnaissance" and intended to provide continuous, high-altitude, day and night, all-weather surveillance of the battlefield, for US and NATO, ground and air commanders during the Cold War. A single-seat, unarmed, high-altitude reconnaissance aircraft, the TR-1A Dragon Lady was designed and manufactured for the USAF by Lockheed Aircraft Corporation's famous "Skunk Works" facility in Palmdale, CA. The first flight of a TR-1A was conducted on 01 August 1980.

The TR-1A Dragon Fly has a long slender, waisted-type fuselage which houses a single, non-afterburning Pratt & Whitney J75-P-13B turbojet engine. The semi-circular engine intakes are located on the sides of the fuselage, well forward of the wing's leading edge and just aft of the cockpit. The engine exhaust nozzle is directly below the vertical stabilizer. The single-seat cockpit has a one-piece clamshell canopy hinged on the right side for pilot ingress and egress. The TR-1A has a unique single main landing gear with twin wheels, which retracts into the fuselage near the wings leading, followed by a small twin-wheel tail gear just below and forward of the vertical stabilizer. The long, equal-tapered wings are mid-mounted on the fuselage and with blunt tips. Slender balancer outrigger gears with small twin-wheels are mounted midway under each wing and jettisoned on take off. Special wing tip fairings serve as skids during landings. The tall vertical stabilizer has an unequal-taper and a square tip; and the equal-tapered horizontal stabilizer is low-mounted on the vertical stabilizer with blunt tips.

The primary imaging sensor payload is the Hughes Advanced Synthetic Aperture Radar System-2 (ASARS-2). A high resolution, multi-mode SAR system it is capable of imaging targets behind enemy lines while orbiting in friendly airspace. Key components of the ASARS-2 hardware, which includes the Electronic Steerable Antenna (ESA), are installed in a specially designed nose of the TR-1A. The ASARS-2 nose is easily identified by the raised bump above the nose cone, which houses the antenna's heat exchanger.

Image 085, TR-1A Dragon Lady with ASARS-2 installed in the nose, identified by the "bump" fairing at the above the forward section of nose for the antenna heat exchanger.

In addition, the TR-1A Dragon Lady carried two "Super Pods", one integrated into each wing approximately 9 ft (2.74 m) from the fuselage. Each pod is 27 ft (8.23 m) long, with a volume of 90 ft3 (2.55 m3) and weighs approximately 1,200 lbs (544 kg) fully loaded. These pods are configured to conduct electronic surveillance using a variety of Communications Intelligence (COMINT) and Electronic Intelligence (ELINT) data collection sensors. A key benefit of the TR-1 program was the ability of the TR-1 system to collect and downlink data in real-time to the TR-1 Ground Station (TRIGS) for immediate processing, exploitation and dissemination

Lockheed delivered the first production TR-1A to the 17th Reconnaissance Wing, Strategic Air Command (SAC) at RAFB Alconbury, UK on 12 February 1983. In March 1985 Hughes delivered and installed the production ASARS-2 in the TR-1A aircraft. The following USAFE based reconnaissance unit was equipped with the TR-1A during the Cold War:

- USAFE, 17th RW (SAC) TR-1A Dragon Lady 1983 - 1992

There are no known TR-1A aircraft on display at this time.

Table 040, TR-1A Dragon Lady Technical and Performance Specifications

DIMENSIONS:				
Wing Span:	103 ft	0.0 in	31.39 m	
Length:	63 ft	0.0 in	19.20 m	
Height:	16 ft	0.0 in	4.88 m	
Wheel Track:	0 ft	0.0 in	0.00 m	
Wing Area:	1000.0 ft²		92.89 m²	
POWERPLANT(S):				
Number of Engines / Designation:	One (1) Pratt & Whitney J75-P-13 Turbojet			
Maximum Power / Thrust per Engine:	17,000 lbs st		7,711 kg st	
FUEL CAPACITY:				
Internal Fuel Capacity:	1,175 US gal		4,447 ltrs	978 Imp gal
External Fuel Capacity:	0 US gal		0 ltrs	0 Imp gal
Total Fuel Capacity:	1,175 US gal		4,447 ltrs	978 Imp gal
WEIGHTS:				
Empty:	15,101 lbs		6,850 kg	
Maximum Take-Off:	40,000 lbs		18,144 kg	
Maximum Wing Loading:	40.0 lbs/ft²		195.3 kg/m²	
PERFORMANCE:				
Max Level Speed at Altitude:	465 mph @ 70,000 ft		748 kmh @ 21,336 m	404 kts @ 70,000 ft
Nominal Cruising Speed:	430 mph		692 kmh	373 kts
Initial Rate of Climb at Sea Level:	5,000 ft/min		1,524 m/min	
Service Ceiling:	80,000 ft		24,384 m	
Nominal Combat Radius:	3,000 mi		4,828 km	2,607 nm
Maximum / Ferry Range:	6,250 mi		10,058 km	5,431 nm

Data File for the TR-1A

F-16A/B(R) Fighting Falcon

Image 086, Dutch AF F-16A(R) Fighting Falcon of the 306 Sq with the Orpheus Reconnaissance Pod. (Photo copyright by Andries Waardenburg)

The F-16A/B(R) Fighting Falcon is the low-level, day and night tactical reconnaissance variant of the F-16A/B Fighting Falcon fighter designed and manufactured for the USAF by General Dynamics Corporation. Ordered by the Royal Netherlands AF to replace the RF-104G Starfighter, the F-16A/B(R) Fighting Falcon was modified to carry the low-altitude Oude Delft Orpheus reconnaissance pod. Externally the aircraft is identical to other F-16A/B Fighting Falcon aircraft. The prototype YF-16A Fighting Falcon first flew on 20 January 1974. This was followed by the first flight of the pre-production F-16A Fighting Falcon on 08 December 1976 and the pre-production F-16B Fighting Falcon on 08 August 1977.

The first flight of a Dutch AF F-16A(R) Fighting Falcon occurred on 27 January 1983.

With an under fuselage air intake and bubble canopy, the F-16A(R) Fighting Falcon resembles the famous P-51 Mustang of WW II. The barrel-type fuselage houses a single, afterburning Pratt & Whitney F100-PW-100 turbofan engine. The large, under fuselage engine intake sits directly below the cockpit and is well forward of the wing's leading edge. A short tubular pitot sensor extends from the conical nose. A one-piece clamshell canopy hinged aft for pilot ingress and egress covers the single-place cockpit. The operational trainer variant designated F-16B(R) Fighting Falcon is identical to the single-seat F-16A(R) except for a tandem, two-place cockpit, for an instructor pilot in the rear seat, which is also covered by a one-piece, clamshell canopy, hinged aft for crew ingress and egress The retractable, tricycle landing gear has a single-wheel nose gear and one wheel on each main gear. There is one hardpoint under the fuselage for the Oude Delft Orpheus reconnaissance pod. The mid-mounted wings blend with the fuselage and highly swept vortex generators near the leading edge. The wings have a tapered leading edge, and are sweptback at an angle of 40° with a straight trailing edge and square tips. There are three underwing hardpoints on each wing for external stores and fuel and one wingtip missile shoe. External fuel is carried in two wing-mounted fuel tanks on the wing's inboard hardpoint, each with a capacity of 370 US gal (1,400 ltr/308 Imp gal). The vertical stabilizer is sweptback with a square tip; and the tapered-straight one-piece horizontal stabilator is mid-mounted on the fuselage with square tips. For improved high-speed maneuverability, there are two ventral fins, canted outboard, mounted below the aft fuselage.

The F-16A/B(R) retains the General Electric M61A1 20 mm multi-barrel cannon in the left wing/body fairing and up to 515 rounds of ammunition. In addition, the F-16A/B(R) Fighting Falcon is capable of carrying bombs and rocket launchers on the wing hardpoints for ground attack missions.

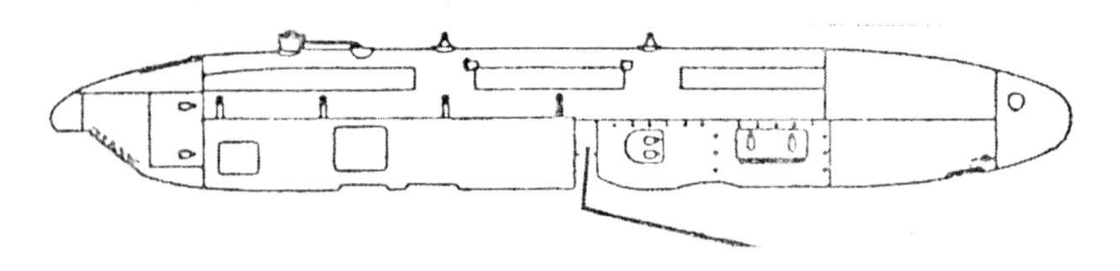

Figure 012, Oude Delft Orpheus reconnaissance pod used on Dutch AF F-16A(R) Fighting Falcons. (Paul Wagner collection)

The F-16A/B(R) Fighting Falcon was modified to carry the Oude Delft Orpheus reconnaissance pod on the aircraft's centerline position. The reconnaissance pod is equipped with five TA-8M cameras; one in the forward-oblique position; two in the low side-oblique position; and two in the high side-oblique positions. In addition, the Oude Delft Orpheus reconnaissance pod also carries an "Old Delft" IRLS-5 sensor.

Image 087, Oude Delft Orpheus reconnaissance pod on the centerline position of a Dutch AF F-16A(R) Fighting Falcon. (Paul Wagner collection) (Photo copyright by Alastair McBean)

A total of eighteen F-16A(R) and two F-16B(R) Fighting Falcon aircraft were delivered to the Royal Netherlands AF at Volkel AB, NL beginning in January 1983.

The F-16A/B(R) Fight Falcons equipped the following Royal Netherlands AF reconnaissance squadron in support of NATO during the Cold War:

- Royal Netherlands AF, 306 Sq F-16A(R) Fighting Falcon 1983 - Present

While there are several F-16A Fighting Falcon aircraft on display throughout the United States and Europe, there are no known F-16A(R) Fighting Falcon aircraft with the Oude Delft Orpheus reconnaissance pod on display at this time.

Table 041, F-16A(R) Fighting Falcon Technical and Performance Specifications

DIMENSIONS:								
Wing Span: (40° sweep / 0° dihedral)	31	ft	0.0	in	9.45	m		
Length:	49	ft	4.0	in	15.04	m		
Height:	16	ft	5.2	in	5.01	m		
Wheel Track:	7	ft	9.0	in	2.36	m		
Wheel Base:	13	ft	1.4	in	4.00	m		
Wing Area:	300.0	ft²			27.87	m²		
POWERPLANT(S):								
Number of Engines / Designation:	One (1)	Pratt & Whitney F100-PW-100 Turbofan						
Maximum Power / Thrust per Engine:	23,810	lbs st			10,800	kg st		
FUEL CAPACITY:								
Internal Fuel Capacity:	1,030	US gal			3,900	ltrs	858	Imp gal
External Fuel Capacity:	1,200	US gal			4,542	ltrs	999	Imp gal
Total Fuel Capacity:	2,230	US gal			8,442	ltrs	1,857	Imp gal
WEIGHTS:								
Empty:	14,567	lbs			6,608	kg		
Maximum Take-Off:	35,400	lbs			16,057	kg		
Maximum Wing Loading:	118.0	lbs/ft²			576.2	kg/m²		
PERFORMANCE:								
Max Level Speed at Sea Level:	915	mph			1,473	kmh	795	kts
Max Level Speed at Altitude:	1,350	mph @			2,173	kmh @	1,172	kts @
	40,000	ft			12,192	m	40,000	ft
Initial Rate of Climb at Sea Level:	42,000	ft/min			12,802	m/min		
Service Ceiling:	50,000	ft			15,240	m		
Nominal Combat Radius:	575	mi			925	km	500	nm
Maximum / Ferry Range:	2,415	mi			3,886	km	2,098	nm

Data File for the F-16A(R) Fighting Falcon

Tornado GR.Mk.1A

Image 088, RAF Tornado GR.Mk.1A of No 13 Sq, which was reactivated at RAFB Honington, UK on 01 January 1990 and received the Tornado GR.Mk.1A less than two months after the fall of the Berlin Wall and the end of the Cold War. (Photo copyright by Alastair McBean)

The Tornado GR.Mk.1A is a two-seat, ground attack and reconnaissance aircraft designed and manufactured for the RAF by Panavia Aircraft GmbH (a German, Italian and British conglomerate). The Tornado GR.Mk.1A is the product of a multinational program initiated in 1968 by the British, German and Italian Ministries of Defense to design and produce a Multi-Role Combat Aircraft (MRCA). The first flight of the Tornado GR.Mk.1 prototype took place on 14 August 1974 and the Tornado GR.Mk.1A first flew on 11 July 1985.

The large rectangular barrel-type fuselage houses twin, afterburning Turbo-Union RB199-34R Mk.101 turbofan engines. The large, square engine intakes are located below and forward of the wing roots, terminating just below the aft cockpit. A short tubular pitot sensor extends from the conical nose. The pilot and navigator sit in a tandem, two-place cockpit covered by a one-piece, clamshell canopy, hinged aft for crew ingress and egress. An in-flight refueling probe receptacle can be installed in a special housing along the right side of the fuselage just below the canopy. The receptacle retracts and is stored in a specially designed fairing when not in use and extends up and out to the side when in use. The retractable tricycle landing gear has a twin-wheel nose gear and one wheel on each main gear. There are hard-points under the fuselage for external stores or fuel. The variable-geometry, shoulder-mounted wings have blunt tips, and a minimum leading edge sweep of 25° and a maximum leading edge sweep of 67° when fully swept. There are two underwing hardpoints for external stores and fuel on each wing. The Tornado GR.Mk.1A can carry one external fuel tank with a maximum capacity of 396 US gal (1,500 ltr/330 Imp gal) on the outboard hardpoint of each wing. The large vertical stabilizer is sweptback with a blunt tip; and the sweptback one-piece horizontal stabilator is mid-mounted on the fuselage with blunt tips. The Tornado GR.Mk.1A carries no internal armament, but is capable of carrying external weapons for ground attack missions.

Image 089, Patch on side of aircraft is for the SLIR sensor and the bump fairing below the fuselage house the IRLS sensor (Photo copyright by Den Pascoe)

For the Tac Recce mission, the Tornado GR.Mk.1A is equipped with an IR sensor suite known as the Tornado Reconnaissance System. This includes a Vinten Linescan 4000 IRLS system in a blister under the forward fuselage, which provides 180° (horizon-to-horizon) cross track coverage. In addition, there is one Vinten SLIR (Side Looking Infrared) sensor installed on each the side of the fuselage above the IRLS sensor. These sensors provide additional high-resolution IR frame imagery perpendicular to the aircraft's line of flight.

The Tornado GR.Mk.1A equipped the following RAF reconnaissance squadron in support of NATO during the Cold War:

- RAF, No.2 Sq — Tornado GR.Mk.1A — 1988 - Present

There are no known Tornado GR.Mk.1 aircraft on display at this time.

Tornado GR.Mk.1A Technical and Performance Specifications

DIMENSIONS:				
Wing Span: [25° to 63° sweep]	45 ft	7.5 in	13.91 m	
Length:	54 ft	10.3 in	16.72 m	
Height:	19 ft	6.3 in	5.95 m	
Wheel Track:	10 ft	2.0 in	3.10 m	
Wheel Base:	20 ft	4.0 in	6.20 m	
POWERPLANT(S):				
Number of Engines / Designation:	Two (2)	Turbo-Union RB199-34R Mk.101 turbofan		
Maximum Power / Thrust per Engine:	14,840 lbs st		6,731 kg st	
FUEL CAPACITY:				
Internal Fuel Capacity:	1,688 US gal		6,389 ltrs	1,406 Imp gal
External Fuel Capacity:	1,980 US gal		7,494 ltrs	1,649 Imp gal
Total Fuel Capacity:	3,668 US gal		13,883 ltrs	3,054 Imp gal
WEIGHTS:				
Empty:	30,620 lbs		13,889 kg	
Maximum Take-Off:	61,620 lbs		27,951 kg	
PERFORMANCE:				
Max Level Speed at Sea Level:	920 mph		1,481 kmh	799 kts
Max Level Speed at Altitude:	1,452 mph @		2,337 kmh	1,261 kts @
Nominal Combat Radius:	863 mi		1,389 km	750 nm
Maximum / Ferry Range:	2,420 mi		3,895 km	2,103 nm

Data File for the Tornado GR.Mk.1A

The Survivors

Of the thousands of tactical reconnaissance aircraft and their variants developed and flown during the Cold War, approximately 400 survive today. Some like the Fiat G91 and the RF-84F Thunder flash exist in large quantities and can be viewed at a variety of locations. Others like the Meteor PR.Mk.10 and the RF-100A Super Sabre have not survived and can no longer be viewed and studied.

The following pages contain detailed listing of known and reported locations where these rare warbirds may be viewed by veterans and enthusiasts alike. However, this listing is only as good as the source data. I have attempted to quantify the information presented by first limiting the source data to what has been reported in the past five years; and by using multiple sources to verify the data presented. This includes information obtained from personal visits, photographs of the aircraft at the reported locations, museum websites, and where practical aerial imagery from sources such as Google Earth.

The first set of tables (Appendix A) list the information in order by aircraft name and/or designation. The second set of tables (Appendix B) list the information by country where the aircraft can be viewed.

Appendix A

Tactical Reconnaissance Aircraft Survivors - Aircraft Listing

A/C	S/N	MUSEUM / DISPLAY	CITY / BASE	STATE	CY	REMARKS
Canberra B.Mk.2	9935	Luftwaffenmuseum	Berlin-Gatow		DE	Used by German Air Force for aerial mapping
Canberra B.Mk.2	9936	Tecknik Museum	Sinsheim		DE	Used by German Air Force for aerial mapping
Canberra PR.MK.3	WE139	Royal Air Force Museum	London		GB	
Canberra PR.MK.3	WF922	Midland Air Museum	Coventry Airport		GB	
Canberra PR.MK.3	WF922		Coventry, Baginton		GB	
Canberra PR.Mk.7	WH773	Gatwick Aviation Museum	Charlwood		GB	
Canberra PR.Mk.7	WH791	Newark Air Museum	Newark		GB	
Canberra PR.Mk.7	WJ821		Bassingbourn		GB	
Canberra PR.Mk.7 (Cockpit)		Newark Air Museum	Newark		GB	
Canberra PR.Mk.7 (Nose)		Bournemouth Aviation Museum	Bournemouth IAP		GB	
Canberra PR.Mk.9	XH131	Kemble Field	Cirencester		GB	
Canberra PR.Mk.9	XH134	Kemble Field	Kemble		GB	
Canberra PR.Mk.9	XH135	Kemble Field	Kemble		GB	
Canberra PR.Mk.9	XH171	Royal Air Force Museum	Cosford		GB	
Canberra PR.Mk.9	XH173	Museo National Aeronautico y Del Espacio	Avendio Pedro Aguirre Cerda		CL	
Canberra PR.Mk.9 (Cockpit)		Cold War Jets Collection	Bruntingthorpe Airfield		GB	
CF-5A Freedom Fighter		Atlantic Canada Aviation Museum	Enfield, Nova Scotia		CA	ONLY SURVIVING CF-5A FREEDOM FIGHTER
CR.12 Phantom II	65-0937	Museo Del Aire	Madrid		ES	Displayed as CR 12-42
CR.12 Phantom II		Museo Del Aire	Madrid		ES	Displayed as CR 12-42
CR.12 Phantom II			Antiguedad		ES	Displayed as CR 12-48
CR.12 Phantom II			Torrejaon AB		ES	Displayed as CR 12-64
CR.12 Phantom II			Torrejaon AB		ES	Displayed as CR 12-55
CR.9 Freedom Fighter		Moron AB	Seville-Moron		ES	Displayed as AR9-060 / 21-55
CR.9 Freedom Fighter		Museo Del Aire	Madrid		ES	Displayed as AR9-062 / 23-62
CR.9 Freedom Fighter		Museo Elder	Las Palmas		ES	Displayed as AR9-053 / 21-50
CR.9 Freedom Fighter			Albacete AB		ES	Displayed as AR9-064 / 212-64
DH-112 Venom FB.MK.1R	J-1603	Tecknik Museum	Sinsheim		DE	Displayed as J-1603
DH-112 Venom FB.MK.1R	J-1627		Bex		CH	
DH-112 Venom FB.MK.1R	J-1628	Tecknik Museum	Sinsheim		DE	
DH-112 Venom FB.MK.1R	J-1630	Verien Fleiger Museum	Altenrhein		CH	
DH-112 Venom FB.MK.1R	J-1632	DeHavilland Aircraft Heritage Center	St. Albans		UK	
DH-112 Venom FB.MK.1R	J-1642	Fleiger Museum Dubendorf	Dubendorf AB		CH	
F-16A Fighting Falcon		Danmark Flyvevabenmuseet	Stauning Lufthavn		DK	
F-16A Fighting Falcon		Musee d'Avions du Palegrv	Perpignan		FR	
F-16A Fighting Falcon		Luchmachht Museum	Soesterberg		NL	Displayed as J-215
F-16B Fighting Falcon		Danmark Flyvevabenmuseet	Stauning Lufthavn		DK	
Fiat G91	MM6417		Treviso-Istrama		IT	
Fiat G91		Butzweilerhof Museum	Cologne		DE	Displayed as 31+78
Fiat G91			Campefordina		IT	
Fiat G91R	MM6377	Malta Aviation Museum	Rabat		MT	
Fiat G91R		Museo Nationale Della Scienza E. Della Tecnic	Milan		IT	Displayed as 2-20
Fiat G91R1	MM6280	Museo Storico dell'Aeronautica Militaire	Vigna di Valle		IT	
Fiat G91R1	MM6282		Forli		IT	
Fiat G91R1A	MM6303		Sassuolo		IT	
Fiat G91R1A	MM6305	San Possidonio Associazionna	Delteland		IT	
Fiat G91R1B	MM6269		San Giovanni Ilarione		IT	
Fiat G91R1B	MM6376		Velo D'Astico		IT	
Fiat G91R1B	MM6389	Museo dell'Aviazione	Cerbaiola		IT	
Fiat G91R1B	MM6390		Stallavena		IT	
Fiat G91R1B	MM6398		Codroipo		IT	
Fiat G91R1B	MM6405	Museo Storico dell'Aeronautica Militaire	Vigna di Valle		IT	
Fiat G91R1B	MM6413		Rivolto		IT	
Fiat G91R3	5444		Alfrasagide		PT	
Fiat G91R3	5445		Sintra AB		PT	
Fiat G91R3	5463		Montijo AB		PT	
Fiat G91R3	5541	Museu du Ar	Alverca		PT	
Fiat G91R3	5542	Junkyard resident	Pombal		PT	
Fiat G91R3	9907	Deutsches Museum	Munich		DE	
Fiat G91R3	9912	Luftwaffenmuseum	Berlin-Gatow		DE	
Fiat G91R3	9939	Musee de L'Air	Paris		FR	
Fiat G91R3	91308	Museu du Ar	Alverca		PT	
Fiat G91R3	30+80		Horta do Douro		PT	
Fiat G91R3	30+83	Carvoeiro School	Carvoeiro		PT	
Fiat G91R3	30+85	Musee de l'Armee et D'Histoire Militaire	Brussels		BE	
Fiat G91R3	30+85		Rothenburg		DE	
Fiat G91R3	30+98		Wittich		DE	
Fiat G91R3	31+01		Oldenberg		DE	
Fiat G91R3	31+35		Obepfaffenhofer		DE	
Fiat G91R3	31+39	Museum fur Luftfarft	Wernigerode		DE	
Fiat G91R3	31+42		Ingolstadt		DE	
Fiat G91R3	31+47	Technikmuseum	Speyer		DE	
Fiat G91R3	31+78		Merseburg		DE	

A/C	S/N	MUSEUM / DISPLAY	CITY / BASE	STATE	CY	REMARKS
Fiat G91R3	31+95	International Luftfarht Museum	Schwenningen am Neckar		DE	
Fiat G91R3	32+15	Luftwaffenmuseum	Berlin-Gatow		DE	
Fiat G91R3	32+43		Savigny Les Beaune		FR	
Fiat G91R3	32+45		Wunstorf		DE	
Fiat G91R3	32+52		Furstenfeldbruck		DE	
Fiat G91R3	32+58		Buseck		DE	
Fiat G91R3	32+64	Technik Museum	Sinsheim		DE	
Fiat G91R3	32+72	Luftwaffenmuseum	Berlin-Gatow		DE	
Fiat G91R3	MM5257		Hermeskeil		DE	
Fiat G91R3	MM6277		Salargius		IT	
Fiat G91R3			Cologne		DE	Dispiayed as 31+29
Fiat G91R3		Musee de L'Epopee et de l'Industrie Aeronautics			FR	
Fiat G91R3			Portimao		PT	
Fiat G91R4	5401		Lisben		PT	
Fiat G91R4	5403		Barro		PT	
Fiat G91R4	5404		Montijo AB		PT	
Fiat G91R4	5407		Parque das Nacoes		PT	
Fiat G91R4	5408		Viseu		PT	
Fiat G91R4	5415		Santa Maria, Azores		PT	
Fiat G91R4	5425		Coviha		PT	
Fiat G91R4	7500	Museum fur Luftfarft	Wernigerode		DE	
Fiat G91R4	35+41	Luftwaffenmuseum	Berlin-Gatow		DE	
Fiat G91T	MM54410	Junkyard resident	Verona Villa Franca		IT	
Fiat G91T	MM6288		Pratica di Mare		IT	
Fiat G91T1	MM54398		Gavalcaselle		IT	
Fiat G91T1	MM54403	Museo dell'Aviazione	Cerbarola		IT	
Fiat G91T1	MM54405	Museo dell'Aviazione	Cerbaiola		IT	
Fiat G91T1	MM54408		Rome		IT	
Fiat G91T1	MM54415		Castellstto		IT	
Fiat G91T1	MM54614	Junkyard resident	Lake Di Garda		IT	Displayed as 60-98
Fiat G91T1	MM6288		Rome		IT	
Fiat G91T1	MM6323	Capital Airport gate guard	Rome		IT	
Fiat G91T1	MM6326	Junkyard resident	Albenga		IT	
Fiat G91T1	MM6344	Museo Storico dell'Aeronautica Militaire	Vigna di Valle		IT	
Fiat G91T1	MM6348		Foggia Amenndola		IT	
Fiat G91T1	MM6359		Pozzolo		IT	
Fiat G91T1	MM6363		Foggia Amenndola		IT	
Fiat G91T1	MM6428		Basiliano		IT	
Fiat G91T1		Junkyard resident	Rome		IT	Displayed as 60-108
Fiat G91T3	9858		Montelimar		FR	
Fiat G91T3	9940	Luftwaffenmuseum	Berlin-Gatow		DE	
Fiat G91T3	9941	Luftwaffenmuseum	Berlin-Gatow		DE	
Fiat G91T3	34+02		Furstenfeldbruck		DE	
Fiat G91T3	34+27		Santo Andre das Tojeiras		IT	
Fiat G91Y	MM579		Pratica di Mare		IT	
Fiat G91Y	MM6292		Vicenza AB		IT	Displayed as 2-22
Fiat G91Y	MM6455		Brindisi Casale		IT	
Fiat G91Y	MM6474		Masera		IT	
Fiat G91Y	MM6487		Belluno		IT	
Fiat G91Y	MM6952		Foggia Amenndola		IT	
Fiat G91Y	MM6959	Museo Storico dell'Aeronautica Militaire	Vigna di Valle		IT	
Fiat G91Y			Carpi		IT	
Harrier GR.Mk.1	XV277	Museum of Flight	East Fortune, Scotland		GB	
Harrier GR.Mk.1	XV798	Bristol Aero Collection, Kemble Field	Cirencester		GB	
Harrier GR.Mk.1		Luftwaffenmuseum	Berlin-Gatow		DE	
Harrier GR.Mk.3	HZ998		Hermeskeil		DE	
Harrier GR.Mk.3	WV752		Blechley Park		GB	
Harrier GR.Mk.3	XV278	Luftwaffenmuseum	Berlin-Gatow		DE	
Harrier GR.Mk.3	XV748	Yorkshire Aviation Museum	Ellvington		GB	
Harrier GR.Mk.3	XV751	Gatwick Aviation Museum	Chartwood		GB	
Harrier GR.Mk.3	XV779		RAFB Wittering		GB	
Harrier GR.Mk.3	XW924		RAFB Cottesmore		GB	
Harrier GR.Mk.3	XZ132		RAFB Cranwell		GB	
Harrier GR.Mk.3	XZ133	Royal Air Force Museum	Duxford		GB	
Harrier GR.Mk.3	XZ966	Cold War Jets Collection	Bruntingthorpe Airfield		GB	
Harrier GR.Mk.3	XZ968	Muckleburgh Collection	Sheringham		GB	
Harrier GR.Mk.3	XZ977	Royal Air Force Museum	London		GB	
Harrier GR.Mk.3	XZ997	Royal Air Force Museum	London		GB	
Harrier GR.Mk.3	ZD668	Planes of Fame Museum, Chino MAP	Chino	CA	US	
Harrier GR.Mk.3		Museo Nacional Aeronautico y Del Espancio	Avendio Pedro Aguirre Cerda		CL	
Harrier GR.Mk.3 (Nose)		Cold War Jets Collection	Bruntingthorpe Airfield		GB	
Harrier T.Mk.2	XW264	Gatwick Aviation Museum	Chartwood		GB	
Harrier T.Mk.4	XW270	Cold War Jets Collection	Bruntingthorpe Airfield		GB	
Harrier T.Mk.4	XW271		RAFB Culdrose		GB	
Harrier T.Mk.4	XZ145		RAFB Culdrose		GB	
Harrier T.Mk.4		Norwich Aviation Museum	Norwich Airport		GB	
Hunter FR.Mk.10	XF426	Royal Air Force Museum	London		GB	
Hunter FR.Mk.10	XG168	Norwich Aviation Museum	Norwich Airport		GB	

A/C	S/N	MUSEUM / DISPLAY	CITY / BASE	STATE	CY	REMARKS
Hunter FR.Mk.10	XJ714	Jet Aviation Preservation Group	Stratford-upon-Avon		GB	
Jaguar GR,Mk.1A	XX108	Royal Air Force Museum	Duxford		GB	
Meteor FR.Mk.9	FF-123	Museo Aeronautico y del Espacio	Quito		EC	Painted in demonstration team colors with homemade canopy ONE OF TWO SURVIVING METEOR FR.MK.5
Meteor FR.Mk.9	VZ608	Newark Air Museum	Newark		GB	Rolls Royce RB108 engine test bed ONE OF TWO SURVIVING METEOR FR.MK.5
Mirage 5BR	BR-04	Florrennes Aviation Museum	Florrennes AB		BE	
Mirage 5BR	BR-10		Beauvechain		BE	Displayed as BR-10
Mirage 5BR	BR-25	Musee Aeronautico	Santiago-Los Carrillos		CL	
Mirage IIIR	336	Musee de L'Air	Paris		FR	
Mirage IIIR	304		Hermeskeil		DE	Displayed as 33-TN
Mirage IIIR			Zruc		CZ	Incorrectly displayed as 304 / 33FN
Mirage IIIRD	356		Ambreneu Airport		FR	Displayed as 33-TE
Mirage IIIRD	364		Epinal-Mirecourt Airport		FR	
Mirage IIIRD		Musee de L'Epopee et de l'Industrie Aeronautics			FR	
Mirage IIIRS	R-2110		Stans		CH	
Mirage IIIRS	R-2112		Tartu		EE	
Mirage IIIRS	R-2116		Stans		CH	
Mirage IIIRS	R-2117	Musee de l'Aviation Militaire de Payerne	Payerne AB		CH	
Mirage IIIRS		Fleiger Museum Dubendorf	Dubendorf AB		CH	
Mirage IIIRS		Musee d'Avions du Palegrv	Perpignan		FR	
Mirage IVP		Le Conservatoire de l'air et de l'Espace d'Antquitqine			FR	
Phantom FGR.Mk.2	XT891	Gate guard	RAFB Coninsby		GB	
Phantom FGR.Mk.2	XV408	Solway Aviation Museum	Carlisle Airport		GB	
Phantom FGR.Mk.2	XV424	Royal Air Force Museum	London		GB	
Phantom FGR.Mk.2	XV470	Royal Air Force Museum	London		GB	
Phantom FGR.Mk.2	XV474	Royal Air Force Museum	Duxford		GB	
Phantom FGR.Mk.2	XV497		Waddington		GB	
Phantom FGR.Mk 2 (Nose)		Norwich Aviation Museum	Norwich Airport		GB	
RB-26C Invader	44-35323	Planes of Fame Museum	Valle	AZ	US	*ONLY SURVIVING RB-26C INVADER*
RB-45C Tornado	48-0017	Strategic Air and Space Museum	Ashland	NE	US	*ONLY SURVIVING RB-45C TORNADO*
RB-57A Canberra	52-1426	Yankee Air Museum	Belleville	MI	US	
RB-57A Canberra	52-1448	Glen L. Martin Aviation Museum	Middle River	MD	US	
RB-57A Canberra	52-1459	Wings of Eagles Discovery Center	Elmira	NY	US	
RB-57A Canberra	52-1467	Glen L. Martin Aviation Museum	Middle River	MD	US	
RB-57A Canberra	52-1475	Museum of Aviation	Warner Robins AFB	GA	US	
RB-57A Canberra	52-1480	Combat Air Museum, Forbes Field	Topeka	KS	US	
RB-57A Canberra	52-1485	Selfridge Military Air Museum	Selfridge ANGB	MI	US	
RB-57A Canberra	52-1488	New England Air Museum	Windsor Locks	CT	US	
RB-57A Canberra	52-1492	Hill Aerospace Museum	Ogden	UT	US	
RB-57A Canberra		National Warplane Museum, Corning MAP	Horseheads	NY	US	
RB-57A Canberra		Commemorative Air Force Museum	Midland	TX	US	
RB-57A Canberra		USAF History and Traditions Museum	Lackland AFB	TX	US	
RB-66B Destroyer	53-0412	Octave Chanute Aerospace Museum	Rantoul	IL	US	
RB-66B Destroyer	53-0431		Florence Regional Airport	SC	US	
RB-66B Destroyer	53-0466	Dyess Linear Air Park	Dyess AFB	TX	US	
RB-66B Destroyer	53-0475	National Museum of the US Air Force	Wright-Patterson AFB	OH	US	
RF-101A Voodoo	41499		Hualieu		TW	
RF-101A Voodoo	41506		Kangshan AFB		TW	
RF-101A Voodoo	54-1503	Hill Aerospace Museum	Ogden	UT	US	
RF-101B Voodoo	59-0483	152nd RG, NV ANG, Reno IAP	Reno	NV	US	*ONLY SURVIVING RF-101B VOODOO*
RF-101C Voodoo	56-0048	Selfridge Military Air Museum	Selfridge ANGB	MI	US	
RF-101C Voodoo	56-0057	Camp Robinson	Little Rock	AR	US	
RF-101C Voodoo	56-0068	Keesler AFB Air Park	Keesler AFB	MS	US	
RF-101C Voodoo	56-0099	Shaw AFB Air Park	Shaw AFB	SC	US	
RF-101C Voodoo	56-0112	Gate guard Gila Bend MAP	Gila Bend	AZ	US	
RF-101C Voodoo	56-0125	Boone National Guard Center	Frankfort	KY	US	
RF-101C Voodoo	56-0130	Gate guard Gila Bend MAP	Gila Bend	AZ	US	
RF-101C Voodoo	56-0135	Maxwell AFB Air Park	Maxwell AFB	AL	US	
RF-101C Voodoo	56-0166	National Museum of the US Air Force	Wright-Patterson AFB	OH	US	
RF-101C Voodoo	56-0187	Cannon AFB Air Park	Cannon AFB	NM	US	
RF-101C Voodoo	56-0214	Pima Air and Space Museum	Tucson	AZ	US	
RF-101C Voodoo	56-0217	George Robert Hall Air Park	Hattiesburg	MS	US	
RF-101C Voodoo	56-0229	Museum of Aviation	Warner Robins AFB	GA	US	Photo is 54-1518 and 5858
RF-101C Voodoo	56-0231	Little Rock AFB	Little Rock	AR	US	
RF-101C Voodoo			Douglas	AZ	US	
RF-101C Voodoo		Paul E. Garber Facility	Suitland	MD	US	
RF-101C Voodoo		Niagara Falls ANGB	Niagara Falls	NY	US	
RF-101C Voodoo		Babe Didrickson Zaharious Memorial Park	Beaumont	TX	US	
RF-101H VooDoo	56-0001	123rd AW, KY ANG, Standiford Field	Louisville	KY	US	*ONE OF TWO SURVIVING RF-101H VOODOOs*
RF-101H VooDoo	56-0011	Pima Air and Space Museum	Tucson	AZ	US	*ONE OF TWO SURVIVING RF-101H VOODOOs*
RF-104G Starfighter	2125	Junkyard resident	Flensburg		DE	
RF-104G Starfighter	2309	Museum fur Luftfarft	Wernigerode		DE	
RF-104G Starfighter	62-12250		Taichung-Chinghuakang		TW	
RF-104G Starfighter	63-8181	Gate guard	Lahr AB		DE	Displayed as 24+38

Air Force Tac Recce Aircraft

A/C	S/N	MUSEUM / DISPLAY	CITY / BASE	STATE	CY	REMARKS
RF-104G Starfighter	D8022	Nordluftfartsmuseum	Bodo		NO	Displayed as B-FN
RF-104G Starfighter	MM6520	San Possidonio Associazionna	Deltaland		IT	
RF-104G Starfighter	MM6632		Loreto		IT	Displayed as 3-25
RF-104G Starfighter			Larissa AB		GR	Displayed as FG6692
RF-104G Starfighter			Rivolto		IT	Displayed as MM6651 / 3-03
RF-104G Starfighter		Luchmachht Museum	Soesterberg		NL	Displayed as D-8022
RF-111A Ardvark	63-9776	Mountain Home Air Park	Mountain Home AFB	ID	US	Displayed as 66-0022, in memory of first **F-111 combat crew KIA** ONLY SURVIVING RF-111A PROTOTYPE
RF-4C Phantom II	62-12200	National Museum of the US Air Force	Wright-Patterson AFB	OH	US	
RF-4C Phantom II	62-12201	Octave Chanute Aerospace Museum	Rantoul	IL	US	
RF-4C Phantom II	63-7745	117th ARW, AL ANGB	Birmingham IAP	AL	US	
RF-4C Phantom II	63-7746	March Field Air Museum	Riverside	CA	US	
RF-4C Phantom II	63-7748	Shaw AFB Air Park	Shaw AFB	SC	US	
RF-4C Phantom II	64-0061	Minnesota Air National Guard Museum	Minneapolis	MN	US	
RF-4C Phantom II	64-0748	Little Rock AFB	Little Rock	AR	US	
RF-4C Phantom II	64-0998	155th ARG, NE ANG	Lincoln	NE	US	
RF-4C Phantom II	64-1000	Rusty Allen Airport	Lago Vista	TX	US	
RF-4C Phantom II	64-1004	Air Force Flight Test Center	Edwards AFB	CA	US	
RF-4C Phantom II	64-1047	National Museum of the US Air Force	Wright-Patterson AFB	OH	US	
RF-4C Phantom II	64-1081	123rd AW, KY ANG, Standiford Field	Louisville	KY	US	
RF-4C Phantom II	65-0886	152nd RG, NV ANG, Reno IAP	Reno	NV	US	
RF-4C Phantom II	65-0903	121st ARW, OH ANG	Rickenbacker ANGB	OH	US	
RF-4C Phantom II	65-0905	Hill Aerospace Museum	Ogden	UT	US	
RF-4C Phantom II	65-0941	Freedom Garden Park	Quartzsite	AZ	US	
RF-4C Phantom II	66-0467	Hill Aerospace Museum	Valdosta	GA	US	
RF-4C Phantom II	66-0469	Hill Aerospace Museum	Ogden	UT	US	
RF-4C Phantom II	66-0903	Strategic Air and Space Museum	Ashland	NE	US	
RF-4C Phantom II	66-0905	Hill Aerospace Museum	Ogden	UT	US	
RF-4C Phantom II	67-0452	Air Force Armaments Museum	Eglin AFB	FL	US	
RF-4C Phantom II	68-0570	Dell Valle Elementary School	Austin	TX	US	
RF-4C Phantom II	68-0587		Hermeskeil		DE	
RF-4C Phantom II	68-0590	Musee de l'Armee et D'Histoire Militaire	Brussels		BE	
RF-4C Phantom II	68-0594	Gowen Field	Boise	ID	US	
RF-4C Phantom II	69-0367	Goodfellow AFB Air Park	Goodfellow AFB	TX	US	
RF-4C Phantom II	69-0372	Air Power Park	Hampton	VA	US	
RF-4C Phantom II		Kelly Field Annex	San Antonio	TX	US	Displayed with non-existant tail number 64-467
RF-4E Phantom II	68-0481		Larissa AB		GR	
RF-4E Phantom II	69-7465	Aviation Park and Plane Museum	Eskisehir		TR	
RF-4E Phantom II	69-7490	Hava Kuvvetleri Muzesi Komutanligi	Ankara		TR	
RF-4E Phantom II	69-7503	Hava Kuvvetleri Muzesi Komutanligi	Ankara		TR	
RF-4E Phantom II	69-7509	Luftwaffenmuseum	Berlin-Gatow		DE	Displayed as 35+62
RF-5A Freedom Fighter	70154	Royal Thai Air Force Museum	Chang Mai		TH	Displayed as TKh 18-3
RF-5A Freedom Fighter	68-9102	Nordluftfartsmuseum	Bodo AB		NO	
RF-5A Freedom Fighter	69-7147	Turkish Aerospace Museum	Istanbul		TR	
RF-5A Freedom Fighter	69-7170	Hellenic Air Force Museum	Dekelia-Tatoi AB		GR	
RF-5A Freedom Fighter	69-9105	Forsvarsels Flysaming	Oslo		NO	
RF-5A Freedom Fighter			Larissa AB		GR	Displayed as 97185 (Decoy Aircraft)
RF-5A Freedom Fighter		Hava Kuvvetleri Muzesi Komutanligi	Ankara		TR	Displayed as 21208 / 3-208
RF-5A Freedom Fighter		Havacylyk Muzesi	Izmir		TR	Displayed as 97156
RF-5A Freedom Fighter			Merzifou		TR	Displayed as 89103
RF-84F Thunderflash	49-2430	National Museum of the US Air Force	Wright-Patterson AFB	OH	US	YRF-84F
RF-84F Thunderflash	51-11253	Luchmachht Museum	Soesterberg		NL	Displayed as P-5
RF-84F Thunderflash	51-11259	155th ARG, NE ANG	Lincoln	NE	US	
RF-84F Thunderflash	51-11260	Ditellandia Air Park	Castel Volturno		IT	May have been scrapped
RF-84F Thunderflash	51-11264	Karup Air Force Museum	Karup AB		DK	Awaiting restoration as C-264
RF-84F Thunderflash	51-11274	Historiske Forening Musseet	Copenhagen		DK	Displayed as C-274
RF-84F Thunderflash	51-11279	117th ARW, AL ANGB	Birmingham IAP	AL	US	
RF-84F Thunderflash	51-11292	188th FG, AR ANG	Fort Smith	AR	US	
RF-84F Thunderflash	51-11293	Dyess Linear Air Park	Dyess AFB	TX	US	
RF-84F Thunderflash	51-16665	Historiske Forening Musseet	Copenhagen		DK	Displayed as KA-D
RF-84F Thunderflash	51-17011	Hellenic Air Force Museum	Dekelia-Tatoi AB		GR	
RF-84F Thunderflash	51-17015		Namur- Suarlee (Temploux)		BE	Displayed as FR-30
RF-84F Thunderflash	51-17041		Furstenfeldbruck		DE	Displayed as BD+119
RF-84F Thunderflash	51-17045	Norsk Flyhistorisk Forening	Stavanger		NO	Displayed as AZ-N
RF-84F Thunderflash	51-17046	Hill Aerospace Museum	Ogden	UT	US	Nose sction only
RF-84F Thunderflash	51-17050	Forsvarsels Flysaming	Oslo		NO	Displayed as AZ-D
RF-84F Thunderflash	51-17051	Forsvarsels Flysaming	Oslo		NO	Displayed as AZ-E
RF-84F Thunderflash	51-17053	Forsvarsels Flysaming	Oslo		NO	Displayed as AZ-G
RF-84F Thunderflash	51-17055	Forsvarsels Flysaming	Oslo		NO	Displayed as AZ-N
RF-84F Thunderflash	51-1896	Selfridge Military Air Museum	Selfridge ANGB	MI	US	
RF-84F Thunderflash	51-1901	Turkish Aerospace Museum	Istanbul		TR	
RF-84F Thunderflash	51-1917	Turkish Aerospace Museum	Istanbul		TR	
RF-84F Thunderflash	51-1922		Spa La Sanveniere		BE	Displayed as FR-27
RF-84F Thunderflash	51-1924	Hava Kuvvetleri Muzesi Komutanligi	Ankara		TR	Displayed as 924
RF-84F Thunderflash	51-1928	Musee d'Avions du Palegrv	Perpignan		FR	
RF-84F Thunderflash	51-1929		Neligh	NE	US	
RF-84F Thunderflash	51-1935		York Municipal Airport	NE	US	

A/C	S/N	MUSEUM / DISPLAY	CITY / BASE	STATE	CY	REMARKS
RF-84F Thunderflash	51-1936	Central Missouri State University	Warrenburg/Skyhaven Airport	MO	US	
RF-84F Thunderflash	51-1940		Villafranca AB		IT	
RF-84F Thunderflash	51-1944	Pima Air and Space Museum	Tucson	AZ	US	
RF-84F Thunderflash	51-1945	Musee de l'Armee et D'Histoire Militaire	Brussels		BE	Displayed as FR-28
RF-84F Thunderflash	52-6778		Hermeskeil		DE	
RF-84F Thunderflash	52-7169	Musee de l'Armee et D'Histoire Militaire	Brussels		BE	Displayed as FR-30
RF-84F Thunderflash	52-7244	Museum of Aviation	Warner Robins AFB	GA	US	Cannot Confirm S/N says Sioux City
RF-84F Thunderflash	52-7249	187th TFG, Donnelly Field ANGB	Montgomery IAP	AL	US	
RF-84F Thunderflash	52-7261	George T. Baker Aviation School, Miami IAP	Miami	FL	US	
RF-84F Thunderflash	52-7262	Walter Soplata Collection	Newbury	OH	US	
RF-84F Thunderflash	52-7295		Munsingen		DE	
RF-84F Thunderflash	52-7339	Museo Dell'Aria 'Nido Delle Aquile			IT	Displayed as MM52-7339
RF-84F Thunderflash	52-7346	Luftwaffenmuseum	Berlin-Gatow		DE	Displayed as EB+344
RF-84F Thunderflash	52-7355	Gate guard	Fliegerhorst Schleswig		DE	Displayed as EB+250
RF-84F Thunderflash	52-7359		Lido d'Jesolo		IT	Displayed as MM52-7459 / 3-04
RF-84F Thunderflash	52-7373		Erding		DE	Displayed as EB+321
RF-84F Thunderflash	52-7375		Manching		DE	Displayed as EB+326
RF-84F Thunderflash	52-7377		Hermeskeil		DE	Displayed as EA+241
RF-84F Thunderflash	52-7379	Deutsches Museum	Munich		DE	Displayed as EB+331
RF-84F Thunderflash	52-7391		San Pelagio		IT	Displayed as MM52-7391 / 3-91
RF-84F Thunderflash	52-7409	117th ARW, AL ANGB	Birmingham IAP	AL	US	
RF-84F Thunderflash	52-7421	Yankee Air Museum	Belleville	MI	US	
RF-84F Thunderflash	52-7458	Museo Storico dell'Aeronautica Militaire	Vigna di Valle		IT	Displayed as MM52-7458 / 3-05
RF-84F Thunderflash	52-7459	Museo dell'Aviazione	Cerbaiola		IT	Displayed as MM52-7459 / 3-54
RF-84F Thunderflash	52-7468		Herakion-Nikos Kazantzakis		GR	
RF-84F Thunderflash	52-7474		Rivolto		IT	Displayed as 3-18
RF-84F Thunderflash	52-8736		Larissa AB		GR	
RF-84F Thunderflash	53-7524	Western Aerospace Museum	Oakland	CA	US	
RF-84F Thunderflash	53-7529	118th AW, TN ANG	Nashville	TN	US	
RF-84F Thunderflash	53-7543	Little Rock AFB	Little Rock	AR	US	
RF-84F Thunderflash	53-7548	Gate guard, Lincoln ANGB	Lincoln	NE	US	
RF-84F Thunderflash	53-7554	Glen L. Martin Aviation Museum	Middle River	MD	US	
RF-84F Thunderflash	53-7570	Enka Junior HS	Chandler	NC	US	
RF-84F Thunderflash	53-7575		Messalongi		GR	
RF-84F Thunderflash	53-7577	Gate guard	Strasbourg AB, France		FR	Displayed as 33-CK
RF-84F Thunderflash	53-7581	Gate guard	Karup AB		DK	Displayed as C-581
RF-84F Thunderflash	53-7583	Gate guard	Larissa AB		GR	
RF-84F Thunderflash	53-7595	American Airpower Museum	Farmingdale	NY	US	
RF-84F Thunderflash	53-7610	Oklahoma State University	Stillwater	OK	US	
RF-84F Thunderflash	53-7619	Gate guard	Bremgarten AB		DE	
RF-84F Thunderflash	53-7636	George Robert Hall Air Park	Hattiesburg	MS	US	
RF-84F Thunderflash	53-7646		Beauvechain		BE	Displayed as FR-32
RF-84F Thunderflash	53-7660		Tripoli		GR	
RF-84F Thunderflash	53-7665		Tatoa		GR	
RF-84F Thunderflash	53-7682		Sedes		GR	
RF-84F Thunderflash	53-7683		Larissa AB		GR	
RF-84F Thunderflash			Beauvechain		BE	Displayed as FR-33
RF-84F Thunderflash			Merseburg		DE	Displayed as EB+368
RF-84F Thunderflash			Schleswig		DE	
RF-84F Thunderflash		Danmark Flyvevabenmuseet	Stauning Lufthavn		DK	Displayed as C-264
RF-84F Thunderflash		Savigny les Beaune Museum	Burgandy		FR	
RF-84F Thunderflash			Lido d'Jesola		IT	
RF-84F Thunderflash		Nordluftfartsmuseum	Bodo AB		NO	
RF-84F Thunderflash			Ozark	AL	US	
RF-84F Thunderflash		Souix City IAP	Souix City	IA	US	
RF-84F Thunderflash			Harlan	IA	US	
RF-84F Thunderflash			Ida Grove	IA	US	
RF-84F Thunderflash		Combat Air Museum, Forbes Field	Topeka	KS	US	
RF-84F Thunderflash			David City	NE	US	
RF-84F Thunderflash			Valley	NE	US	
RF-84F Thunderflash		Commemorative Air Force Museum	Midland	TX	US	
RF-84K Thunderflash	52-7259	National Museum of the US Air Force	Wright-Patterson AFB	OH	US	
RF-84K Thunderflash	52-7265	Planes of Fame Museum, Chino MAP	Chino	CA	US	
RF-84K Thunderflash	52-7266	Wings over the Rockies Aviation and Space Mu	Denver	CO	US	
RT-33A Shooting Star	56141	Royal Thai Air Force Museum	Chang Mai		TH	Displayed as TF 11-5
RT-33A Shooting Star	53-5322		Traviso-Istrana		IT	Displayed as MM53-5322 / 51-76
RT-33A Shooting Star	53-5396	Gate guard	65 Deposito Aeronautico Taranto		IT	Displayed as MM53-5396
RT-33A Shooting Star	53-5430		Gioia del Coll		IT	Displayed as MM53-5430
RT-33A Shooting Star	53-5587	Flying Tigers Air Museum	Brookston/Tico		IT	Displayed as MM53-5587
RT-33A Shooting Star	53-5594	Museo Storico dell'Aeronautica Militaire	Vigna di Valle		IT	Displayed as MM53-5594 / 9-35
RT-33A Shooting Star	53-5668		Cagliari-Elmas		IT	Displayed as MM53-5594 / 9-36
RT-33A Shooting Star	53-5795		Rivolto		IT	Displayed as MM53-5795
RT-33A Shooting Star	54-1543	Turkish Aerospace Museum	Istanbul		TR	Displayed as 8-543
RT-33A Shooting Star	54-1548	Aviation Park and Plane Museum	Eskisehir		TR	
RT-33A Shooting Star		Military Honor Park, Michiana Regional Airort	South Bend		IN	Incorrectly displayed with US Navy TV-2 serial number
RT-33A Shooting Star		Pole Air Museum	Sintra		PT	Displayed as 1918
Saab J29OF Tunnan			Fliegerhorst Volgler		AT	ONE OF TWO SURVIVING SAAB J29OF TUNNAN

A/C	S/N	MUSEUM / DISPLAY	CITY / BASE	STATE	CY	REMARKS
Saab J29OF Tunnan	29588		Graz-Thalerof		AT	*ONE OF TWO SURVIVING SAAB J29OF TUNNAN*
Saab RF-35 Draken	AR-105	Karup Air Force Museum	Karup AB		DK	
Saab RF-35 Draken	AR-107	Newark Air Museum	Newark		GB	
Saab RF-35 Draken	AR-112	Gate guard	Karup AB		DK	
Saab RF-35 Draken	AR-120	Nordluftfartsmuseum	Bodo		NO	
Saab RF-35 Draken		Danmark Flyvevabenmuseet	Stauning Lufthavn		DK	
Saab S29C Tunnan	29929	Lulea AB	Kallax		SE	
Saab S29C Tunnan	29937	Lulea AB	Kallax		SE	
Saab S29C Tunnan	29945		Kareby		SE	
Saab S29C Tunnan	29969	Vasteras Flygmuseum, Vasteras AB	Hasslo		SE	
Saab S29C Tunnan	29970	Flygvapenmuseum Malmen	Linkoping AB		SE	
Saab S29C Tunnan	29974	Vasteras Flygmuseum, Vasteras AB	Hasslo		SE	
Saab S32C Lansen	32940		Nylcoping AB		SE	
Saab S35E Draken	35931	Fire and Rescue Facility guard	Karup AB		DK	Displayed as F21-60
Saab S35E Draken	35952		Lules-Kaliax		SE	
Saab SF37 Viggen	37974		Hermeskeil		DE	
Swift FR,Mk.5	WK277/N	Newark Air Museum	Newark		GB	*ONE OF TWO SURVIVING SWIFT FR.MK.5*
Swift FR,Mk.5	WK281	Tangmere Military Aviation Museum	Chichester		GB	*ONE OF TWO SURVIVING SWIFT FR.MK.5*

Appendix B

Tactical Reconnaissance Aircraft Survivors - Location Listing

A/C	S/N	MUSEUM / DISPLAY	CITY / BASE	STATE	CY	REMARKS
AUSTRIA						
Saab J29OF Tunnan			Fliegerhorst Voigler		AT	*ONE OF TWO SURVIVING SAAB J29OF TUNNAN*
Saab J29OF Tunnan	29588		Graz-Thalerof		AT	*ONE OF TWO SURVIVING SAAB J29OF TUNNAN*
BELGIUM						
Mirage 5BR	BR-10		Beauvechain		BE	Displayed as BR-10
RF-84F Thunderflash	53-7646		Beauvechain		BE	Displayed as FR-32
RF-84F Thunderflash			Beauvechain		BE	Displayed as FR-33
Fiat G91R3	30+85	Musee de l'Armee et D'Histoire Militaire	Brussells		BE	
RF-4C Phantom II	68-0590	Musee de l'Armee et D'Histoire Militaire	Brussels		BE	
RF-84F Thunderflash	51-1945	Musee de l'Armee et D'Histoire Militaire	Brussels		BE	Displayed as FR-28
RF-84F Thunderflash	52-7169	Musee de l'Armee et D'Histoire Militaire	Brussels		BE	Displayed as FR-30
Mirage 5BR	BR-04	Florennes Aviation Museum	Florrennes AB		BE	
RF-84F Thunderflash	51-		Namur- Suarlee (Temploux)		BE	Displayed as FR-30
RF-84F Thunderflash	51-1922		Spa La Sanveniere		BE	Displayed as FR-27
CANADA						
CF-5A Freedom Fighter		Atlantic Canada Aviation Museum	Enfield, Nova Scotia		CA	*ONLY SURVIVING CF-5A FREEDOM FIGHTER*
CHILE						
Harrier GR.Mk.3		Museo Nacional Aeronautico y Del Espancio	Avendio Pedro Aguirre Cerda		CL	
Canberra PR.Mk.9	XH173	Museo National Aeronautico y Del Espacio	Avendio Pedro Aguirre Cerda		CL	
Mirage 5BR	BR-25	Musee Aeronautico	Santiago-Los Carrilos		CL	
CZECH REPUBLIC						
Mirage IIIR			Zruc		CZ	Incorrectly displayed as 304 / 33FN
GERMANY						
Canberra B.Mk.2	9935	Luftwaffenmuseum	Berlin-Gatow		DE	Used by German Air Force for aerial mapping
Fiat G91R3	9912	Luftwaffenmuseum	Berlin-Gatow		DE	
Fiat G91R3	32+15	Luftwaffenmuseum	Berlin-Gatow		DE	
Fiat G91R3	32+72	Luftwaffenmuseum	Berlin-Gatow		DE	
Fiat G91R4	35+41	Luftwaffenmuseum	Berlin-Gatow		DE	
Fiat G91T3	9940	Luftwaffenmuseum	Berlin-Gatow		DE	
Fiat G91T3	9941	Luftwaffenmuseum	Berlin-Gatow		DE	
Harrier GR.Mk.1		Luftwaffenmuseum	Berlin-Gatow		DE	
Harrier GR.Mk.3	XV278	Luftwaffenmuseum	Berlin-Gatow		DE	
RF-4E Phantom II	69-7509	Luftwaffenmuseum	Berlin-Gatow		DE	Displayed as 35+62
RF-84F Thunderflash	52-7346	Luftwaffenmuseum	Berlin-Gatow		DE	Displayed as EB+344
RF-84F Thunderflash	53-7619	Gate guard	Bremgarten AB		DE	
Fiat G91R3	32+58		Buseck		DE	
Fiat G91		Butzweilerhof Museum	Cologne		DE	Displayed as 31+78
Fiat G91R3			Cologne		DE	Displayed as 31+29
RF-84F Thunderflash	52-7373		Erding		DE	Displayed as EB+321
RF-104G Starfighter	2125	Junkyard resident	Flensburg		DE	
RF-84F Thunderflash	52-7355	Gate guard	Fliegerhorst Schleswig		DE	Displayed as EB+250
Fiat G91R3	32+52		Furstenfeldbruck		DE	
Fiat G91T3	34+02		Furstenfeldbruck		DE	
RF-84F Thunderflash	51-		Furstenfeldbruck		DE	Displayed as BD+119
Fiat G91R3	MM5257		Hermeskeil		DE	
Harrier GR.Mk 3	HZ998		Hermeskeil		DE	
Mirage IIIR	304		Hermeskeil		DE	Displayed as 33-TN
RF-4C Phantom II	68-0587		Hermeskeil		DE	
RF-84F Thunderflash	52-6778		Hermeskeil		DE	
RF-84F Thunderflash	52-7377		Hermeskeil		DE	Displayed as EA+241
Saab SF37 Viggen	37974		Hermeskeil		DE	
Fiat G91R3	31+42		Ingolstadt		DE	
RF-104G Starfighter	63-8181	Gate guard	Lahr AB		DE	Displayed as 24+38
RF-84F Thunderflash	52-7375		Manching		DE	Displayed as EB+326
Fiat G91R3	31+78		Merseburg		DE	
RF-84F Thunderflash			Merseburg		DE	Displayed as EB+368
Fiat G91R3	9907	Deutsches Museum	Munich		DE	
RF-84F Thunderflash	52-7379	Deutsches Museum	Munich		DE	Displayed as EB+331
RF-84F Thunderflash	52-7295		Munsingen		DE	
Fiat G91R3	31+35		Obepfaffenhofer		DE	
Fiat G91R3	31+01		Oldenberg		DE	
Fiat G91R3	30+85		Rothenburg		DE	
RF-84F Thunderflash			Schleswig		DE	
Fiat G91R3	31+95	International Luftfarht Museum	Schwenningen am Neckar		DE	
Fiat G91R3	32+64	Technik Museum	Sinsheim		DE	
Canberra B Mk.2	9936	Tecknik Museum	Sinsheim		DE	Used by German Air Force for aerial mapping

A/C	S/N	MUSEUM / DISPLAY	CITY / BASE	STATE	CY	REMARKS
DH-112 Venom FB.MK.1R	J-1603	Tecknik Museum	Sinsheim		DE	Displayed as J-1603
DH-112 Venom FB.MK.1R	J-1628	Tecknik Museum	Sinsheim		DE	
Fiat G91R3	31+47	Technikmuseum	Speyer		DE	
Fiat G91R3	31+39	Museum fur Luftfarft	Wernigerode		DE	
Fiat G91R4	7500	Museum fur Luftfarft	Wernigerode		DE	
RF-104G Starfighter	2309	Museum fur Luftfarft	Wernigerode		DE	
Fiat G91R3	30+98		Wittich		DE	
Fiat G91R3	32+45		Wunstorf		DE	
DENMARK						
RF-84F Thunderflash	51-	Historiske Forening Musseet	Copenhagen		DK	Displayed as C-274
RF-84F Thunderflash	51-	Historiske Forening Musseet	Copenhagen		DK	Displayed as KA-D
Saab S35E Draken	35931	Fire and Rescue Facility guard	Karup AB		DK	Displayed as F21-60
Saab RF-35 Draken	AR-112	Gate guard	Karup AB		DK	
RF-84F Thunderflash	53-7581	Gate guard	Karup AB		DK	Displayed as C-581
RF-84F Thunderflash	51-	Karup Air Force Museum	Karup AB		DK	Awaiting restoration as C-264
Saab RF-35 Draken	AR-105	Karup Air Force Museum	Karup AB		DK	
F-16A Fighting Falcon		Danmark Flyvevabenmuseet	Stauning Lufthavn		DK	
F-16B Fighting Falcon		Danmark Flyvevabenmuseet	Stauning Lufthavn		DK	
RF-84F Thunderflash		Danmark Flyvevabenmuseet	Stauning Lufthavn		DK	Displayed as C-264
Saab RF-35 Draken		Danmark Flyvevabenmuseet	Stauning Lufthavn		DK	
ECUADOR						
Meteor FR Mk 9	FF-123	Museo Aeronautico y del Espacio	Quito		EC	Painted in demonstration team colors with homemade canopy ONE OF TWO SURVIVING METEOR FR.MK.5
ESTONIA						
Mirage IIIRS	R-2112		Tartu		EE	
FRANCE						
Mirage IIIRD	356		Ambrerieu Airport		FR	Displayed as 33-TE
RF-84F Thunderflash		Savigny les Beaune Museum	Burgandy		FR	
Mirage IIIRD	364		Epinal-Mirecourt Airport		FR	
Fiat G91T3	9858		Montelimar		FR	
Fiat G91R3	9939	Musee de L'Air	Paris		FR	
Mirage IIIR	336	Musee de L'Air	Paris		FR	
F-16A Fighting Falcon		Musee d'Avions du Palegrv	Perpignan		FR	
Mirage IIIRS		Musee d'Avions du Palegrv	Perpignan		FR	
RF-84F Thunderflash	51-1928	Musee d'Avions du Palegrv	Perpignan		FR	
Fiat G91R3	32+43		Savigny Les Beaune		FR	
RF-84F Thunderflash	53-7577	Gate guard	Strasbourg AB, France		FR	Displayed as 33-CK
Mirage IVP		Le Conservatoire de l'air et de l'Espace d'Antquitqine			FR	
Fiat G91R3		Musee de L'Epopee et de l'Industrie Aeronautics			FR	
Mirage IIIRD		Musee de L'Epopee et de l'Industrie Aeronautics			FR	
GREECE						
RF-5A Freedom Fighter	69-7170	Hellenic Air Force Museum	Dekelia-Tatoi AB		GR	
RF-84F Thunderflash	51-	Hellenic Air Force Museum	Dekelia-Tatoi AB		GR	
RF-84F Thunderflash	52-7468		Herakion-Nikos Kazantzakis		GR	
RF-84F Thunderflash	53-7583	Gate guard	Larissa AB		GR	
RF-104G Starfighter			Larissa AB		GR	Displayed as FG6692
RF-4E Phantom II	68-0481		Larissa AB		GR	
RF-5A Freedom Fighter			Larissa AB		GR	Displayed as 97185 (Decoy Aircraft)
RF-84F Thunderflash	52-8736		Larissa AB		GR	
RF-84F Thunderflash	53-7683		Larissa AB		GR	
RF-84F Thunderflash	53-7575		Messalongi		GR	
RF-84F Thunderflash	53-7682		Sedes		GR	
RF-84F Thunderflash	53-7665		Tatoa		GR	
RF-84F Thunderflash	53-7660		Tripoli		GR	
ITALY						
RT-33A Shooting Star	53-5396	Gate guard	65 Deposito Aeronautico Taranto		IT	Displayed as MM53-5396
Fiat G91T1	MM6326	Junkyard resident	Albenga		IT	
Fiat G91T1	MM6428		Basiliano		IT	
Fiat G91Y	MM6487		Belluno		IT	
Fiat G91Y	MM6455		Brindisi Casale		IT	
RT-33A Shooting Star	53-5587	Flying Tigers Air Museum	Brookston/Tico		IT	Displayed as MM53-5587
RT-33A Shooting Star	53-5668		Cagliari-Elmas		IT	Displayed as MM53-5594 / 9-36
Fiat G91			Campefordina		IT	
Fiat G91Y			Carpi		IT	
RF-84F Thunderflash	51-	Ditellandia Air Park	Castel Volturno		IT	May have been scrapped
Fiat G91T1	MM5441		Castelisitto		IT	
Fiat G91R1B	MM6389	Museo dell'Aviazione	Cerbaiola		IT	
Fiat G91T1	MM5440	Museo dell'Aviazione	Cerbaiola		IT	
Fiat G91T1	MM5440	Museo dell'Aviazione	Cerbaiola		IT	
RF-84F Thunderflash	52-7459	Museo dell'Aviazione	Cerbaiola		IT	Displayed as MM52-7459 / 3-54
Fiat G91R1B	MM6398		Codroipo		IT	
Fiat G91R1A	MM6305	San Possidonio Associazionna	Deltaland		IT	

A/C	S/N	MUSEUM / DISPLAY	CITY / BASE	STATE	CY	REMARKS
RF-104G Starfighter	MM6520	San Possidonio Associazionna	Deltaland		IT	
Fiat G91T1	MM6348		Foggia Amenndola		IT	
Fiat G91T1	MM6363		Foggia Amenndola		IT	
Fiat G91Y	MM6952		Foggia Amenndola		IT	
Fiat G91R1	MM6282		Forli		IT	
Fiat G91T1	MM5439		Gavalcaselle		IT	
RT-33A Shooting Star	53-5430		Gioia del Coll		IT	Displayed as MM53-5430
Fiat G91T1	MM5461	Junkyard resident	Lake Di Garda		IT	Displayed as 60-98
RF-84F Thunderflash			Lido d'Jesola		IT	
RF-84F Thunderflash	52-7359		Lido d'Jesolo		IT	Displayed as MM52-7459 / 3-04
RF-104G Starfighter	MM6632		Loreto		IT	Displayed as 3-25
Fiat G91Y	MM6474		Masera		IT	
Fiat G91R		Museo Nationale Della Scienza E. Della Tecnica	Milan		IT	Displayed as 2-20
Fiat G91T1	MM6359		Pozzolo		IT	
Fiat G91T	MM6288		Pratica di Mare		IT	
Fiat G91Y	MM579		Pratica di Mare		IT	
Fiat G91R1B	MM6413		Rivolto		IT	
RF-104G Starfighter			Rivolto		IT	Displayed as MM6651 / 3-03
RF-84F Thunderflash	52-7474		Rivolto		IT	Displayed as 3-18
RT-33A Shooting Star	53-5795		Rivolto		IT	Displayed as MM53-5795
Fiat G91T1		Junkyard resident	Rome		IT	Displayed as 60-108
Fiat G91T1	MM5440		Rome		IT	
Fiat G91T1	MM6288		Rome		IT	
Fiat G91T1	MM6323	Capital Airport gate guard	Rome		IT	
Fiat G91R3	MM6277		Salargius		IT	
Fiat G91R1B	MM6269		San Giovanni Ilarione		IT	
RF-84F Thunderflash	52-7391		San Pelagio		IT	Displayed as MM52-7391 / 3-91
Fiat G91T3	34+27		Santo Andre das Tojeiras		IT	
Fiat G91R1A	MM6303		Sassuolo		IT	
Fiat G91R1B	MM6390		Stallavena		IT	
RT-33A Shooting Star	53-5322		Traviso-Istrana		IT	Displayed as MM53-5322 / 51-76
Fiat G91	MM6417		Treviso-Istrama		IT	
Fiat G91R1B	MM6376		Velo D'Astico		IT	
Fiat G91T	MM5441	Junkyard resident	Verona Villa Franca		IT	
Fiat G91Y	MM6292		Vicenza AB		IT	Displayed as 2-22
Fiat G91R1	MM6280	Museo Storico dell'Aeronautica Militaire	Vigna di Valle		IT	
Fiat G91R1B	MM6405	Museo Storico dell'Aeronautica Militaire	Vigna di Valle		IT	
Fiat G91T1	MM6344	Museo Storico dell'Aeronautica Militaire	Vigna di Valle		IT	
Fiat G91Y	MM6959	Museo Storico dell'Aeronautica Militaire	Vigna di Valle		IT	
RF-84F Thunderflash	52-7458	Museo Storico dell'Aeronautica Militaire	Vigna di Valle		IT	Displayed as MM52-7458 / 3-05
RT-33A Shooting Star	53-5594	Museo Storico dell'Aeronautica Militaire	Vigna di Valle		IT	Displayed as MM53-5594 / 9-35
RF-84F Thunderflash	51-1940		Villafranca AB		IT	
RF-84F Thunderflash	52-7339	Museo Dell'Aria 'Nido Delle Aquile			IT	Displayed as MM52-7339
			MALTA			
Fiat G91R	MM6377	Malta Aviation Museum	Rabat		MT	
			NETHERLANDS			
F-16A Fighting Falcon		Luchmachht Museum	Soesterberg		NL	Displayed as J-215
RF-104G Starfighter		Luchmachht Museum	Soesterberg		NL	Displayed as D-8022
RF-84F Thunderflash	51-	Luchmachht Museum	Soesterberg		NL	Displayed as P-5
			NORWAY			
RF-104G Starfighter	D8022	Nordluftfartsmuseum	Bodo		NO	Displayed as B-FN
Saab RF-35 Draken	AR-120	Nordluftfartsmuseum	Bodo		NO	
RF-5A Freedom Fighter	68-9102	Nordluftfartsmuseum	Bodo AB		NO	
RF-84F Thunderflash		Nordluftfartsmuseum	Bodo AB		NO	
RF-5A Freedom Fighter	69-9105	Forsvarsels Flysaming	Oslo		NO	
RF-84F Thunderflash	51-	Forsvarsels Flysaming	Oslo		NO	Displayed as AZ-D
RF-84F Thunderflash	51-	Forsvarsels Flysaming	Oslo		NO	Displayed as AZ-E
RF-84F Thunderflash	51-	Forsvarsels Flysaming	Oslo		NO	Displayed as AZ-G
RF-84F Thunderflash	51-	Forsvarsels Flysaming	Oslo		NO	Displayed as AZ-N
RF-84F Thunderflash	51-	Norsk Flyhistorisk Forening	Stavanger		NO	Displayed as AZ-N
			PORTUGAL			
Fiat G91R3	5444		Alfrasagide		PT	
Fiat G91R3	5541	Museu du Ar	Alverca		PT	
Fiat G91R3	91308	Museu du Ar	Alverca		PT	
Fiat G91R4	5403		Barro		PT	
Fiat G91R3	30+83	Carvoeiro School	Carvoeiro		PT	
Fiat G91R4	5425		Coviha		PT	
Fiat G91R3	30+80		Horta do Douro		PT	
Fiat G91R4	5401		Lisben		PT	
Fiat G91R3	5463		Montijo AB		PT	
Fiat G91R4	5404		Montijo AB		PT	
Fiat G91R4	5407		Parque das Nacoes		PT	
Fiat G91R3	5542	Junkyard resident	Pombal		PT	
Fiat G91R3			Portimao		PT	
Fiat G91R4	5415		Santa Maria, Azores		PT	

A/C	S/N	MUSEUM / DISPLAY	CITY / BASE	STATE	CY	REMARKS
RT-33A Shooting Star		Pole Air Museum	Sintra		PT	Displayed as 1918
Fiat G91R3	5445		Sintra AB		PT	
Fiat G91R4	5408		Viseu		PT	
			SPAIN			
CR.9 Freedom Fighter			Albacete AB		ES	Displayed as AR9-064 / 212-64
CR.12 Phantom II			Antiguedad		ES	Displayed as CR 12-48
CR.9 Freedom Fighter		Museo Eider	Las Palmas		ES	Displayed as AR9-053 / 21-50
CR.12 Phantom II	65-0937	Museo Del Aire	Madrid		ES	Displayed as CR 12-42
CR.12 Phantom II		Museo Del Aire	Madrid		ES	Displayed as CR 12-42
CR.9 Freedom Fighter		Museo Del Aire	Madrid		ES	Displayed as AR9-062 / 23-62
CR.9 Freedom Fighter		Moron AB	Seville-Moron		ES	Displayed as AR9-060 / 21-55
CR.12 Phantom II			Torrejaon AB		ES	Displayed as CR 12-64
CR.12 Phantom II			Torrejaon AB		ES	Displayed as CR 12-55
			SWEDEN			
Saab S29C Tunnan	29969	Vasteras Flygmuseum, Vasteras AB	Hasslo		SE	
Saab S29C Tunnan	29974	Vasteras Flygmuseum, Vasteras AB	Hasslo		SE	
Saab S29C Tunnan	29929	Lulea AB	Kallax		SE	
Saab S29C Tunnan	29937	Lulea AB	Kallax		SE	
Saab S29C Tunnan	29945		Kareby		SE	
Saab S29C Tunnan	29970	Flygvapenmuseum Malmen	Linkoping AB		SE	
Saab S35E Draken	35952		Lules-Kallax		SE	
Saab S32C Lansen	32940		Nylcoping AB		SE	
			SWITZERLAND			
DH-112 Venom FB.MK.1R	J-1630	Verien Fleiger Museum	Altenrhein		CH	
DH-112 Venom FB.MK.1R	J-1627		Bex		CH	
DH-112 Venom FB.MK.1R	J-1642	Fleiger Museum Dubendorf	Dubendorf AB		CH	
Mirage IIIRS		Fleiger Museum Dubendorf	Dubendorf AB		CH	
Mirage IIIRS	R-2117	Musee de l'Aviation Militaire de Payerne	Payerne AB		CH	
Mirage IIIRS	R-2110		Stans		CH	
Mirage IIIRS	R-2116		Stans		CH	
			TAIWAN			
RF-101A Voodoo	41499		Hualieu		TW	
RF-101A Voodoo	41506		Kangshan AFB		TW	
RF-104G Starfighter	62-		Taichung-Chinghuakang		TW	
			THAILAND			
RF-5A Freedom Fighter	70104	Royal Thai Air Force Museum	Chang Mai		TH	Displayed as TKh 18-3
RT-33A Shooting Star	56141	Royal Thai Air Force Museum	Chang Mai		TH	Displayed as TF 11-5
			TURKEY			
RF-4E Phantom II	69-7490	Hava Kuvvetleri Muzesi Komutanligi	Ankara		TR	
RF-4E Phantom II	69-7503	Hava Kuvvetleri Muzesi Komutanligi	Ankara		TR	
RF-5A Freedom Fighter		Hava Kuvvetleri Muzesi Komutanligi	Ankara		TR	Displayed as 21208 / 3-208
RF-84F Thunderflash	51-1924	Hava Kuvvetleri Muzesi Komutanligi	Ankara		TR	Displayed as 924
RF-4E Phantom II	69-7465	Aviation Park and Plane Museum	Eskisehir		TR	
RT-33A Shooting Star	54-1548	Aviation Park and Plane Museum	Eskisehir		TR	
RF-5A Freedom Fighter	69-7147	Turkish Aerospace Museum	Istanbul		TR	
RF-84F Thunderflash	51-1901	Turkish Aerospace Museum	Istanbul		TR	
RF-84F Thunderflash	51-1917	Turkish Aerospace Museum	Istanbul		TR	
RT-33A Shooting Star	54-1543	Turkish Aerospace Museum	Istanbul		TR	Displayed as 8-543
RF-5A Freedom Fighter		Havacylyk Muzesi	Izmir		TR	Displayed as 97156
RF-5A Freedom Fighter			Merzifou		TR	Displayed as 89103
			UNITED KINGDOM			
Canberra PR Mk.7	WJ821		Bassingbourn		GB	
Harrier GR.Mk.3	WV752		Blechley Park		GB	
Canberra PR.Mk.7 (Nose)		Bournemouth Aviation Museum	Bournemouth IAP		GB	
Canberra PR.Mk.9 (Cockpit)		Cold War Jets Collection	Bruntingthorpe Airfield		GB	
Harrier GR.Mk.3	XZ966	Cold War Jets Collection	Bruntingthorpe Airfield		GB	
Harrier GR.Mk.3 (Nose)		Cold War Jets Collection	Bruntingthorpe Airfield		GB	
Harrier T.Mk.4	XW270	Cold War Jets Collection	Bruntingthorpe Airfield		GB	
Phantom FGR.Mk.2	XV406	Solway Aviation Museum	Carlisle Airport		GB	
Canberra PR.Mk.7	WH773	Gatwick Aviation Museum	Charlwood		GB	
Harrier GR.Mk.3	XV751	Gatwick Aviation Museum	Charlwood		GB	
Harrier T.Mk.2	XW264	Gatwick Aviation Museum	Charlwood		GB	
Swift FR,Mk.5	WK281	Tangmere Military Aviation Museum	Chichester		GB	ONE OF TWO SURVIVING SWIFT FR.MK.5
Harrier GR.Mk.1	XV798	Bristol Aero Collection, Kemble Field	Cirencester		GB	
Canberra PR.Mk.9	XH131	Kemble Field	Cirencester		GB	
Canberra PR.Mk.9	XH171	Royal Air Force Museum	Cosford		GB	
Canberra PR.MK.3	WF922	Midland Air Museum	Coventry Airport		GB	
Canberra PR.MK.3	WF922		Coventry, Baginton		GB	
Harrier GR.Mk.3	XZ133	Royal Air Force Museum	Duxford		GB	
Jaguar GR,Mk.1A	XX108	Royal Air Force Museum	Duxford		GB	
Phantom FGR.Mk.2	XV474	Royal Air Force Museum	Duxford		GB	
Harrier GR.Mk.1	XV277	Museum of Flight	East Fortune, Scotland		GB	
Harrier GR.Mk.3	XV748	Yorkshire Aviation Museum	Ellvington		GB	
Canberra PR.Mk.9	XH134	Kemble Field	Kemble		GB	

A/C	S/N	MUSEUM / DISPLAY	CITY / BASE	STATE	CY	REMARKS
Canberra PR.Mk.9	XH135	Kemble Field	Kemble		GB	
Canberra PR.MK.3	WE139	Royal Air Force Museum	London		GB	
Harrier GR Mk.3	XZ977	Royal Air Force Museum	London		GB	
Harrier GR Mk.3	XZ997	Royal Air Force Museum	London		GB	
Hunter FR.Mk.10	XF426	Royal Air Force Museum	London		GB	
Phantom FGR.Mk.2	XV424	Royal Air Force Museum	London		GB	
Phantom FGR.Mk.2	XV470	Royal Air Force Museum	London		GB	
Canberra PR.Mk.7	WH791	Newark Air Museum	Newark		GB	
Canberra PR.Mk.7 (Cockpit)		Newark Air Museum	Newark		GB	
Meteor FR.Mk.9	VZ608	Newark Air Museum	Newark		GB	Rolls Royce RB108 engine test bed ONE OF TWO SURVIVING METEOR FR.MK.5
Saab RF-35 Draken	AR-107	Newark Air Museum	Newark		GB	
Swift FR,Mk.5	WK277/N	Newark Air Museum	Newark		GB	*ONE OF TWO SURVIVING SWIFT FR.MK.5*
Harrier T.Mk.4		Norwich Aviation Museum	Norwich Airport		GB	
Hunter FR.Mk.10	XG168	Norwich Aviation Museum	Norwich Airport		GB	
Phantom FGR.Mk.2 (Nose)		Norwich Aviation Museum	Norwich Airport		GB	
Phantom FGR.Mk.2	XT891	Gate guard	RAFB Coninsby		GB	
Harrier GR.Mk.3	XW924		RAFB Cottesmore		GB	
Harrier GR.Mk.3	XZ132		RAFB Cranwell		GB	
Harrier T.Mk.4	XW271		RAFB Culdrose		GB	
Harrier T.Mk.4	XZ145		RAFB Culdrose		GB	
Harrier GR.Mk.3	XV779		RAFB Wittering		GB	
Harrier GR.Mk.3	XZ968	Muckleburgh Collection	Sheringham		GB	
DH-112 Venom FB.MK.1R	J-1632	DeHaviliand Aircraft Heritage Center	St. Albans		GB	
Hunter FR.Mk.10	XJ714	Jet Aviation Preservation Group	Stratford-upon-Avon		GB	
Phantom FGR.Mk.2	XV497		Waddington		GB	
UNITED STATES						
RF-4C Phantom II	63-7745	117th ARW, AL ANGB	Birmingham IAP	AL	US	
RF-84F Thunderflash	51-	117th ARW, AL ANGB	Birmingham IAP	AL	US	
RF-84F Thunderflash	52-7409	117th ARW, AL ANGB	Birmingham IAP	AL	US	
RF-101C Voodoo	56-0135	Maxwell AFB Air Park	Maxwell AFB	AL	US	
RF-84F Thunderflash	52-7249	187th TFG, Donnelly Field ANGB	Montgomery IAP	AL	US	
RF-84F Thunderflash			Ozark	AL	US	
RF-84F Thunderflash	51-	188th FG, AR ANG	Fort Smith	AR	US	
RF-101C Voodoo	56-0231	Little Rock AFB	Little Rock	AR	US	
RF-4C Phantom II	64-0748	Little Rock AFB	Little Rock	AR	US	
RF-101C Voodoo	56-0057	Camp Robinson	Little Rock	AR	US	
RF-84F Thunderflash	53-7543	Little Rock AFB	Little Rock	AR	US	
RF-101C Voodoo			Douglas	AZ	US	
RF-101C Voodoo	56-0112	Gate guard Gila Bend MAP	Gila Bend	AZ	US	
RF-101C Voodoo	56-0130	Gate guard Gila Bend MAP	Gila Bend	AZ	US	
RF-4C Phantom II	65-0941	Freedom Garden Park	Quartzsite	AZ	US	
RF-101C Voodoo	56-0214	Pima Air and Space Museum	Tucson	AZ	US	
RF-101H VooDoo	56-0011	Pima Air and Space Museum	Tucson	AZ	US	*ONE OF TWO SURVIVING RF-101H VOODOOs*
RF-84F Thunderflash	51-1944	Pima Air and Space Museum	Tucson	AZ	US	
RB-26C Invader	44-	Planes of Fame Museum	Valle	AZ	US	*ONLY SURVIVING RB-26C INVADER*
Harrier GR.Mk.3	ZD668	Planes of Fame Museum, Chino MAP	Chino	CA	US	
RF-84K Thunderflash	52-7265	Planes of Fame Museum, Chino MAP	Chino	CA	US	
RF-4C Phantom II	64-1004	Air Force Flight Test Center	Edwards AFB	CA	US	
RF-84F Thunderflash	53-7524	Western Aerospace Museum	Oakland	CA	US	
RF-4C Phantom II	63-7746	March Field Air Museum	Riverside	CA	US	
RF-84K Thunderflash	52-7266	Wings over the Rockies Aviation and Space Museum	Denver	CO	US	
RB-57A Canberra	52-1488	New England Air Museum	Windsor Locks	CT	US	
RF-4C Phantom II	67-0452	Air Force Armaments Museum	Eglin AFB	FL	US	
RF-84F Thunderflash	52-7261	George T. Baker Aviation School, Miami IAP	Miami	FL	US	
RF-4C Phantom II	66-0467	Hill Aerospace Museum	Valdosta	GA	US	
RB-57A Canberra	52-1475	Museum of Aviation	Warner Robins AFB	GA	US	
RF-101C Voodoo	56-0229	Museum of Aviation	Warner Robins AFB	GA	US	Photo is 54-1518 and 5656
RF-84F Thunderflash	52-7244	Museum of Aviation	Warner Robins AFB	GA	US	Cannot Confirm S/N says Sioux City
RF-84F Thunderflash			Harlan	IA	US	
RF-84F Thunderflash			Ida Grove	IA	US	
RF-84F Thunderflash		Souix City IAP	Souix City	IA	US	
RF-4C Phantom II	68-0594	Gowen Field	Boise	ID	US	
RF-111A Ardvark	63-9776	Mountain Home Air Park	Mountain Home AFB	ID	US	Displayed as 66-0022, in memory of first F-111 combat crew KIA ONLY SURVIVING RF-111A PROTOTYPE
RB-66B Destroyer	53-0412	Octave Chanute Aerospace Museum	Rantoul	IL	US	
RF-4C Phantom II	62-	Octave Chanute Aerospace Museum	Rantoul	IL	US	
RT-33A Shooting Star		Military Honor Park, Michiana Regional Airort	South Bend	IN	US	Incorrectly displayed with US Navy TV-2 serial number
RB-57A Canberra	52-1480	Combat Air Museum, Forbes Field	Topeka	KS	US	
RF-84F Thunderflash		Combat Air Museum, Forbes Field	Topeka	KS	US	
RF-101C Voodoo	56-0125	Boone National Guard Center	Frankfort	KY	US	
RF-101H VooDoo	56-0001	123rd AW, KY ANG, Standiford Field	Louisville	KY	US	*ONE OF TWO SURVIVING RF-101H VOODOOs*
RF-4C Phantom II	64-1081	123rd AW, KY ANG, Standiford Field	Louisville	KY	US	

A/C	S/N	MUSEUM / DISPLAY	CITY / BASE	STATE	CY	REMARKS
RB-57A Canberra	52-1446	Glen L. Martin Aviation Museum	Middle River	MD	US	
RB-57A Canberra	52-1467	Glen L. Martin Aviation Museum	Middle River	MD	US	
RF-84F Thunderflash	53-7554	Glen L. Martin Aviation Museum	Middle River	MD	US	
RF-101C Voodoo		Paul E. Garber Facility	Suitland	MD	US	
RB-57A Canberra	52-1426	Yankee Air Museum	Belleville	MI	US	
RF-84F Thunderflash	52-7421	Yankee Air Museum	Belleville	MI	US	
RB-57A Canberra	52-1485	Selfridge Military Air Museum	Selfridge ANGB	MI	US	
RF-101C Voodoo	56-0048	Selfridge Military Air Museum	Selfridge ANGB	MI	US	
RF-84F Thunderflash	51-1896	Selfridge Military Air Museum	Selfridge ANGB	MI	US	
RF-4C Phantom II	64-0061	Minnesota Air National Guard Museum	Minneapolis	MN	US	
RF-84F Thunderflash	51-1936	Central Missouri State University	Warrenburg/Skyhaven Airport	MO	US	
RF-101C Voodoo	56-0217	George Robert Hall Air Park	Hattiesburg	MS	US	
RF-84F Thunderflash	53-7636	George Robert Hall Air Park	Hattiesburg	MS	US	
RF-101C Voodoo	56-0068	Keesler AFB Air Park	Keesler AFB	MS	US	
RF-84F Thunderflash	53-7570	Enka Junior HS	Chandler	NC	US	
RB-45C Tornado	48-0017	Strategic Air and Space Museum	Ashland	NE	US	ONLY SURVIVING RB-45C TORNADO
RF-4C Phantom II	66-0903	Strategic Air and Space Museum	Ashland	NE	US	
RF-84F Thunderflash			David City	NE	US	
RF-4C Phantom II	64-0998	155th ARG, NE ANG	Lincoln	NE	US	
RF-84F Thunderflash	51-	155th ARG, NE ANG	Lincoln	NE	US	
RF-84F Thunderflash	53-7548	Gate guard, Lincoln ANGB	Lincoln	NE	US	
RF-84F Thunderflash	51-1929		Neligh	NE	US	
RF-84F Thunderflash			Valley	NE	US	
RF-84F Thunderflash	51-1935		York Municipal Airport	NE	US	
RF-101C Voodoo	56-0187	Cannon AFB Air Park	Cannon AFB	NM	US	
RF-101B Voodoo	59-0483	152nd RG, NV ANG, Reno IAP	Reno	NV	US	ONLY SURVIVING RF-101B VOODOO
RF-4C Phantom II	65-0886	152nd RG, NV ANG, Reno IAP	Reno	NV	US	
RB-57A Canberra	52-1459	Wings of Eagles Discovery Center	Elmira	NY	US	
RF-84F Thunderflash	53-7595	American Airpower Museum	Farmingdale	NY	US	
RB-57A Canberra		National Warplane Museum, Corning MAP	Horseheads	NY	US	
RF-101C Voodoo		Niagara Falls ANGB	Niagara Falls	NY	US	
RF-84F Thunderflash	52-7262	Walter Soplata Collection	Newbury	OH	US	
RF-4C Phantom II	65-0903	121st ARW, OH ANG	Rickenbacker ANGB	OH	US	
RB-66B Destroyer	53-0475	National Museum of the US Air Force	Wright-Patterson AFB	OH	US	
RF-101C Voodoo	56-0166	National Museum of the US Air Force	Wright-Patterson AFB	OH	US	
RF-4C Phantom II	62-	National Museum of the US Air Force	Wright-Patterson AFB	OH	US	
RF-4C Phantom II	64-1047	National Museum of the US Air Force	Wright-Patterson AFB	OH	US	
RF-84F Thunderflash	49-2430	National Museum of the US Air Force	Wright-Patterson AFB	OH	US	YRF-84F
RF-84K Thunderflash	52-7259	National Museum of the US Air Force	Wright-Patterson AFB	OH	US	
RF-84F Thunderflash	53-7610	Oklahoma State University	Stillwater	OK	US	
RB-66B Destroyer	53-0431		Florence Regional Airport	SC	US	
RF-101C Voodoo	56-0099	Shaw AFB Air Park	Shaw AFB	SC	US	
RF-4C Phantom II	63-7748	Shaw AFB Air Park	Shaw AFB	SC	US	
RF-84F Thunderflash	53-7529	118th AW, TN ANG	Nashville	TN	US	
RF-4C Phantom II	68-0570	Dell Valle Elementary School	Austin	TX	US	
RF-101C Voodoo		Babe Didrickson Zaharious Memorial Park	Beaumont	TX	US	
RB-66B Destroyer	53-0466	Dyess Linear Air Park	Dyess AFB	TX	US	
RF-84F Thunderflash	51-	Dyess Linear Air Park	Dyess AFB	TX	US	
RF-4C Phantom II	69-0367	Goodfellow AFB Air Park	Goodfellow AFB	TX	US	
RB-57A Canberra		USAF History and Traditions Museum	Lackland AFB	TX	US	
RF-4C Phantom II	64-1000	Rusty Allen Airport	Lago Vista	TX	US	
RB-57A Canberra		Commemorative Air Force Museum	Midland	TX	US	
RF-84F Thunderflash		Commemorative Air Force Museum	Midland	TX	US	
RF-4C Phantom II		Kelly Field Annex	San Antonio	TX	US	Displayed with non-existant tail number 64-467
RB-57A Canberra	52-1492	Hill Aerospace Museum	Ogden	UT	US	
RF-101A Voodoo	54-1503	Hill Aerospace Museum	Ogden	UT	US	
RF-4C Phantom II	65-0905	Hill Aerospace Museum	Ogden	UT	US	
RF-4C Phantom II	66-0469	Hill Aerospace Museum	Ogden	UT	US	
RF-4C Phantom II	66-0905	Hill Aerospace Museum	Ogden	UT	US	
RF-84F Thunderflash	51-	Hill Aerospace Museum	Ogden	UT	US	Nose sction only
RF-4C Phantom II	69-0372	Air Power Park	Hampton	VA	US	

Appendix C

Acronyms

AB	-	Air Base
AFB	-	Air Force Base
AFHRA	-	Air Force Historical Research Agency
AKG	-	Auklarungsgeshwader (German AF Reconnaissance Wing)
ANG	-	Air National Guard
ANGB	-	Air National Guard Base
ASARS	-	Advanced Synthetic Aperture Radar
CAF	-	Canadian Armed Forces
EFW	-	Federal Aircraft Factory
ESA	-	Electronic Steerable Radar
Esc	-	Escadrille (Belgium AF Squadron)
Esc	-	Escudaron (Spanish AF Squadron)
Esk	-	Eskadrille (Royal Danish AF Squadron)
FB	-	Fighter Bomber
FGR	-	Fighter Ground Attack Reconnaissance
fl	-	focal length
FP	-	Fighter Photographic Reconnaissance
FR	-	Fighter Reconnaissance
ft	-	feet
GR	-	Ground Attack Reconnaissance
IFF	-	Identification Friend and Foe
Imp gal	-	Imperial gallon
in	-	inch
IR	-	Infrared
IRLS	-	Infrared Linescanner
JRP	-	Jaguar Reconnaissance Pod

kg st	-	kilogram static thrust
kg	-	kilogram
km	-	kilometer
kmh	-	kilometers per hour
kts	-	knots
lbs st	-	pounds static thrust
lbs	-	pounds
ltr	-	liters
LOROP	-	Long Range Optical
LRMTS	-	Laser Ranging and Marked Target Seeking
m	-	meter
Mk	-	Mark
mm	-	millimeter
mph	-	miles per hour
MRCA	-	Multi-Role Combat Aircraft
NATO	-	North Atlantic Treaty Organization
nm	-	nautical mile
NMUSAF	-	National Museum of the USAF
OCU	-	Operational Conversion Unit
PACAF	-	Pacific Air Command
PR	-	Photographic Reconnaissance
PW	-	Pratt and Whitney
R	-	Reconnaissance
RAF	-	Royal Air Force
RAFB	-	Royal Air Force Base
RB	-	Reconnaissance Bomber
RF	-	Reconnaissance Fighter
RS	-	Reconnaissance Squadron
RT	-	Reconnaissance Trainer
RWR	-	Radar Warning Receiver
SAC	-	Strategic Air Command
SAR	-	Synthetic Aperture Radar
SLAR	-	Side Looking Airborne Radar
Sq	-	Squadron
Tac Recce	-	Tactical Reconnaissance
TAC	-	Tactical Air Command
TEREC	-	Tactical Electronic Reconnaissance
TR	-	Tactical Reconnaissance
TRIGS	-	TR-1 Ground Station
TRS	-	Tactical Reconnaissance Squadron
TRW	-	Tactical Reconnaissance Wing
UK	-	United Kingdom
US	-	United States

US gal	-	US gallons
USAAF	-	US Army Air Force
USAF	-	United States Air Force
USAFE	-	United States Air Force Europe
V/STOL	-	Vertical/Short Take-Off and Landing
WW II	-	World War II

Appendix D

Glossary

Afterburner	- System to increase the thrust of a jet engine for short periods by injecting raw fuel for burning downstream of the turbine, also known as engine reheat
Anhedral	- The downward inclination of an airplane's wing, normally specified in degrees of dihedral
Arrester Hook	- A retractable hook lowered by a carrier-based aircraft
Barrel Fuselage	- Fuselage with an internal engine(s) and an engine intake in the fuselage nose, on the sides of the fuselage, or in the wing roots
Bicycle Landing Gear	- Tandem main gear under the fuselage with small outrigger gears near the wing tips
Blunt Tips	- Wing and stabilizer tips, which have a continuous curved or rounded tip
Blunt Tips	- Wing and stabilizer tips, which have straight edges with rounded corners
Bubble Canopy	- A canopy molded in one piece with no external bracing
Bypass Ratio	- For a turbofan engine, it is the ratio of the air that goes around the engine versus the air that goes through the core or turbine

Cabin	- An enclosed compartment in an aircraft for crewmembers
Canopy	- A transparent hood, covering or enclosure
Chord	- The straight line distance between the leading and trailing edge of the wing or stabilizer
Cigar Fuselage	- Fuselage that has no internal engine and an enclosed cabin or cockpit
Clamshell Canopy	- A one-piece canopy cover that is hinged on the side, front or rear for crewmember ingress and egress
Compartment	- The compartment in an aircraft to accommodate the pilot or other crewmembers and usually covered by a moveable canopy
Delta Wing	- A wing with a swept leading edge and straight trailing edge
Depression Angle	- the angle between the optical axis of the camera or direction the radar antenna is pointing relative the horizon (0° depression angle)
Dihedral	- The upward inclination of an airplane's wing, normally specified in degrees of dihedral
Dorsal Spine	- A distinct ridge or spine on the back or top portion of the fuselage
Drag Chute	- A deceleration parachute normally installed in a fairing below the vertical stabilizer at the rear of the aircraft
Electronic Reconnaissance	- the detection, identification, evaluation, and location of foreign non-communications electromagnetic radiations
Engine Nacelle	- A separate streamlined enclosure, normally located within or below a wing, to house an aircrafts engine
Engine Reheat	- System to increase the thrust of a jet engine for short periods by injecting raw fuel for burning downstream of the turbine, also known as afterburning

Fairing	- An auxiliary part of the exterior structure to reduce drag or streamline the aircraft
Fillet	- A faired surface that smoothes the flow of air at an internal angle as at a wing root
Focal Length (fl)	- Focal length is the distance as measured from the lens to the film.
Foreplanes	- Small wings normally located on the fuselage above and ahead of the main wings to improve maneuverability
Framing Camera	- An aerial camera designed to take a series of overlapping frames of imagery. Most framing cameras have a square image format.
Fuselage	- Main body of the aircraft to which the wings and tails are attached
Greenhouse	- Colloquial term for the framed hood or canopy over cockpit
Hardpoints	- Fixed stations above or below the wings, or under the fuselage for mounting external stores or fuel tanks
High-Mounted Wing	- The wing/horizontal stabilizer is mounted near or at the top of the fuselage or vertical stabilizer
Horizontal Stabilator	- One piece, all moving horizontal stabilizer
Horizontal Stabilizer	- Fixed horizontal tail surface of the aircraft mounted on the fuselage or vertical stabilizer
Imperial Gallon (Imp gal)	- An Imperial gallon is a British standard for measuring liquid and is equal to 1.2009 US gallons, 4.546 liters or 153.7 US liquid ounces
Inch (in)	- An inch is a US standard for measuring distance and is equal to 25.4 millimeters
Infrared Linescanner	- An Infrared sensor that scans narrow strips directly below the aircraft and records the results as a continuous unbroken image while the sen-

sor is operating

Infrared Sensor - A thermal sensor which uses a scanner to detect infrared emissions, converts the infrared energy into an electrical signal, and converts the signal to visible light and records it on ordinary black and white aerial film.

Kilogram (kg) - A kilogram is a European metric standard for measuring weight and is equal to 2.2046 pounds or 35.3 US ounces

Kilometer (km) - A kilometer is a European metric standard for measuring distance and is equal to 0.62137 statute miles, 0.5396 nautical miles or 3,280.8 feet

Liter (ltr) - A liter is a European metric standard for measuring liquid and is equal to 0.26418 US gallons, 0.21998 Imperial gallons or 33.8 US ounces

Low-Mounted Wing - The wing/horizontal stabilizer is mounted near or at the bottom of the fuselage or vertical stabilizer

Meter (m) - A meter is a European metric standard for measuring distance and is equal to 3.281 feet

Mid-Mounted Wing - The wing/horizontal stabilizer is mounted at the midpoint between the top and the bottom of the fuselage or vertical stabilizer

Millimeter (mm) - A millimeter is a European metric standard for measuring distance and is equal to 0.03937 inches

Moveable Canopy - A canopy cover that slides aft for crewmember ingress and egress

Nacelle Fuselage - A fuselage with or without and engine on an aircraft with a twin boom tail section

Nautical Mile (NM) - A nautical mile is a British standard for measuring distance and is equal to 1.1508 miles, 1.8532 kilometers or 6,076.1 feet

Nose	- The foremost part of the fuselage
Oblique Camera Position	- An installation normally associated with framing cameras that provides coverage of the area ahead of the aircraft's line of flight and/or off to either side. The depression angle for cameras in the oblique positions varied based on the aircraft, camera, and lens focal length.
Panoramic Camera	- A aerial camera, normally a framing camera, installed in the vertical position, with a scanning lens with a wide angular field of view from 60° to 180° (horizon-to-horizon) to provide increased lateral coverage along the aircraft' line of flight. The field of view is dependent on the camera, lens focal length and operating mode.
Photoflash Bomb	- A bomb designed to produce a brief and intense illumination for medium altitude night photography
Photoflash Cartridge	- a pyrotechnic cartridge designed to produce a brief and intense illumination for low altitude night photography
Piston Engine	- Internal combustion engine, which drives a propeller to provide power or thrust for an aircraft
Pitot-Static Pressure Sensor	- Thin tubular sensor normally mounted on the nose or a wing tip and is the source for air pressure for the aircraft altimeter, vertical speed indicator and airspeed indicator
Pound (lb)	- A pound is a US standard for measuring weight and is equal to 0.4536 kilograms or 16 US ounces
Refueling Probe	- Fixed or movable structure used as an in-flight refueling receptacle
Refueling Receptacle	- Fixed receptacle on top the fuselage normally located behind the cockpit for in-flight refueling
Rotatable Camera	- Normally one camera, which can

be, rotated manually or mechanically, by remote control into a variety of positions or depression angles

Saw Tooth Leading Edge - A wing leading edge with a broken or uneven appearance

Shoulder Mounted Wing - The wing is mounted midway between the top and middle of the fuselage

Side Looking Airborne Radar - airborne radar viewing at right angles to the axis of the vehicle, which produces a presentation of the terrain or moving targets

Split Vertical Camera Position - A pair of framing cameras, mounted side-by-side and tilted slightly off the vertical axis so to provide increased lateral coverage along the aircraft's line of flight a some overlap in between the two cameras coverage directly below the aircraft track.

Square Tips - Wing and stabilizer tips, which have straight edges with sharp corners

Stall Fence - Small vertical fin(s) located on a wing to improve aerodynamics and stability

Static Pressure Port - short tubular sensor attached to a small fairing and normally mounted on the side of the fuselage, and is the source for air pressure for the aircraft altimeter, vertical speed indicator and airspeed indicator

Static Thrust - maximum force or pressure exerted by an aircraft engine, static on the ground and measured in units of pounds or kilograms

Statute Mile (mi) - A statute mile is a US standard for measuring distance and is equal to 0.8689 nautical miles, 1.6093 kilometers or 5,280 feet

Stovepipe Fuselage - A tubular fuselage with an internal engine, full nose engine intake and aft engine exhaust

Straight Wing - The wing or stabilizer leading and

trailing edges are straight, parallel and perpendicular to the fuselage

Straight-Tapered Wing - The wing or stabilizer leading edge is straight and perpendicular to the fuselage and the trailing edge is straight, but not perpendicular to the fuselage, so the wing diminishes in chord from the root to the tip

Swept Wing - A wing or stabilizer whose leading and trailing edges are farther aft at the tip, than at the root, normally specified in degrees and minutes of sweep

Synthetic Aperture Radar (SAR) - High-resolution radar system and associated processing techniques that synthetically increases the antenna's size or aperture to improve the azimuth resolution using the same pulse compression techniques adopted for radar collection and processing in the range direction

Tactical Reconnaissance - Data collection and the subsequent processing, interpretation, and distribution of derived intelligence concerning terrain, weather, the enemy's force structure, movement, strength, disposition, capability, actual or potential lines of communication and other enemy resources that could affect the tactical situation

Tapered Wing - The wing or stabilizer leading and trailing edges are straight, but not perpendicular to the fuselage so the wing diminishes in chord from the root to the tip

Tapered-Straight Wing - The wing or stabilizer leading edge is straight, but not perpendicular to the fuselage and the trailing edge is straight and is perpendicular to the fuselage, so the wing diminishes in chord from the root to the tip

Tricycle Landing Gear	- Nose wheel is located ahead of the main landing gear
Trimetrogon Configuration	- A configuration of three framing cameras that provide horizon-to-horizon coverage with approximately 14° of cross-track overlap
Turbofan Engine	- A variation of the gas turbine or jet engine, which derives some of its thrust from air and fuel mixture passing through the turbine, but with some of the incoming air passing through the fan and bypassing, or going around the engine, like the air through a propeller. The air that going through the fan has a velocity slightly higher from the free stream, so the turbofan gets some of its thrust from the core and some of it from the fan.
Turbojet Engine	- A variation of the gas turbine or jet engine, which derives its thrust from air and fuel mixture passing through the turbine and normally, used for high speed combat aircraft
US Gallon (US gal)	- A gallon is a US standard for measuring liquid and is equal to 0.8327 Imperial gallons, 3.785 liters, or 128 US liquid ounces
Variable Geometry Wing	- A wing whose leading swept can be varied in flight
Ventral Fin	- Small fin mounted under the fuselage for increased maneuverability or stability
Vertical Camera Position	- Any framing camera with a fixed depression angle of 90°
Vertical Stabilizer	- Fixed vertical tail surface of the aircraft (fin)
Waisted Fuselage	- Normally associated with delta wing aircraft, the "waisted" fuselage usually presents a coke bottle or hourglass shape when viewed from above
Wheel Base	- For an aircraft with a tricycle land-

ing gear, the wheelbase refers to the distance from the center of the axle of the nose landing gear strut to the center of the axle of the main landing gear strut

Wheel Track - For an aircraft, wheel track refers to the distance between the main landing gear as measured from the outside edge of the outer wheels on the two main landing gear struts

Wing Root Intakes - Engine intakes located in the wing roots of an aircraft wing

Appendix E

Bibliography

A-26 Invader in action, Jim Mesko, Squadron/Signal Publications, Aircraft Number 134, 1993

Air Force Characteristics Summary, RF-101A Voodoo, 01 September 1960

Air Force Characteristics Summary, RF-84F Thunderflash, 09 October 1953

Air Force Guide 1, Addendum 103, Characteristics Summary, RB-66B Destroyer, November 1972

Air Force Guide 1, Addendum 47, Characteristics Summary, RF-104G Starfighter, February 1963

Air Force Guide 1, Addendum 65, Characteristics Summary, RF-101C Voodoo, July 1964

Air Force Guide 1, Addendum 69, Characteristics Summary, RF-4C Phantom II, January 1965

Air Force Guide 2, Volume-1, Addendum 37, Standard Aircraft Characteristics, RF-101C Voodoo, June 1964

Air Force Guide 2, Volume-1, Addendum 40, Standard Aircraft Characteristics, RB-66B Destroyer, June 1965

Air Force Guide 2, Volume-1, Addendum 54, Standard Aircraft Characteristics, RF-104G Starfighter, August 1972

Air Force Guide 2, Volume-1, Addendum 55, Standard Aircraft Characteristics, RF-4C Phantom II, January 1973

Air Force Manual 200-50, Volume-I, Imagery Interpretation Handbook, December 1967

Air Force Manual 200-50, Volume-II, Imagery Interpretation Handbook, December 1967

Air Force Manual 50-40, Aircraft Recognition Manual, June 1962

Air Force Standard Aircraft Characteristics, RF-84F Thunderflash, 20 June

1956
Aircraft Museums Directory, European, Bob Ogden, Battle of Britain Prints International, Limited, 1978
Aircraft Museums, USA and Canada, 22nd Edition, Michael A. Blaugher, February 2004
All-Weather Reconnaissance Capability with the AN/UPD-6 Side-Looking Radar System, Goodyear Aerospace Corporation, August 1971
B-57 Canberra in action, Jim Mesko, Squadron/Signal Publications, Aircraft Number 77, 1986
Boeing/BAe Harrier, Warbird Tech Series Volume 21, Dennis R. Jenkins, Specialty Press, 1998
British Fighter since 1912, The, Francis K. Mason, Naval Institute Press, 1992
Dassault Mirage F1, Aerofax Minigraph 17, René J. Francillon, Aerofax, Inc, 1986
Defence Intelligence Agency Manual 57-25-100, Major World Aircraft Recognition Guide (Excluding US and USSR), 15 January 1977
Encyclopedia of World Airpower, The, Bill Gunston, Crescent Books, 1981
F-100 Super Sabre in action, Larry Davis and David Menard, Squadron/Signal Publications, Aircraft Number 190, 2003
F-101 Voodoo Detail and Scale, Volume 21, Bert Kinzey, Airlife Publishing Limited, 1986
F-104 Starfighter Detail and Scale, Volume 38, Bert Kinzey, Airlife Publishing Limited, 1991
F-4 Phantom II in action, Larry Davis, Squadron/Signal Publications, Aircraft Number 65, 1984
F-5 Freedom Fighter in action, Lou Drendel, Squadron/Signal Publications, Aircraft Number 38, 1980
F-84 Thunderjet in action, Larry Davis and David Menard, Squadron/Signal Publications, Aircraft Number 61, 1983
Harrier in action, Don Linn, Squadron/Signal Publications, Aircraft Number 58, 1982
Hawker Hunter in action, Glenn Ashley, Squadron/Signal Publications, Aircraft Number 121, 1992
Hawker Hunter, Biography of a thoroughbred, Francis K. Mason, Patrick Stephens, Cambridge, 1981
Jane's All the World's Aircraft 1954-1955, McGraw-Hill
Jane's All the World's Aircraft 1957-1958, McGraw-Hill
Jane's All the World's Aircraft 1960-1961, McGraw-Hill
Jane's All the World's Aircraft 1963-1964, McGraw-Hill
Jane's All the World's Aircraft 1964-1965, McGraw-Hill
Jane's All the World's Aircraft 1965-1966, McGraw-Hill
Jane's All the World's Aircraft 1966-1967, McGraw-Hill

Jane's All the World's Aircraft 1967-1968, McGraw-Hill
Jane's All the World's Aircraft 1969-1970, McGraw-Hill
Jane's All the World's Aircraft 1971-1972, McGraw-Hill
Jane's All the World's Aircraft 1985-1986, McGraw-Hill
Jane's All the World's Aircraft 1988-1989, McGraw-Hill
Jane's All the World's Weapon Systems 1973-1974, McGraw-Hill
Jane's All the World's Weapon Systems 1976-1977, McGraw-Hill
Jane's All the World's Weapon Systems 1979-1980, McGraw-Hill
Jane's American Fighting Aircraft of the 20th Century, Mallard Press
Jane's Battlefield Surveillance Systems 1993-1994, McGraw-Hill
Jane's Battlefield Surveillance Systems 1998-1999, McGraw-Hill
Lockheed Aircraft since 1913, René J. Francillon, Naval Institute Press, 1987
Lockheed F-104 Starfighter, Steve Pace, Motorbooks International, 1992
Lockheed F-104 Starfighter, Warbird Tech Series Volume 38, Jim Upton, Specialty Press, 2003
Lockheed P-80/F-80 Shooting Star, A Photo Chronicle, David R. McLaren, Schiffer Military/ Aviation History, 1996
Lockheed U-2 in action, Larry Davis, Squadron/Signal Publications, Aircraft Number 58, 1988
Lockheed U-2R/TR-1, Aerofax Minigraph 28, Jay Miller and Chris Pocock, Aerofax, Inc, 1988
McDonnell Douglas Aircraft since 1920: Volume II, René J. Francillon, Naval Institute Press, 1990
McDonnell Douglas F-4 Phantom II, Robert F. Dorr, Osprey Publishing Limited, 1984
McDonnell RF-4 Variants, Aerofax Minigraph 13, Jay Miller, Aerofax, Inc, 1984
Meteor in action, Glenn Ashley, Squadron/Signal Publications, Aircraft Number 152, 1995
P-80 Shooting Star and T-33/F-94 in action, Larry Davis, Squadron/Signal Publications, Aircraft Number 40, 1980
Planning and Flying the Mission with the AN/APQ-102A Side Looking Radar, Goodyear Aerospace Corporation, April 1967
Reconnaissance Handy Book for the Tactical Reconnaissance Specialist, McDonald Douglas Corporation, 1982
Reconnaissance Reference Manual, McDonald Douglas Corporation, 1969
Republic F/RF-84F Thunderstreak/Thunderflash, Ernest R. McDowell, Arco Publishing Company, Inc, 1970
SAAB Aircraft since 1937, Hans G. Andersson, Putnam Aeronautical Books, 1989
Standard Aircraft Characteristics, RF-101A Voodoo, 01 September 1960
Supermarine Aircraft since 1914, C.F. Andrews and E.B. Morgan, Naval Institute Press, 1981

Tactical Electronic Reconnaissance (TEREC) AN/ALQ-125 System Summary, Litton AMECOM, April 1981
Textbook of Radar Interpretation, Volume I, Basic Radar and Imaging Principles, Goodyear Aerospace Corporation, December 1966
UPD-8 All-Weather Radar Reconnaissance, Goodyear Aerospace
United States Air Force Fact Sheet, F-4C/RF-4C Phantom II, July 1965
USAF Information Sheet, Operation Sun Run, 1957
USAF Series RB-66B Aircraft Flight Handbook, T.O. 1B-66(R)B-1
USAF Series RF-101A Aircraft Flight Handbook, T.O. 1F-101(R)(Y)A-1
USAF Series RF-104G Aircraft Flight Handbook, T.O. 1F-104G-1
USAF Series RF-4C Aircraft Flight Handbook, T.O. 1F-4(R)C-1
USAF Series RT-33A Aircraft Flight Handbook, T.O. 1T-33(R)A-1
Venom, De Havilland Venom and Sea Venom, The Complete History, David Watkins, Sutton Publishing Limited, 2003
Vinten 70 mm Reconnaissance Cameras and Lenses, W. Vinten Military Division
World Aircraft Combat Aircraft 1945-1960, Enzo Angelucci and Paolo Matricardi, Sampson and Low, 1980

Appendix F

International Country Codes

AT - Austria (Republic of)
BE - Belgium (Kingdom of)
CA - Canada
CH - Switzerland (Swiss Confederation)
CL - Chile (Republic of)
CZ - Czech Republic
DE - Germany (Federal Republic of)
DK - Denmark (Kingdom of)
EC - Ecuador (Republic of)
ES - Spain (Kingdom of)
FI - Finland (Republic of)
FR - France (French Republic)
GB - United Kingdom (Great Britain, Northern Ireland, Scotland, Wales)
GR - Greece (Hellenic Republic)
IT - Italy (Italian Republic)
MT - Malta
NL - Netherlands (Kingdom of the)
NO - Norway (Kingdom of)
PL - Poland (Republic of)
PT - Portugal (Portuguese Republic)
SE - Sweden (Kingdom of)
TR - Turkey (Republic of)
UK - United Kingdom
US - United States (United States of America)

Appendix - G

US State Postal Codes

AK - Alaska
AL - Alabama
AR - Arkansas
AZ - Arizona
CA - California
CO - Colorado
CT - Connecticut
DC - District of Columbia (Washington DC)
DE - Delaware
FL - Florida
GA - Georgia
HI - Hawaii
IA - Iowa
ID - Idaho
IL - Illinois
IN - Indiana
KS - Kansas
KY - Kentucky
LA - Louisiana
MA - Massachusetts
MD - Maryland
ME - Maine
MI - Michigan
MN - Minnesota
MO - Missouri
MS - Mississippi
MT - Montana
NC - North Carolina
ND - North Dakota
NE - Nebraska
NH - New Hampshire
NJ - New Jersey
NM - New Mexico
NV - Nevada
NY - New York
OH - Ohio
OK - Oklahoma
OR - Oregon
PA - Pennsylvania
RI - Rhode Island
SC - South Carolina

SD - South Dakota
TN - Tennessee
TX - Texas
UT - Utah
VA - Virginia
VT - Vermont
WA - Washington
WI - Wisconsin
WV - West Virginia
WY - Wyoming

About the Author

Paul is a retired US Air Force Chief Master Sergeant with more than twenty years experience as a multi-sensor Imagery Analyst. His career includes twelve years in tactical reconnaissance, eleven of which were in Germany, with assignments to the 17th and 38th TRS, and Intelligence Directorate of HQ USAFE. As the Intelligence Branch Chief for Tactical Reconnaissance, Paul developed and managed tactical reconnaissance Imagery Analyst operational and training requirements; was the HQ USAFE Intelligence representative to NATO's Imagery Reconnaissance and Intelligence Working Party; and an active member of several multi-national working groups and committees. Following retirement Paul has managed research, development and testing of high-resolution, multi-frequency SAR imaging technologies, and the DOD's annual Tri-Service Radar Symposium

Paul is an advocate for the use of multi-sensor imaging technologies to support non-invasive archeological research, environment monitoring, disaster planning and relief. In October 1993 Paul co-authored an Article for Earth Observation Magazine entitled "Airborne Imaging used to Monitor the great Flood of '93".

Paul has a Bachelors Degree in Business Administration, with a major in management from Cleary University, and an Associates Degree in Applied Science from the Community College of the Air Force with a major in Intelligence and Imagery Analysis.

Image 090m The author at Zweibrucken AB, GE in June 1983